0148202

KT-486-065

0335
25.95

F LY
(Sch)

HAROLD BRIDGES LIBRARY
S. MARTIN'S COLLEGE
LANCASTER

0393702057

Single in a
Married World

A NORTON PROFESSIONAL BOOK

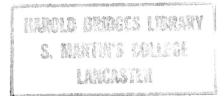
HAROLD BRIDGES LIBRARY
S. MARTIN'S COLLEGE
LANCASTER

Single in a Married World

A Life Cycle Framework for Working with the Unmarried Adult

NATALIE SCHWARTZBERG
KATHY BERLINER
DEMARIS JACOB

The Clinical Project on Singlehood

W.W. NORTON & COMPANY • NEW YORK • LONDON

Credit for quote in Epilogue: Copyright © 1994 by The New York Times Company. Reprinted by permission.

Copyright © 1995 by Natalie Schwartzberg, Kathy Berliner, and Demaris Jacob.

All rights reserved.

Printed in the United States of America

First Edition

Manufacturing by Haddon Craftsmen, Inc.

For information about permission to reproduce selections from this book, write to
Permissions, W. W. Norton & Company, Inc., 500 Fifth Avenue, New York, NY 10110.

Library of Congress Cataloging-in-Publication Data

Schwartzberg, Natalie.
    Single in a married world : a life cycle framework for working with the unmarried adult / Natalie Schwartzberg, Kathy Berliner, Demaris Jacob
        p.   cm.
    "A Norton professional book."
    Includes bibliographical references and index.
    ISBN 0-393-70205-7
    1. Single people—United States—Psychology. 2. Single people—Counseling of—United States. I. Berliner, Kathy. II. Jacob, Demaris. III. Title.
HQ800.4.U6S35   1995
305.9′0652—dc20   95-30991   CIP

W. W. Norton & Company, Inc., 500 Fifth Avenue, New York, NY 10110
W. W. Norton & Company, Ltd., 10 Coptic Street, London WC1A 1PU

1 2 3 4 5 6 7 8 9 0

To all the single people who told us their stories. Their ideas, struggles, and creative solutions will help other single people find their way
in a married world.

Contents

Foreword   ix
   Betty Carter
Acknowledgments   xi

I. A MULTICONTEXTUAL FRAMEWORK FOR SINGLEHOOD

1   The "Problem" of Singlehood   3
2   The Couples Culture and the Single Adult   13
3   Culture and Family   30

II. A LIFE CYCLE MODEL FOR THE SINGLE ADULT

4   An Overview of the Life Cycle   51
5   Young Adulthood: The "Not Yet Married" Phase   58
6   The Thirties: Entering the "Twilight Zone" of Singlehood   69
7   The Forties to Mid-Fifties: Developing Alternative Scripts 82
8   The Fifties to Failing Health: Putting It All Together   99
9   Elderly Phase: Between Failing Health and Death   117
10 Single and Gay: Issues and Opportunities   125

III. CLINICAL APPLICATIONS

11 The Twenties: Bob's Story   149
12 The Thirties: Susan's Story   157

13   Midlife: George's Story   173
14   Later Life: Lina's Story   187
15   Stories from Gay and Lesbian Singles   202

Epilogue   215
References   217
Index   223

Foreword

THE AUTHORS OF THIS BOOK, Natalie Schwartzberg, Kathy Berliner, and Dee Jacob, have recognized the growing population of single people who until now have been relegated to the margins of a society in which marriage not only is the norm but is presented as the *only* "healthy" solution to the existential dilemmas of life. And the selling of marriage as the "solution" continues in spite of all the facts and statistics that show it to be an institution experiencing deep troubles.

We could write this off as just one more example of the power of the majority to set the norms, if there weren't such a high toll in human suffering involved, and if we therapists weren't such a big part of the problem. How often have we colluded with single clients' view of themselves as necessarily flawed *because they are not married*, and let development of self in the service of "finding a mate" stand as a legitimate goal of therapy? How ready are we to base our work with clients on the premise that a satisfying, creative, full life is not dependent on marital status?

It has been a thought-provoking and arresting experience at The Family Institute of Westchester, where, like everywhere else, almost all of the staff and trainees are (or have been) married, to hear the questions, the discussion, and the reevaluations emanating from the Singles Project over the last few years. Married therapists are usually unaware of the powerful negative impact of societal messages and the organization of social institutions — including the family and the mental health establishment — on the single person. The social context in which the single person operates moves to exclude him or her from full, authentic membership in the larger community and continues to reinforce a "flawed" self-definition. The authors rightly underscore the necessity for both therapist and client to question these dominant messages *and* to realize their impact on the meaning single clients give to their lives.

Rescuing the single adult from the life cycle limbo of being seen as biding time "between families," the authors extend and deepen the multicontextual life cycle framework I have developed over the past several years. They have fleshed out the emotional tasks specific to single life at each phase of the life cycle, and illustrated what clinical work with this life cycle model is about through extensive clinical cases. Their conceptualization will help therapists move away from the view that full emotional development is not possible outside of marriage.

I think readers of this work will find, as I did, that they will bring a new and life-enhancing theoretical framework to their clinical work with single clients.

Betty Carter
Director, Family Institute of Westchester

Acknowledgments

OF THE MANY PEOPLE who are owed a debt of gratitude for helping with this book, most particularly we would like to thank Betty Carter. As the director of the Family Institute of Westchester, she has been our mentor in formulating the ideas that are the foundation of the book. We also want to acknowledge two of the original members of the Singles Clinical Project: Shirley Wilmers and Larry Torrisi, whose thoughts, efforts, and good companionship helped enormously in the conceptualization of our thinking about single people. A number of colleagues have been invaluable in giving feedback and suggestions. They include Pat Colucci, Ed Dunne, Claudio Bepko, Barbara Rothenberg, Tom Johnson, Walter Alvarez, Miriam Shere, and Al Spordone. We are indebted to Martin Hanfling, Bill Tilles, Anna Tilles, Jonathan Tilles, Michelle Spirn and Amnon Goldstein for their support, encouragement, and advice. We also thank Susan Munro, our editor, for her belief in our ideas about single people.

Single in a
Married World

I

A MULTICONTEXTUAL FRAMEWORK FOR SINGLEHOOD

The "Problem" of Singlehood

ANN, AGE 35, is the only unmarried one of her four siblings. She comes from a working-class family where marriage is highly valued. It has been the way for daughters to leave home, the way for sons to show responsibility, and the evidence to her parents that they have done their job. While Ann no longer lives at home, her "not yet married" status has kept her in a "not quite adult" position in the family. Her thirty-fifth birthday is experienced with a mixture of panic and depression as she anticipates moving into a "never married" category. When she evaluates her life, she attributes both her depression and a lack of focus or success at work to the absence of a significant relationship in her life. Despite the emotional turmoil in her siblings' marriages, she romanticizes marriage as the thing that would make her life work. She assumes it is a personal failing that she has not married. Her siblings did it. Why can't she? Because, for her, single status is a sign of a serious problem, she consults a therapist. Perhaps therapy will help her get married.

•••

JOANNE, A 40-YEAR-OLD free-lance journalist, has had a series of interesting relationships that lasted several years at a time, but ultimately felt too restraining to her career aspirations. She has decided that she is "not the marrying kind," but wonders what the price for this will be. Can she really say her career has been worth it as she watches her friends marry and have children, and join a "community" she has no access to? Who will take care of her in her old age if there is no spouse or children? She wonders if her parents' stormy relationship is to blame for putting her outside the norm. She has decreased her interaction with family members as she has felt their questions regarding marriage shift from friendly teasing to anxious pressure. Her circle of friends is also constantly shifting, as her life experience diverges from her peers who marry. Her attempts to create a good life, as a result, are often hampered as her sense of isolation increases and she feels that she is out of the mainstream. Because turning forty seems like the point of no return regarding marriage and family, she consults a therapist. Maybe she could make some personal changes to make marriage more acceptable.

•••

PETER COMES TO THERAPY because he is in danger of losing his job. He has been placed on probation for excessive absences and suspected alcohol abuse. In fact, the celebration of his fiftieth birthday led to a weeklong binge, where he lost contact with everyone. He sees his problem as a growing depression regarding career choice and the use of alcohol to medicate the unhappiness. While Peter does not immediately identify his single status as a problem, he describes a life he believes shaped by default of not marrying. As the only unmarried child in the family of four, he helps out by living with his ailing father. The oldest, he dreads family events where his younger sisters show off their families. Feeling out of step with his friends, now mostly married, he further isolates himself. Because he was afraid to commit himself to marriage several years ago, when the opportunity presented itself, he believes he is not capable of marriage.

Whether actually articulated as the presenting problem for therapy or not, being single has become a problem to be addressed in therapy for these three clients. They have used marital status to evaluate their lives and, based on this measure, wonder if there is something lacking. Whether pursuing or distancing from marriage, they all find themselves in a reactive position to one of our culture's major yardsticks for normality. While men and women may experience it differently, marriage is a marker for the culture, family, and self in the expected progression from dependency to adulthood. Its presence or absence becomes a comment on how far along we are. This comment, however, is not value free. If the milestone of marriage has not been achieved by a certain time, which can vary with the individual, family, or culture, it can have a profound impact on our sense of place in the surrounding social milieu, our position in the family, and our evaluation of self.

As long as marriage is our standard, single people are pushed to the margins of a married world (Simon, 1987). Even when this is considered a temporary position, as it is by most, it affects how single adults view their next life steps. Other markers of adulthood are often postponed, such as buying a house, having children, or planning for retirement, as they are seen as relevant only in the context of couplehood. Because there is no commonly agreed on blueprint for adults who remain single, their life course can look different from that of their married counterparts.

Feeling "deviant" with regards to marital status creates an added burden. In response to societal and family pressure to marry and this sense of deviance, one may make marital status an organizing feature of one's life, and then view the rest of one's life through this lens. A standard of adult development that emphasizes marriage and a traditional family only reinforces marriage as a gate to adulthood and does little to inform us about what makes a good life for single people. This lack of information can make it difficult to move out of a reactive position to the "standard" and find a comfortable definition of self as a single person.

This book is about helping our single clients create a different map for their lives that is not about waiting to be married, a map about developing an authentic life whether marriage occurs or not. We are defining single people as those who have never married or spent a majority of their adult life single. While even a short marriage may decrease the sense of stigmatization of being single, for the most part the issues remain the same. Newly divorced, widowed, and single people with children also will find common cause in our discussion, but addressing their specific issues and the way they change the single experience is beyond the scope of this book.

SINGLE IN A MARRIED WORLD

People are single for a variety of reasons, with their single status representing a wide array of experience and choice. Both the number of people staying single and the portion of some part of adult life spent single are growing due to various factors. According to the 1991 census report, 78% of men were unmarried at age 24, as opposed to only 53% single at age 24 in 1960. The rates for woman unmarried at 24 have increased from 28% in 1960 to 61% in 1991 (Bureau of the Census, 1992), suggesting a trend in delaying marriage. With the rate of divorce in first marriages almost 50% (Glick, 1984), and that in second marriages even higher, we cannot assume that marriage lasts a lifetime. A significant number of people experiences single status at some phase of life. This is particularly true for women, who outlive most men and have a decreasing pool of eligible marital partners as they age (Hicks & Anderson, 1989). The Women's Movement has also helped to expand the economic opportunities for women, making them less dependent on a husband.

While all these changes have certainly made being single more common, and while there have been enormous changes in what is an acceptable lifestyle, remaining single beyond a certain age is extremely uncomfortable for both men and women in America. We live in a world of couples and families, where singlehood really only has meaning in relation to marriage: it is the absence of marriage (Stein, 1981). When single status is used to categorize someone, to sum up his or her experience, the situation is automatically placed on a continuum, with marriage as the anchor point. A person is not yet married and therefore in the transitional phase of moving toward marriage, or has failed to get married and consequently in the decline away from marriageability. Either of these two positions defines a person as incomplete or missing something that is yet to happen or won't happen.

While the meaning and function of marriage may have changed over time, marriage as an institution has always been one of the main organizers of social relationships between the couple and society and between men and women. Marriage not only represents a desire for intimacy, but also has much greater meaning beyond the romantic joining of two people. It creates the context for the sanctioned way of expressing sexuality, raising children, and becoming part of the family-oriented community that is the norm of our society. Selecting a spouse often fixes where one fits in the social structure with respect to class and economics. This has been very significant for women, who have until recently been defined by the status of their spouses, as their own access to social and economic power has been limited. Mate choice also sends a message to the family about the desire for sameness or differentness from one's family of origin. Marrying outside the religion or ethnic group, for example, can be an attempt to set a boundary and influence the structure of the relationship between generations (Friedman, 1982).

Because marriage takes on meaning beyond the relationship of the couple, it is not surprising that being or remaining single at different stages of one's life is a complex experience, which goes beyond the phenomenon of just being alone. For the majority of people and for the culture as a whole, couplehood remains the desired state (Staples & Johnson, 1993). Even in the face of a 50% divorce rate for first marriages, most people want to marry and in fact do marry at some time in their lives. The absence of marriage leaves the adult in undefined territory, where there is no legitimate social role beyond a certain age. Almost all of our stereotypes about singles are negative, ranging from irresponsible and selfish to unfit or pathological. Without the structural shift of marriage to change one's place in the larger community, the single adult can feel locked into age-inappropriate roles (forever young or early spinsterhood) as expectations regarding behavior are shaped by single status.

Single women of any age continue to be viewed as sexual threats to the social comfort of a coupled society, as symbolized by the discrimination against and exclusion of single women from social clubs (Holloway, 1993). Whatever referent power is assigned women from their spouses is inaccessible to single women. While a single woman may have more opportunity to devote herself to career and money-making without the encumbrance of a spouse or children, she will still make less money than her male counterpart and, when in her twenties and thirties, be assumed to be less serious in her work, just waiting to marry (Holder & Anderson, 1989).

A single man beyond a certain age also suffers from a decrease in status and power, as he is seen as less stable or as not fitting the corporate model of family man. Without a woman, his masculinity may also become suspect, further decreasing his status (Gordon & Meth, 1990). The societal view of a single person as outside the normal social frame of reference is furthered by the devaluation of a single person's social network. When it is dismissed as part of a single scene and therefore merely transient, it is seen as less important than family as a source of social definition and of long-term support. This lack of validation from the mainstream culture imparts a sense of deviance, which may seriously limit the single person's ability to feel life is, at present, authentic or to envision other options beyond marriage for creating a rich, rewarding life.

SINGLE IN THE WORLD OF THE FAMILY

In addition to experiencing oneself as out of step with the wider society, the adult who remains single beyond the standard age range may also feel out of step with the norms of his or her own family. The family, perhaps the most powerful context influencing one's life (Carter & McGoldrick, 1989), not only transmits cultural messages but also transforms them to fit the particular generational legacies regarding the meaning and role of marriage that are specific to each family. The filters of ethnicity, class, race, and gendered expectations, as well as the unique multigenerational processes that have shaped the family, all contribute to the particular way the family responds when a family member remains single beyond young adulthood.

Most families define the eventual marriage of the children as part of the natural evolution of the family. It can signal to parents that they have successfully reared their children to "mature adulthood," especially in the eyes of the surrounding culture. The change in status from single to married often provides the impetus or context to realign relationships from parent/child to adult/adult, which then has an impact on all family relationships. Within the family, the shift from child to adult can be more difficult to negotiate without the boundary making ritual of marriage and the creation of a new nuclear family. A grown child's choice to remain single may also be experienced by the parents as a comment on their marriage. Opting not to marry may indeed feel like a reaction to whatever cautionary tales parents may have imparted about the impact of marriage on their lives. When both generations react to singlehood as a default status, it becomes an organizing construct in the family relationships.

MARRIAGE AS A LIFE CYCLE TASK

For many, marriage represents a personal life goal accomplishment. Although people can and do marry at any stage of their lives, the expectation persists that first marriages should take place in early adulthood, as part of the initiation into adulthood. While in fact the meaning and desire for marriage change over one's life, when the developmental milestone of achieving marriage in early adulthood is missed, it shapes the way other adult developmental markers are approached, such as developing financial viability apart from the family of origin.

Because gender training in managing the world presupposes a division of labor (and access to money and power) between heterosexual couples, certain adult tasks may be overemphasized or underemphasized by the single adult. Men, for example, generally have fewer skills and experience in developing and maintaining strong friendship networks. Indeed, much of their "gender training" has been to define masculinity as synonymous with autonomy and a denial of emotional needs. Combined with the homophobia or heterosexism many men in our culture experience (Lehne, 1976), this training makes male friendships elusive. Many men identify their wives or girl friends as their best friends, which suggests their reliance on women's greater ability to foster an intimate connection with others (Pasick, 1990). It is not surprising, then, that single men's social supports are much less substantial than single women's. This lack of connectedness has been correlated with greater mental and physical health problems for men on their own (Bernard, 1982).

Because finance is a male preserve, women frequently are not trained to take their finances seriously and therefore postpone financial planning. In our experience, women are less apt to buy a home for themselves, where men will do it as investment regardless of marital status. Society's judgment of where men and women should put their energies is also colored by gender expectations. We generally don't question a man's focus on career, while we might see a hardworking career woman as overcompensating for not having a family or not being suitable for family life. High achieving women are frequently seen as hard-bitten, while successful men are thought to be good catches. When marriage is viewed as one of the primary indicators of adulthood, not only may other accomplishments be delayed, but they may also be called into question, devalued, or dismissed as compensatory.

Whether it is experienced negatively or positively, being single at various life stages has an impact on how the rest of one's life path unfolds. Not understanding this impact and the different kinds of needs it generates — for example, for a wider circle of friends, or to make decisions on one's own about issues seen as couple or husband/wife decisions — is often what contributes to the single adult's feeling frozen in time. While marriage and parenthood provide many automatic structures and rituals to locate one's life along a fairly predictable life course, singlehood has very few signposts to mark the trail. Consider how many of our standard rituals and celebrations in daily life are centered around the formation and progression of the family. Because there is an expected time frame for marriage, and biological limits on the age for women to have children, for some the single status may become a hurdle to cross before other developmental issues are addressed. When this happens, the need to cross the hurdle becomes the focus in one's adult life. Rather than broaden the themes in the life story to include other definitions and developments of self, the life story becomes about the single status.

SINGLEHOOD AS AN ISSUE FOR THERAPY

This sense of being stuck and a general discomfort with singlehood often spurs a request for therapy. Despite the "problem" with singlehood emanating from many sources, such as marginalization by society, deviation from family expectations, lack of available partners, or a sense of dislocation in time, the single state is often experienced as a personal problem or failure because marriage is presumed to be a "natural" step in one's life. If the single adult is not blamed or does not blame him or herself, then family background is the "cause." Singlehood, in and of itself, becomes the "evidence" of immaturity or troubled family life. It is striking how this sense of personal or familial shortcoming and the anxiety it engenders take over the evaluation of one's life.

Because both therapist and client are embedded in the cultural context and share the collective anxiety of the culture, therapist and client may have difficulty separating themselves from the larger cultural ambivalence about the single state. This ambivalence flows from an overall confusion or disagreement over what constitutes a healthy adult and general intolerance of those outside of the mainstream. As a result, both therapist and client are constantly positioning themselves in reaction to the dominant discourse regarding singlehood. Together they struggle with the internalization of the cultural messages. This positioning leads to many therapeutic dilemmas that must be addressed when working with the single adult.

Let's return to the earlier vignettes for a moment. In each, we see a negative sense of self shaped by a social status viewed as inauthentic. In the first, Ann's intense feelings about singlehood are colored by her belief that her marital status is a personal failure. For her, marriage is the only desired goal and proof of health. This definition of the problem and the solution presents the therapist with a number of issues right from the beginning. The first is perhaps a familiar one, that the solution is in some way the problem. When there is such intense focus on marriage and forming a relationship, the resultant anxiety dooms the project from the start. But because marriage is a socially sanctioned goal, and because it appears to answer one's needs for intimacy and companionship, any attempt to move off the goal may be experienced as confirmation that the therapist thinks, yes, the client is in some way unmarriageable. Shifting the focus to trying to find a good life as a single person is like asking someone to live with a terminal illness or handicap. At the same time, working on the goal of forming a good relationship with a mate also confirms the single adult's sense that there is something wrong with her for not already being married. Ann, like many others, may show self-defeating behavior in relationships that interferes with her goal of marriage. The dilemma for the therapist becomes how to address problems in the client's relationships without making marriage the prize. This means that other relationships besides the longed-for partner relationship must be valued and used as arenas to learn and practice intimacy and the development of self.

Joanne's discomfort with her single status presents other aspects of the problem of being single in our culture. While she may feel that she has a good life, her assumptions about herself get called into question when others respond to her life as transient. Questions such as "When are you getting married?" or "What kind of wedding do you want?" place an emphasis on the future rather than the present. It is often difficult for both client and therapist to validate the present when there are so few positive role models of single people across the life span. Both therapist and client are in new territory. With someone like Joanne who values her work, both therapist and client need to counteract the tendency to look at relationships and career as two separate worlds.

Joanne also comes to therapy wrestling with the potential absence in her life of children in the context of a partnered relationship. Because men can father children until quite late in life, they can delay dealing with this aspect of remaining single. In reality, it is not an issue that gets dealt with once and for all—and then the client moves on. Like the absence of marriage, the absence of children has different meanings at each phase of the life cycle; it may recur as an issue, requiring different kinds of interventions.

For Joanne, as for many single people, a significant determinant of the quality of single life is whether there is a viable context for pleasurable sexual relationships, either in a friendship or in a committed relationship. Not having an outlet for one's sexual expression can reinforce the less than adult sense of self.

Working with Peter would present many of the same treatment dilemmas, as well as other issues specific to single men. Peter, for example, is much more comfortable discussing his problems at work than his emotional isolation. The latter feels more like his dirty little secret because, loneliness seems so unmanly. With work such a major source of identity for a man, it cannot be pushed aside; yet, the gender prescriptions must be challenged to increase the arenas for connection to the world.

As discussed before, most men don't know how to reach out to others, and because they often use sex as the bridge to intimacy (Meth, 1990a), end up limiting the range of possible relationships.

SHIFTING THE MEANING OF SINGLEHOOD

In this book, we have tried to place these therapeutic dilemmas into a multicontextual framework, a concept developed by Betty Carter (1994) to take into account the wider system, the family system, and the family life cycle. In doing so, we hope to broaden the issues of singlehood beyond the totally personal meaning that most people attach to it. Our thinking regarding the single adult and the therapy that follows from it are also based on Murray Bowen's family systems theory (Bowen, 1978), as expanded by Betty Carter and Monica McGoldrick to include the family life cycle and the broader societal context (Carter & McGoldrick, 1989).

The first step is to understand how the meanings of marriage and therefore of singleness are influenced by the economic and political times. Chapter 2 will look in more detail at this, particularly as depicted by the popular culture. When an understanding of wider cultural issues informs the therapy, options open up for both the therapist and the single client. Chapter 3 looks closely at how the meaning of marital status operates within a multigenerational context, with examples of how differences in cultural background help structure the individual and family experience. The next section of the book presents a modification of the family life cycle that takes into account the differences in development that are created in the single person's life when the "expected" life course does not unfold. Having a sense of options in one's own growth — with or without marriage — is key

HAROLD BRIDGES LIBRARY
S. MARTIN'S COLLEGE
LANCASTER

in expanding the sense of choice regarding marriage or singlehood. Section III presents clinical examples of our work with single clients through different stages of the life cycle.

Throughout this book we talk about a way of doing therapy that addresses all three levels of reaction to singlehood—the personal, the familial, and the societal. While attempting to depathologize singleness, we do not discount the desire for connectedness in relationships or trivialize the discomfort of being out of the mainstream. As family therapists, we locate the single adult in the multigenerational flow of the family, as well as in the developing family life cycle. Yet we acknowledge the differences that are created in life cycle development when a major milestone is not experienced within the expected time frame. Ultimately, we propose a model for thinking about singlehood that moves it out of a marginal limbo. This will, we hope, enable single adults to experience their life as authentic in the present whether marriage is in the future or not.

The Couples Culture
and the Single Adult

PEOPLE LIVING AND WORKING within a larger social system tend to evaluate themselves by the criteria of that system. By that standard, single people, living in a culture in which the majority of people are married, cannot help but evaluate their lives in relationship to the institution of marriage. As a result their definitions of self must always lack a quality that the larger system values. To understand the full scope of how this negative attribute affects people, it is important to examine the meaning that the dominant culture assigns to marriage.

As family therapists we know that it is important to look at the themes and relationships in previous generations to understand how our own parents developed their ideas and abilities to parent. Similarly, to understand the values Americans presently hold about marriage and family, we need to look to previous generations to see how these ideas evolved.

This chapter will look at how marriage and family were seen from the fifties through the nineties, since World War II and its aftermath continue to influence our culture today.

THE 1950s: REALIZATION OF
THE AMERICAN DREAM

Of all the influences on Americans in the 1950s, the needs of the expanding post-war economy had the most profound impact on people's lives. The immediate pressure for women to leave the workplace so that men returning from combat could regain their jobs translated into newsreels and movies of women doing their patriotic duty of rearing children and baking apple pies. Employment opportunities in an expanding economy enabled middle-class men with ambition to move up the professional ladder and blue-collar workers to find stable employment. Because of the "family wage system," in which men's salaries were supposed to support the entire family, the social structure of men working and women tending the home fires became an almost a universal ideal. This structure became a goal symbolizing upward mobility. In fact, men took pride in the fact that their wives did not have to work (Ehrenreich, 1983).

Although the society accepted this ideal wholeheartedly, it locked women and men into a somewhat unfortunate financial interdependency. Women were dependent on men to raise their standard of living, since even if they did work their wages would not support them. This, in fact, upped the ante for women to marry. Although men were also expected to marry, many were fearful of what was then experienced as lifetime responsibility, since the full burden of family finances weighed heavily on them (Ehrenreich, 1983).

Nevertheless, expectations to marry and fulfill oneself completely through this process were extremely high. Marriage was idealized, to say the least. "Patriotism, prosperity, and parenthood reigned" (Lang, 1991). By 1957, in fact, 96% of Americans of marriageable age were married (Eisler, 1986). Americans in the 1950s were focused on marrying, having children and raising them. "The increase was most spectacular among college women; they were abandoning careers to bear four, five and six or more children," wrote historian William Manchester (1973, p. 22).

Education for women began to slide. Only 35% of college students were women, compared with 40% before World War II. Of those who did go to college during this period two-thirds dropped out, including our previous First Lady, Barbara Bush. Most dropped out to help their husbands in their careers or "headed off in search of greener husband hunting territories" (Lang, 1991, p. 34).

The value placed on marriage during the 1950s was completely new. At no time in the history of the United States had there been such an emphasis on finding all of life's satisfactions within the nuclear family (Coontz, 1992). Since this notion was supported in every area of public life, single people felt particularly out of the mainstream and acutely disadvantaged during this era. Television, the powerful infant of the 1950s, both picked up messages from the culture and profoundly influenced it as well. Situation comedies proliferated, glorifying white middle-class suburban life. *Leave it to Beaver, Ozzie and Harriet, Father Knows Best* — all reflected families who were happy in their "intactness" and in the upwardly mobile suburbs.

The messages to marry, to propagate, to acquire more possessions, and to advance one's social status were everpresent. Even the much adored and seemingly innocuous *I Love Lucy* show advanced this notion. Underlying the pranks and get-rich schemes were clear expectations that Lucy, Desi, and the Mertzes were couples who were on their way. *The Honeymooners* and *The Life of Riley* also depicted families who laughed and bantered but clearly aimed to raise their social class (Taylor, 1989). The middle-class wisdom of these shows implied that there was enough to go around in a society rooted in benign, happy, traditional family life.

Single people weren't the only group that the popular culture did not reflect. People of color and homosexuals were almost completely invisible. Despite the fact that 25% of American families were poor, these shows reflected only the "good life." The American economy needed the ever constant expectation for people to move into the middle class, with acquisition of the material goods that reflected this status. The message was both overt in advertisements for shiny new cars, homes, and appliances, and covert in television storylines implying that consumerism was good (Coontz, 1992).

The needs of the expanding economy were serviced by the proliferation and purchases of consumer goods. Nearly the entire increase in the gross national product in the mid 1950s, in fact, was due to increased spending on consumer durables and residential construction, mostly for nuclear families (May, 1988).

What emerged from this pressured push for marriage, family, and consumerism was a distinct focus on what was "normal." Supporting the correctness of traditional family life came the entrance of "experts" into American consciousness. Turning for advice to baby books, marriage manuals, and even psychoanalytic literature, Americans became consumers of "observed self consciousness" (Ehrenreich & English, 1978). The psychological material available to the public very much supported the notion of home and family as "developmental tasks." In 1953 psychologist R. J. Havinghurst conceptualized eight tasks of early adulthood. The list affected the consciousness of the nation, and as such was repeated for the next three decades in many different forms and by many different representatives of the culture. It included the following: (1) selecting a mate, (2) learning to live with a marriage partner, (3) starting a family, (4) rearing children, (5) managing a home, (6) getting started in an occupation, (7) taking on civic responsibilities, and (8) finding a congenial social group (Ehrenreich, 1983).

Marriage became proof of maturity, the only acceptable way to move into the adult world. Deviations in performing this transitional task became pathological, a term that made its way from psychoanalytic literature into the popular culture. Ehrenreich (1983) cites Dr. Paul Popenjoe, who appeared regularly in *The Ladies Home Journal*, where he blamed bachelorhood on "emotional immaturity and infantile fixations" and referred to unmarried women as biological inferiors and discards who do not offer good matrimonial prospects. Is it any wonder that in 1957, 80% of Americans polled said that people who chose not to marry were "sick, neurotic, and immoral" (Coontz, 1992).

The experts who defined the "correct way" to live very much supported the American dream. This dream locked the culture into such rigid notions of psychological correctness that it influenced Americans for decades to come. Images of proper living denied the actual diversity in America, particularly the significant amount of poverty in this country. The dream persisted despite the fact that many people were living in circumstances that excluded them from being part of it. At a time when ethnic and racial minorities were almost entirely excluded from the gains of the white middle class, for example, many people did not have a "household to manage."

Marriage, a family, and a home were definitely equated with normalcy. The fact that after the losses in World War II not everybody could have an available potential partner was never an issue for the popular mythology of the day.

Sexual mores in the 1950s were quite restrictive and were based on a double standard between women and men. Women, who were supposed to save themselves for marriage bore the responsibility to hold the sexual line, whereas it was considered natural for men to be sexually aggressive. These sexual mores were not only unequal but also quite confusing, and ultimately led to a profusion in early marriages (Coontz, 1992).

The conformity of American society in the 1950s clearly left very little room for those people who remained single. Not only did single people experience themselves as peripheral to the larger society, but they were also very much aware that they were labeled as deviants. This was particularly true for women. As Ehrenreich and English wrote about the typical single woman, "She might be brilliant, famous, visibly pleased with herself, successful in every way—but the judgment hung over her that she had failed as a woman" (1978, p. 287).

Interestingly enough, the conformity of "normal life" didn't suit everyone. The popularity of books like *The Man in the Grey Flannel Suit*, for example, reflected a growing discomfort with massive conformity. The 1957 cult film, *The Invasion of the Body Snatchers*, satirized the paranoid McCarthy era. Both works depicted people in the culture as automated creatures locked into a soulless life. The startling popularity of Elvis Presley's overt sexuality reflected some of the dissatisfaction with the restrictions of this era.

Despite the evidence of these dissatisfactions, as well as a sense of emptiness beneath the dream, the American mainstream persisted with this dream far into the turbulence of the next decade.

THE 1960s: WHAT THE REVOLUTION WAS ALL ABOUT AND HOW IT AFFECTED OUR NOTIONS OF FAMILY

The coming of age of the greatest number of young people in this century during the 1960s was felt with tremendous force throughout the United States. The convulsions this society experienced during this era were no doubt influenced by the millions of young people moving into adulthood at this time. Authors offered a myriad of explanations for the dismemberment of the social structure, ranging from the permissiveness of the parents of the Dr. Spock generation to the revolutionary impact of books like *The Greening of America* (Michener, 1993). There is no question, however, that the 1960s saw the underpinnings of the basic values of American life become "unglued."

While young people were witnessing an adult world attempting to conform to somewhat rigid moralistic values of family life, they were also being barraged with information from the media that presented outright contradictions to these values. In the larger community, events were developing which, thanks to television, were exploding into the livingrooms of this country. Civil rights confrontations, previously written about in newspapers, were now being observed by people as they happened. The sight of African-American civil rights marchers being hosed and clubbed by law enforcement officials brought into question the legitimacy of authority for many young adults (Coontz, 1992).

Not only were the overt actions of the law enforcement officials open to question, but the underlying issues that were being confronted also exposed the hypocrisy of the status quo. The civil rights that were being demanded, in fact, were already supposed to be the law of the land!

In November of 1963 President John F. Kennedy was brutally murdered. Here was a President who not only appealed to the youth of the country by his appearance and demeanor but also involved them in building a new society. After seeing this terrible event repeated over and over on their television sets, people then witnessed the violent and unlawful death of the man who was accused of Kennedy's murder. Less than five years later, Martin Luther King, the humanist and proponent of nonviolent protest, was also murdered. The pain and confusion following these tragedies set the stage for a major societal upheaval in response to the expansion of an extremely unpopular war.

The American buildup in Vietnam, which started in the administration of President John Kennedy, continued and expanded throughout the decade of the 1960s. This war was different from World War II, since the issues were much more confusing to many people. When people actually witnessed the battles on their television sets, it was impossible to ignore the horrors of war. As the 1960s became the 1970s, this war, which exacted a high cost in American and Vietnamese lives, showed no sign of abating. It became, in fact, a symbol of misguided policy and outright betrayal by the government. Many soldiers who had enlisted with the idea of saving the world from Communism became painfully disillusioned (Tischler, 1989).

For the first time since World War II, significant numbers of citizens resisted the government's judgment and profoundly questioned its morality. The nation was deeply divided about this war, with older adults joining with young people in questioning the status quo. Conflicts between deeply patriotic people and those who nevertheless questioned the authority of the government changed the idea of the consumer society's moral correctness forever (Coontz, 1992).

The family had been the focus of the moral integrity of the nation in the fifties. With the ethical structure of the entire nation in question, the moral structure of the family also came under attack. The gender role structure that had been the basis for the traditional family of the 1950s began to loosen. Betty Friedan's landmark book, *The Feminine Mystique*, published in 1963, opened up minds to feminist thinking. Its huge popularity represented the fact that American women were ready for this change. Certainly many people—both men and women—were stifled and disillusioned by the marriages of the 1950s (Coontz, 1992).

During the sixties women entered the work force in significant numbers. Many families needed two wages to support the consumer lifestyles they had created. Increased awareness of the limits of women's positions in the 1950s marriages, along with growing financial power, opened the way to new feminist thought.

Schooled in the civil rights and anti-war movements, early feminists were ready to question the holy grail of the gender-based social structure. In consciousness-raising groups, books and magazine articles, women questioned the old facts of family life. "The immutable maternal instinct, the sanctity of 'vaginal orgasms' as representative of female emotional maturity, the child's need for exclusive mothering, the theory of female masochism, all the shibboleths of mid-century psychomedical theory, shriveled in the light of feminist thinking" (Ehrenreich & English, 1978, p. 315).

Whether or not women developed their thinking as feminists, the questioning of gender stereotypes affected the families of our nation in many powerful ways. Certainly complete acceptance of the status quo of family life was a thing of the past.

Equally significant to the feminist revolution, and in many ways interwoven with it was the sexual revolution. The growth of a significant counterculture who rebelled against what they saw as the hypocrisy of the older generation's values had a profound impact on the wider culture. Not only did this culture reject materialism, but in rejecting rigid moral values it also opened up possibilities for much more liberal sexual mores. The development and more widespread use of birth control methods made sexual activity outside of marriage more acceptable (Coontz, 1992).

Later in the decade, this openness affected the homosexual movement as well, as gay men and lesbians began to question the exclusive definition of sexual freedom in terms of heterosexuality. Societal repression of homosexual activity had severely affected the expression of sexuality in their community, since most of the time they could not be open. In 1969, riots occurred at the Stonewall bar in New York City's Greenwich Village; this marked a turning point, with more gays and lesbians becoming defiantly activist (Silverstein, 1991). Gradually more rights were secured than ever before, although homosexuals continued to be marginalized in the larger society. Nevertheless, the successes of these efforts led to more pride and ultimately to increased openness in the gay community (see Chapter 10).

The many changes in gender relationships and sexual openness affected family life in somewhat contradictory ways. While these trends created more flexibility in family relationships, people were left struggling to sort out new roles.

Certainly there has been much backlash to the Women's Movement, ranging from outright media attacks against the new order to major marital imbalances that left people feeling confused and uncertain (Faludi, 1991). Such backlash to the changing roles of men and women did not, however, stop the changes. It just added uneasiness to the shifting social structure. Many questions were being asked — with few answers.

Violence continued to envelop the nation, with the deaths of the leaders of the decade: Bobby Kennedy, Medgar Evers, and Malcolm X. With the continued escalation of the Vietnam War, and the devastation that was witnessed, a pervasive cynicism enveloped the nation. Everything that was previously associated with their parents' morality was seen as suspect by young people. The symbolism of many anti-war movement slogans, like "Make Love Not War," suggested that previous generations hypocritically concerned themselves with chastity as a moral issue but permitted violence. Many of the young acted out their disillusionment by dropping out of middle-class lives and becoming involved with open sex and drugs. This confrontation of the entire moral and social structure led people to seriously questioning the "holy grail" of family life. As a result, many young adults chose other options than marriage or else married later in life.

For the first time, people began spending a significant period of time on their own and away from their families. As a result, a sizable singles population developed (Coontz, 1992). This population, having few role models, developed its own unique value structure and its own set of mores. Somewhat more liberated than their counterparts in the 1950s, they nevertheless continued to experience alienation from the larger society.

A singles industry quickly developed in response to this alienation. It provided a proliferation of activities geared to the supposed tastes of this population. This industry provided both a guide to a lifestyle heretofore unknown (and certainly unheralded) and an image that was often distorted and difficult to emulate. The groundbreaking *Sex and the Single Girl* by Helen Gurley Brown (1962) was an early contribution to the development of an image that was both liberating and misleading. Most single girls as well as single boys of the 1960s were hard-pressed to imitate the sexual prowess of the images suggested.

Guidelines for men and women had previously been clear. The new expectations were confusing at best and, for those who remained single, almost nonexistent. The single people of the 1960s shared the uneasiness of the times. The old structure had been rejected, but there were no new rules to follow.

THE 1970s: AMERICA MOVES INTO HARD TIMES

The shifts in family structure that started in the 1960s continued and escalated throughout the next decade. Although there were many factors contributing to these changes, one significant precipitant was the deteriorating economic climate.

The country's move into a series of deep recessions brought unemployment for many, and for others severe drops in "real income." Coontz notes that "between 1929 and 1932, during the Great Depression, per capita income fell by 27%. Between 1973 and 1986, the median income of families headed by a person under 30 fell by almost the same amount" (1992, p. 261).

This financial devastation, obviously, played havoc with people's lives. Typically, it was felt most severely by people who could least afford it — people who had limited educational opportunities and limited prospects. The poverty rate for young married couples with children doubled between 1973 and 1988 (Coontz, 1992).

Economic instability placed additional pressures on families, increasing stressors on marriages and parenting. Even those people who managed to maintain their living standards felt more pressed for quality time with their families, since they had to focus more on work. Government cutbacks fell hard on the blue-collar occupations and urban regions, which particularly affected African-American communities (Zinn & Eitzen, 1987). Despite the perceptions of the rest of the world, clearly the era of middle-class aspirations for everyone in America was over.

It was no longer possible for most families to be supported by one wage earner. Although in the 1970s 78% of married women under age 45 said they believed it was better for men to earn the family living and women to be homemakers, the decline in the family's "real income" made two wage earners a necessity (Van Horn, 1988). Unprecedented numbers of mothers entered the labor force in the 1970s, bringing the growth rate of women in the labor force to 41% (Van Horn, 1988). Obviously, the numbers of working women in families had a tremendous impact on the structure of marriage and family life.

For African-Americans the changes had to do mainly with the increased stresses that financial hardships had on family life. Because of the labor practices where black workers often filled the jobs left by white workers, black workers lost their jobs when the economy dipped. As a result, this community suffered severe financial setbacks during this period. The long historical pattern of role sharing between husband and wife, however, served as a buffer and support against this harsh reality (Staples & Johnson, 1993).

In Caucasian families the family structure had been traditionally based on the man being the wage earner and the woman remaining at home rearing the children. When women moved into the economic marketplace, profound changes were experienced in the operations of family life. The changing responsibilities between husbands and wives placed pressure on marriages, since household chores were now added to marital systems with very little time to spare. With women now working outside of the home, many were still responsible for household tasks. More of these chores were shared by husbands, but rarely at a level commensurate with the number of hours women put in at work.

Although women inevitably wound up working what actually could be considered a double shift, the amount of selfhood they gained by employment outside of the home not only was experienced as a profound source of satisfaction but also promoted changes in the power relationships between husbands and wives (Hochschild & Machung, 1989). The feminist movement in this country was strengthened by these changes and provoked even further shifts in the way women and men operated together. In marriages this took the form of challenging long-term roles.

Jessie Bernard's 1982 book, *The Future of Marriage*, reflected the questions people were having about roles in marriages. Her research on marriage, for example, indicated that women and men experienced this institution very differently. Marriage was experienced so differently, in fact, that one could almost say that there were two separate marriages—"his" marriage and "hers" (Bernard, 1982). Bernard pointed out that, even though men might rail against marriage, on the whole they experienced it as a much more satisfying institution than did women. The women who were interviewed, for the most part, reported a lowering of life satisfactions in marriage. This was due to the differences between what they expected in the married state and what they actually experienced. They were generally not prepared to deal with the unacknowledged expectations to conform to their husband's demands, as well as the abrupt lowering of status between the courtship period and the married state.

Contrary to the messages from the larger society that marriage was the only viable state for women, single women fared much better in terms of mental and physical health than their married counterparts. Single men, on the other hand, fared much worse than married men on measures of mental and physical health.

Bernard's book supported the notion that the traditional family and gender structure was no longer meeting the needs of men and, particularly, women. As the economy increasingly required two working parents, it necessitated drastic alterations in family life.

While these societal shifts changed family structure, they also changed the expectations and behavior of single adults. Not only were single people questioning conventional interactions in dating behavior, but they were also looking beyond tradition to see what changed expectations meant for future marriages. While there were no wholesale transformations, people started challenging time-honored gender roles prescribing active and passive positions for men and women. Standards that were previously unquestioned were now uncertain. Who calls for a date? Who pays? What would a potential partner think if you broke the rules? While these questions certainly added more anxiety to dating, they also opened up possibilities for new behavior.

Economic pressures and changing role relationships certainly played havoc with families during the 1970s. The divorce rate practically doubled in this decade, profoundly affecting the forms and expectations of family life (Ehrenreich, 1983). Divorced people had few guideposts to follow and often functioned within complex logistical and legal requirements. While financial supports, child-care arrangements, and single-parent authority issues were of primary concern, these newly single adults needed to be with other singles and reentered the dating world.

Suddenly, a new group of single people entered the consciousness of the American culture. More previously married single people, many with children, became visible. Not only did these people have to balance all of the complications of single-parent families, but they also had to manage dating relationships. Even with organizations like Parents Without Partners, many found themselves too overwhelmed with responsibilities to negotiate in a singles world. For these single people and their families, there were no role models. Few people knew how to balance their own adult needs while also meeting the needs of their children. While remarrying seemed like a solution for many people, few were prepared for the problems this would introduce (McGoldrick & Carter, 1989).

Meanwhile, the problems in the economy resulted in delayed first marriages. When people did marry, most delayed having children, so that fewer children were born overall. In the 1970s women reproduced at a record low rate of 1.7 babies each (Lang, 1991). At the same time, the numbers of women achieving college degrees increased dramatically, enabling women to enter the work force on a different level from previous generations. There was an overall awareness that the economy had permanently changed and that women were now expected to participate in families as "breadwinner."

In 1978, I (NS) recall speaking to a colleague who was the father of a young woman. He remarked that he knew things were changing when he began to worry that his daughter may not have chosen the right occupation to make a living. In contrast, he recalled his father worrying that his daughter might not be able to marry and find somebody to take care of her. Many people shared my colleague's sense of change. There was a certain amount of anxiety present in the larger society, a sense that the simpler times were gone forever. The Watergate crisis and the subsequent resignation of the President of the United States added a sense of disillusionment to the frustrations involved with the downturn in the economy.

With less free time available, the American people turned to television for easy and inexpensive entertainment. Television not only reflected the anxieties and disillusionment of the times but had its own effects. In television narratives the concerns of the time were articulated and, in the particular ways of television, resolved. In contrast to the harmonious families of the 1950s and 1960s, domestic life of the 1970s comedies and dramas was in turmoil. Shows that depicted minority families and divorced families, as well families with more serious problems, entered the livingrooms of America. In the sitcoms of this era characters tended to represent social issues, and the arguments that took place reflected the tensions between tradition and modernity, between women and men, between generations, classes, and social groups (Taylor, 1989).

The anger that lay beneath the surface in past decades opened up as a result of the financial setbacks in this era, as well as the dismantling of many of the social controls. This was expressed in the comedies of this period, and in many ways had a cathartic effect. The immense popularity of the *All in the Family* and other shows centered on social issues spoke to the need for this kind of public airing of previously hidden topics (Taylor, 1989).

Equally relevant to this era were the shows portraying work families.

The success of *The Mary Tyler Moore* show and *M*A*S*H* generated a series of shows with occupational settings. Essentially, what these shows accomplished was a shift in focus from the traditional family to a benign surrogate work family. Characters in these sitcoms were provided with the stability and nurturance in the workplace that was missing from the vision of "home" in the 1970s (Taylor, 1989).

Television depicted strong, competent women for the first time, illustrating the possibility of women surviving well on their own. It also gave the message that single people could be happy and were capable of forming surrogate families. These shows accurately picked up the mood of this era. Responding to people's need for new guidelines to follow, they illustrated ways one could survive without traditional home and family life.

Difficult as it was to live through this era, many positive changes seem to have occurred. Movements to expand the rights of previously disenfranchised groups were successful and many laws were enacted to pave the way for social equality. The rights of unmarried couples and gays and lesbians were expanded, reducing the state's power to define normalcy (Coontz, 1992).

Some of the changes that started in the 1960s moved to a different level. Sexual relationships outside of marriage were not seen as a revolution anymore, but became an accepted part of normal life. People no longer entered marriages primarily for the purpose of sexual gratification. At the same time, people who remained single were freer to satisfy these needs.

At the end of this era, the structure of marriage seemed to have been changed permanently. Many different family forms were considered normal, including a large and growing singles population. Single people were no longer hidden. They were now reflected in television and movies, and industries that catered to them were blossoming.

THE 1980s: THE BOOM YEARS

The economics of the 1980s divided the larger society along class lines, widening the gap between the "haves" and the "have-nots" to an unprecedented degree. After a recession in 1982, the country gradually moved into an economic recovery. This recovery, however, did not raise the living standards across the board. In fact, the government figures showing rising averages obscured the growing polarization of incomes. In 1987 income inequality was greater than at the height of the earlier recession. Opportunities for those in the poorer sectors of society decreased rapidly as half of the new jobs created in the 1980s paid a wage lower than the poverty figure for a family of four. (Mishel & Frankel, 1991). As economic and social safety nets unraveled, more people fell into the ranks of the poor; moreover, 40% of the poor had incomes less than half the amount designated as poverty level by the federal government (Whitman, 1990).

The "haves," although financially successful, in many cases felt their level of achievement was precarious. Some were making money at young ages and living in tremendously inflated ways, while others were struggling with multiple jobs and pressured living situations.

The value of "making it" in American society is shared across races and classes. When so many struggling people witnessed others making enormous amounts of money in activities unrelated to providing any kind of goods or services, it affected the moral consciousness of the country. The reaction to Wall Street speculators, corporate raiders, HUD bandits, and S&L criminals was, unfortunately, that only "suckers" worked for low salaries. In fact, it was a fitting commentary on the times that Tom Wolfe's "morality play" book, *Bonfire of the Vanities*, became the smash hit of the 1980s.

Coontz (1992) commented that the cynicism this kind of economic climate engendered in people was acted out in the withdrawal of interest in community support. The developing family found itself trying to survive in a sea of pressures and cynicism — far from ideal for healthy functioning. At the same time, the country's political swing to the right brought with it exhortations to return to "traditional family values." Many of the country's ills were placed on "the decaying family."

Although attitudes had moved in a conservative direction, it didn't change the tide of divorce. The 1991 demographic statistics, reflecting family structural changes of the 1980s, indicated that one-fifth of white children, one-third of hispanic children, and one-half of black children were living in "mother only" homes (Ahrons, 1994). Alternative family structures and alternative lifestyles were here to stay.

The gay and lesbian movement brought many inequities of the larger system into focus, and while the overall culture may have shifted to the right, some legal decisions were being made to protect these minorities (Adam, 1987).

Later in the decade, when the economy had taken a severe downturn, many middle- and lower-class families were affected, as jobs were cut back and people laid off. Economic tensions once again opened the way for blaming the deterioration of the family for the country's ills. The result of this mood was a backlash against any movement that was seen as "destroying" the American family. The backlash was directed against any number of so-called deviant populations: "selfish parents" who divorced rather than rear the children in a two-parent home, gays, singles, "militant African-Americans," and finally, women who embraced feminist values. These women were seen as fundamentally to blame for abandoning the ethic of care that was the backbone of American family life (Faludi, 1991).

The television world attempted to illustrate some of the issues of the period by portraying varieties of domestic life in the United States. Workplace shows were vastly different from before. *Cagney and Lacy, Thirtysomething, L.A. Law,* and finally, *Hill Street Blues* all reflected the moral confusions of the day. Not only were there pulls between career and home life, but the job itself presented moral ambiguities not previously presented on television. Gone was the workplace as a benign substitute for a confusing family life.

The unprecedented success of *The Cosby Show*, which aired in 1984 and ran to the end of the decade and beyond, represented the national hunger for normalcy and structure. In the Cosbys, we have an example of a family surviving the political and economic times in great style. The Cosbys, in fact, represent a return to an intact family, but with some slight variance from 1950. Mother works in an equally prestigious job as father, but, of course, has all the time in the world for her husband and children. Parents return to an all-knowing position, and the world was right again for one half-hour on Thursday evenings (Taylor, 1989).

THE 1990s

The world of the 1990s was certainly not all right. This decade opened with bitter struggles being fought over abortion rights, minority rights, and governmental apportionment of money, with all sides claiming the moral high ground. The presidential election of 1992 embodied that struggle, with the battleground being over the values and problems of American families. Society again focused on family values rather than the deterioration of the economic underpinnings of these families.

Certainly the constant, open struggle over what is normal and what is abnormal in living situations in the 1990s is quite different from the decades immediately after World War II, when none but the most rigid picture of home and intact family life was considered proper. There was not even room for a difference of opinion in this arena, much less open warfare.

The large numbers of single people now living in this country are mostly centered in large urban areas. They are living at a time when families are no longer seen as idealized containers of civilization. The traditional family appears to be under question in all areas, particularly when the media portrays alternative types of families as viable options. In fact, tradition in general is being questioned.

The singles population, incorporating huge numbers of previously married people, is growing larger and much more visible. One would think that this would be the ideal time for single people to live. Nevertheless, single people continue to feel alienated from the larger society, and those who enter therapy in the 1990s still feel acutely aware of their "differentness." Many still long for the safety, normalcy, and connectedness of married life. The reason for this apparent anomaly is important to understand.

Unfortunately, no matter how much the traditional foundations of our society have changed, there are substantial lags in the establishment of institutional structures that truly support a lifestyle deviant from mainstream culture. Also, despite appearances, the media has lagged in wholeheartedly endorsing a singles lifestyle. While a multitude of different family forms do proliferate, on television the underlying subtexts in these programs, as well as within the accompanying advertisements, support the 1990s version of venerated love and marriage.

Too many single people are still being portrayed as silly, as in the TV show *Seinfeld*, vulnerable, as in the movie *Single White Female*, or predatory, as in *Pacific Heights*. Nowhere can single people, heterosexual or homosexual, observe role models who are thoughtful and well developed people.

Not only have there been inadequate role models for single people to observe in the media, but there has also been few role models within the main institutions that organize adult life in American culture. In fact, for the most part these institutions — *work, spirituality, and community* — are still organized around marriage and family. This is not immediately obvious, since when small changes are reported in the news it gives the overall impression that major changes are happening (Williams, 1994). As a result, single people wind up blaming themselves for not achieving a connected and meaningful life.

Most work systems, for example, are subtly organized around a premise of family life. Christmas parties, dinner dances, and corporate picnics are typically arranged with the wife or husband in mind. As people move up in work systems, the enormous responsibilities of executives are almost impossible to manage without a "spousal support staff" working behind the scenes to arrange for dinner parties, car pooling, and maintaining contacts with relatives.

The fact that women's salaries continue to be lower than men's across the nation keeps single women in the uncomfortable position of not quite being able to make it on their own. This fact continues to place women in the position of needing to marry to raise their standard of living.

Although they enjoy income possibilities that exceed those of women, men's work life may still be affected by their single status. In a survey of fifty major corporations in 1981, for example, 80% of the heads of responding companies stated that single executives tended to make snap judgments, and 25% said that singles were less stable than married people (Stein, 1981). Although these stereotypes continue to change as companies become less conservative, many singles still perceive themselves to be on the outside of informal work structures.

Since the work system is highly significant to single people as a source of livelihood and as a socialization network, potential problems in this area can become quite threatening to their well-being. When, as too often is the case, work systems are not sensitive to their needs, single people feel different, excluded and sometimes even exploited.

For example, as more companies are relying on a mobile work force, single people are seen as being more transient than their married counterparts. Since friendship networks are the most important support systems single people have outside of work, they risk the disruption of their major emotional supports when asked to move alone to another city. When businesses are not sensitive to this issue, single people can easily experience themselves as dispensable.

The lack of sensitivity to the needs of single people can also be seen in church communities. Although more and more religious institutions, particularly in urban areas, are becoming aware of their single members, few are aware of what single people require to feel included.

Certainly, negative messages about sexuality outside of the institution of marriage target single people. A less apparent but equally important message, however, is that there is usually no clear path for the single person to follow as a member of the church community. When the rhythm of formal religious life is centered around marriage and birth, single people experience themselves on the outside of life's important events. The more single people feel that their needs are not reflected by the institutions in which they participate, the more they feel peripheral to society. People may not be immediately aware of how much this sense of marginality affects their well-being.

In this same light, the fact that the culture exalts family forms that are not accessible to single people trivializes the world in which they live. The most important adult emotional connections single people have are often with their friends. As Willa Cather wrote, "Only solitary people know the full joys of friendship. Others have their families, but to a solitary and an exile his friends are everything" (in Holland, 1992). The friendship networks single people develop are experienced as every bit as important as blood relatives, but are not treated this way by the institutions in which they participate.

This message is echoed by the families from which single people emerge. The friendship system is seen by most families as secondary—one which should be sacrificed if a blood relative is in need. Parents, emerging from the more rigid value structures of the 1950s and 1960s, continue to believe that their job has not been completed until their children are "safely married." Their children's ability to form loving and committed friendship systems is not enough evidence of their successful negotiation of the adult world. As a result, single adults get messages from all around that their lives are incomplete.

In one sense single people are no longer invisible, since their lives are now depicted in television and in movies. Advertisements show sexy singles meeting each other in exotic places, and companies are putting out food products that can be consumed by "one." At the same time the real needs of single people to be validated as complete people and to participate fully in the institutions of society are not being met. As long as they experience their lives as peripheral to the important "goings on" in the world, they will experience their state as painful — one which must be changed at any cost.

3

Culture and Family

RICHARD CAME OF AGE in the sixties, when marriage was not on the mind of most of his peers. He had several long-term relationships but never married. He had some regrets about this but overall valued his flexibility and freedom. His parents had, he felt, been remarkably tolerant of this — they even jokingly called his dog their grandchild. That is, until his father had a heart attack. In the aftermath and recovery, both parents, in their separate ways, began anxiously questioning his plans for the future and expressed concern about when he would settle down. It was news to him that he wasn't "settled."

Why would Richard's parents react in this way? Despite shifts in the wider society's feelings about singlehood, which this family had accommodated, the meaning of such charged issues as marital status change for a family over time. The change may be precipitated by an event such as Richard's father's heart attack, which may then trigger issues based on the family's own idiosyncratic history and ethnic and racial heritage.

For example, both parents had been the rebels in their family. His father had eschewed his parents' Jewish orthodoxy and his mother had left behind her what she saw as a rigid Catholic upbringing. Their marriage had been a cause célèbre, creating a cut-off in both extended families. For them an intense marriage had been the way to repair the wound of the disconnection from family. The crisis of the father's heart attack and possible death shook the balance in the family. The anxiety about the father's health became focused on Richard's marital status and lack of future family.

In Chapter 2 we talked about how the social and political context influences the family, and how the family's structure, roles, and gender expectations are often a mirror of societal values. In this chapter we look at two things: (1) how the family's own history as an emotional system and its multigenerational legacies become a filter for the wider cultural messages, and (2) how other spheres of influence, such as race, ethnicity, and class, contribute to this context.

The family system and the culture in which it is embedded are not really separable with respect to understanding a family's experience. They form a reciprocal system, where culture shapes family and then family experience shapes the fit with the culture. The family also influences what aspects of the culture are continued. In an ongoing process, culture and family together define the rules of family life and patterns of relating. This is particularly clear when we look at families who are in a one-down position with respect to the dominant culture and have had to cope with the effects of racism and economic disadvantage. Family structure and process are inextricably shaped by these realities (Boyd-Franklin, 1989). Given the age in which we live, we cannot talk about cultural context as one-dimensional or homogeneous; instead we must recognize the diversity of influences on the family (Szapocznik & Kurtines, 1993). For the purposes of clarity regarding our theoretical base, however, we have separated our discussion of family process from our discussion of culture.

FAMILY

When we talk about family, we are using the theoretical perspective developed by Murray Bowen (1978), which describes the family as a natural system, spanning several generations, which functions with both order and predictability in its relationships. His concepts of triangles, differentiation, fusion, and anxiety form the basis for our thinking about how the emotional system of the family operates. The concepts also indicate points of entry for therapy. Our use of these concepts, which we will discuss below, has also been greatly influenced by others who have elaborated and expanded Bowen's work. Foremost are Carter and McGoldrick (1989), who in their conceptualization of the family life cycle have provided a structure to understand the movement of families from generation to generation (vertical), as well as across time (horizontal). This overlay of the family life cycle on Bowen theory is key in understanding the impact of living a life that does not follow the "expected" or usual life course. Carter and McGoldrick have also contributed to our inclusion of issues of gender (Walters, Carter, Papp, & Silverstein, 1988), ethnicity, race, and class (McGoldrick, Pearce, & Giordano, 1982), when we consider the meaning of situations for families as well as parameters and consequences of change.

Family as an Emotional System

Bowen's family systems theory defines the multigenerational family as the primary unit of emotional influence in the life of the individual. Unlike other systems that the individual may be part of, membership in a family is not voluntary, except by marriage, and cannot be given up when dissatisfaction arises (Carter & McGoldrick, 1989). This creates a unique interconnectedness among family members and a boundary that defines the family as a discrete unit. Within that unit, there is also a balance or reciprocity in relationships, such as overfunctioning and underfunctioning, which reflects the interdependence of emotional functioning. In this way the functioning of one person is best understood by looking at the functioning of those around him or her (Kerr & Bowen, 1988).

Richard's dilemma shows how the field of emotional influence spans several generations. What happens in one generation — for example, between Richard's parents and grandparents — influences how particular issues such as the meaning of marriage are negotiated between Richard and his parents, which in turn affects Richard's own feelings about his marital status.

Triangles

When issues are unresolved in one generation, patterns of relating are transmitted from one generation to the next through a system described by Bowen as emotional triangling (Kerr & Bowen, 1988). In that process, when a conflict cannot be resolved between two people, it gets detoured through a third as a tension-reducing maneuver. The third can be a person, such as a child or a lover, or a thing like work or substance abuse. When spread among three relationships, the anxiety is now easier to manage. Because it feels better, this maneuver becomes self-reinforcing, and the original two begin to rely on the third member or thing in the triangle. Indeed, each relationship becomes dependent on the others (Herz Brown, 1991). While diffusing the anxiety is helpful in the short run, in the long term it prevents the twosome from resolving their issues and adds rigidity their relationship. Entrenched issues are usually an indication of a triangle. Because anxiety is infectious, one triangle is rarely enough to stabilize a relationship, and so interlocking triangles form.

When marital status is a loaded issue in a family, it is usually held in place with a series of interlocking triangles, originating with the primary triangle of a child with parents. Holding the social or cultural context aside for a moment, let us look at Tom, who is still distraught over a year after the breakup with his girlfriend. In addition to mourning the loss of the relationship as it was, he can't give up the idea of what it was supposed to lead to — marriage and children. Tom's inability to come to terms with the breakup is held in place by the role the girlfriend played in the relationship with his parents. As long as he was marriage bound, his parents could focus their energies on his future family and the upcoming roles they would play as in-laws and grandparents. During the relationship, his girlfriend had already taken on the role of fielding phone calls from his parents and managing family get-togethers. Without the relationship, Tom falls back into his old position in the parental triangle, where involvement in his life has been a longstanding tension-reducing maneuver by his parents in managing their own relationship.

Anxiety is the key ingredient in the activation of a triangle, and usually signals a disruption or potential change in a two-person relationship where there are different ideas about the need for closeness or distance. The role of the triangle is to stabilize the closeness/distance negotiation. The launching of the young adult into adulthood, as our example above illustrates, is a time in a family's life where the anxiety about changes in the parent-child relationship may activate a triangle. Leaving home for marriage, and finding a spouse to become a third leg of the triangle, is the most common and accepted method of defusing the anxiety that can arise when a young adult leaves home. When marriage does not occur, the quest for marriage often becomes part of the triangle.

The process of triangulation is stopped when one person in the triangle takes responsibility for his or her functioning rather than involving another or making someone else responsible, while at the same time staying emotionally connected to the other parts of the triangle (Kerr & Bowen, 1988). Cut-offs don't end triangles. The ability to take responsibility for oneself and find one's own voice in the midst of others is related to the level of emotional separateness, which Bowen defines as differentiation (Bowen, 1978).

Differentiation

The concept of differentiation is the cornerstone of Bowen theory, in that it describes the process of defining self in a system. As a lifelong endeavor, it represents managing the dynamic tension between the counterbalancing life forces of togetherness and separateness. At high levels of differentiation, or one end of the continuum, it is the ability to define one's own thoughts and feelings as one's own in the context of significant relationships and around important issues (Bowen, 1978; Kerr & Bowen, 1988). This implies being separate enough to know one's own thoughts and sufficiently

emotionally connected to want to handle the risk and anxiety of communicating them.

Balancing the need for togetherness and the need for separation is affected by what Bowen calls the emotional system, which keeps family members connected and responsive to each other, and the intellectual system,
which allows one to take a step back from feelings and make choices about
how one wants to respond. The emotional system governs the reactive or
automatic response to the emotional field of others and often overrides the
quest for individuality. When differentiation is low, the emotional system
outweighs the intellectual system. Feeling is about fusion, where one person's feelings cannot be separated from another. This can be expressed
as maintaining consensus, constant conflict, or no contact at all (pseudo
autonomy). At higher levels of differentiation, operating in the intellectual
system allows for emotional closeness but without dependence and the need
for acceptance (Kerr & Bowen, 1988).

We find differentiation to be a useful concept because it emphasizes that
individuality or emotional separateness really has meaning only in relation
to others. Movement toward higher levels of differentiation is an interpersonal, multigenerational process which is accomplished by getting to know
all the players in the family on a personal basis, unbiased by other family
members' relationship with them. This involves exploration of the family
system as a way to clarify issues, tap resources in understanding one's own
position in the family, and move out of triangles. In the process, it helps to
locate the individual as a responsible actor, rather than just as a "cog" in
the system.

Horizontal and Vertical Movement in Families

The patterns of interaction that are transmitted across generations through
triangles are also shaped by the process of family development, in which
the family as a unit adapts to predictable and unpredictable events that
occur throughout the life span. The idea that the family itself has a life
cycle means that we must look not only at the developmental stages of the
members of the nuclear family unit and how they influence other members,
but also at the development of the family as a unit, as a unifying structure
that sets the context for the development of the members. That context
includes the influence of at least three generations at any one time, with the
concerns of one generation often reverberating through others. So there are
not just individual tasks and transition points but also family transitions to
negotiate, all of which affect the family unit in the future. In addition,
family development is not limited to the immediate family but is influenced
by the multigenerational experience; that is, how the nuclear family negoti-

ates life cycle transitions is reflective of how life cycle transitions were handled in previous generations (Carter & McGoldrick, 1989).

Understanding both the emotional system and the family life cycle creates our frame of reference when we think about the meaning of marriage — and therefore singlehood — for a family. Both the multigenerational transmission and the developmental course of the family tell us how and why a family might organize its interaction around an issue like marital status, why some life cycle transitions are more problematic than others, and how the emotional issues are communicated across generations.

Role of Anxiety

Whether marital status is or is not an issue for a family is largely determined by the flow of anxiety in the emotional system of the family. Carter and McGoldrick (1989) describe anxiety in a family as having both a vertical and a horizontal direction. The vertical flow caries the myths, the "shoulds," the labels and attitudes, and prescriptions for behavior that make up patterns of relating and functioning across generations. The horizontal flow carries the anxiety created as the family moves through time, coping with expected life cycle transitions. It also reflects the anxiety from other events that change the unfolding of the life cycle, such as illnesses or deaths, as well as changes in the surrounding culture like the changing role of women or the emergence of AIDS as a public health issue.

For many families, stress is created when marriage does not occur in the expected time frame on the horizontal axis. This then causes a fluctuation in the unfolding of the family life cycle, affecting the developmental tasks of the adult child, the parents, and possibly the siblings. If, for example, marriage has been equated with the natural transition away from the parental home to adulthood, the family may have to struggle to find other ways to realign the relationship between parent and young adult. This may be particularly difficult with daughters when they have not been raised to have an adulthood outside the context of marriage and where competence has been defined by the ability to attract a man and serve others.

When marriage equals adulthood, parents may use it as a way to decrease their financial and emotional support of the adult child, freeing up resources for their later life stages such as marriage without children and retirement. For the adult child, marriage may be the only "legitimate" way to set up boundaries around one's own life. Siblings who are married may expereince increased pressure to have children, so that the parents can join the ranks of their peers as grandparents. When family members can find other ways to realign their roles with one another as well as the surrounding community, the decision to marry or not can become more reality-based and less the anxious centerpiece to family interaction. Handling this kind of transition without marriage will be described in greater detail in the next section, which deals specifically with life cycle issues of the single adult.

Unpredictable life cycle events like divorce in parental marriage may also increase stress for the family around delayed or no marriage of the adult child. The parents, for example, may feel concerned that the "failure" of their own marriage may have caused their children's single status. Or, if the issues in the divorce remain unresolved, the adult child may be caught in a reactive position that either romanticizes or damns marriage. Illness in a parent is another example of a life cycle event that can be the catalyst for an overemphasis on marriage. Marriage becomes the "goal" to accomplish before the parent dies.

As we discuss in Chapter 10 on gay and lesbian single adults, the process of coming out to oneself and one's family alters what would be the normative unfolding of the life cycle. Forming relationships, for example, is usually kept separate, if not secret, from the family (Berzon, 1988). When the gay or lesbian single adult has not come out to the family, the family may increase the pressure for a relationship or marriage, to avoid confronting the adult child's possible homosexuality.

The above are examples of how events in the nuclear family can shape the reaction of a family system to an issue like marital status. If there is anxiety regarding marital status coming from the historical, vertical axis as well, the stress a family experiences around the single status of an adult child will be magnified tenfold. It then has the potential to create a disruption in the life cycle transition (Bowen, 1978; Carter & McGoldrick, 1989).

For example, one woman who felt like a failure for not marrying and could only focus on this deficit rather than enhancing the quality of her life in other areas learned about the stigmatized position and ostracism of her unmarried aunt. This helped her understand how loaded the issue of marriage was in the extended family. In another family, the desertion of the family by the paternal grandfather created increased pressure by the father on the sons to prove responsibility through marital commitments. The eldest son had quite predictably never made a commitment to job or relationship.

In these cases, the family history complicated the resolution of the immediate developmental tasks and refocused the family on loaded issues that carried meaning from the past. In each, the previous generation had difficulty in negotiating a life transition. That experience then either served as a model of behavior or became intensified through the process of triangulation, so that the immediate generation had similar difficulties (Carter & McGoldrick, 1989). When the degree of anxiety around an issue, lik marital status, is particularly intransigent, it is most likely predictive of a larger family issue.

Wider Culture

When we talk about culture in this section, we are particularly looking at the influence of ethnicity (because, except for Native Americans, we are a nation of immigrants) and race (because it significantly divides our society), with an eye to how class and gender operate in these contexts. While it is difficult to separate culture from the emotional operating system of the family, it is important to understand how anxiety around singlehood in a family can be related to significant cultural prescriptions about marriage. An examination of the family map needs not only to trace the patterns of triangulation and reactivity around marital status through the wider family and the life cycle, but also to look at the ethnic, racial, or class contexts that help define the family's experience.

In doing so, however, it is important to keep in mind, as we said earlier, that the influence of culture is not static and that it does not exist in a void. It is affected by many variables, including time in history and fit with the larger social forces, particularly economic, which define a group's experience (Steinberg, 1989). In fact, it has been argued by some that class and economic opportunity drive behavior more accurately than cultural norms, although culture may be invoked to explain behavior (Gans, 1962; Steinberg, 1989). In either case, class and ethnicity intersect in influencing the importance of certain values and identity (McGoldrick & Rohrbaugh, 1987). Variables associated with degree of ethnic identity include greater educational attainment and higher occupational status, with each negatively correlated with ethnicity. The notion of symbolic or voluntary ethnicity, where there is selectivity about the traditions one maintains, has been used to explain the role that ethnicity takes on with increased social mobility (Gans, 1979). It no longer shapes day-to-day life but is invoked to maintain a social identity without alienating one from other groups.

In addition to the interplay between class and ethnicity, experience with the dominant culture's mores affects the role and importance of cultural values among different family members. For example, the first generation since immigration is more likely to be connected to the ethnic norms of the country they came from through language or traditions than succeeding generations who have greater exposure to the mainstream culture. Whether the family lives in a community or neighborhood with shared cultural norms will also determine the salience of the group norms (McGoldrick & Rohrbaugh, 1987). What defines a person's culture can also change over the course of the life span. The culture of the homosexual community, for example, may assume larger influence, overriding other aspects of one's background, such as ethnicity, class, or even race. With these variables in mind, it is easy to see how cultural values change in importance for families, as well as take on different meaning for individuals in the same family.

As a cultural context, race differs significantly from ethnicity because of its visibility and, in the case of African-Americans, because of the circumstances of their immigration, slavery. The history of racism and oppression in this country is an everpresent factor in the issue of cultural roots versus assimilation. Mainstream society has never been welcoming to the majority of African-Americans.

Culture, class, and race also affect men and women differently. The gendered expectations of patriarchy create commonalities for men and women even in the face of real differences between groups. To address these commonalities, however, it is important not to lose the track of the way the specific group experience shapes the circumstances or the form of oppression that patriarchy asserts over people's lives. The oppression of white women, for example, is not the same as for black women. The experiences of middle-class women and working-class or poor women are materially different enough to influence their perspective regarding their power position in society (Cole, 1995). While almost all women across ethnic lines appear to have less status, the actual roles, rules, and arenas of power will vary widely from one ethnicity to the next (McGoldrick, Garcia-Preto, Hines, & Lee, 1989). Our perspective is that culture is the fabric, gender is the thread. To pick out the thread one must have a good knowledge of the fabric.

Because of the many variables that contribute to shaping culture, understanding the role of culture in a family's life is a complicated process. The process of mapping the influences may in itself be as important as the specific content that emerges. As individuals become aware that culture has a role in shaping the life of the family, they see the "big picture" and begin to make some sense out of the details of their lives and the hows and whys of the family emotional system (McGoldrick et al., 1982).

Since marriage often symbolizes the first step in the continuation of the family and therefore the culture of the family, it is not OK, per se, in any group to remain single (Staples & Johnson, 1993). What aspect of singlehood the family reacts to most, however, will vary according to the different norms of the defining culture of the family. In some families, there may be more concern about the single adult being on one's own, apart from the protection of family; for other families, the fact of no marriage and children brings shame to parents who feel they have failed in their role. Because the norms help organize the content and form of the reaction to singlehood, attaching them to aspects of a family's culture can help detoxify personal reactions and increase the single adult's ability to respond in a differentiated manner.

CULTURAL THEMES

Rather than providing a comprehensive guide to all the ethnic, class, or racial variations that inform the family regarding single status (see McGold-rick et al., 1982), let us give a number of examples to illustrate the importance of attending to the impact of the cultural context as part of the therapeutic process. In the following vignettes, we highlight four cultural themes that may become relevant to a family in its reactions to a difference such as prolonged singlehood: (1) the definition of family, (2) the meaning of marriage (both as a rite of passage and as part of a group's cultural and religious history), (3) pathways to adulthood, and (4) relationship with the dominant culture. In discussing these themes, we don't mean to fall back on the generalizations that make culture seem monolithic. As we have discussed before, even within a group, culture is heterogeneous. Our intention is, rather, to look at how culture intersects with family emotional process and takes on greater importance when the stress level increases.

Definition of Family

By this we mean who is considered family, whether it is just immediate relatives, or several generations as in Italian families, or even one's ancestors as in Asian families. It may mean extended family including fictive kin as is common in black families, or just the nuclear family in WASP households. How the family is defined influences the role of marriage in the overall life of the family. For example, in cultures where the individual is secondary to the needs of the family (Italian or Asian), and each generation is connected to the ones before, marriage is not about the creation of a new family but about the continuatiion of a line (usually the male line). Marriage symbolizes stability and continuity and provides a social identity (Mindel, Habenstein, & Wright, 1988). Conversely, not marrying is often seen as counterproductive or as a betrayal to the perpetuation of the family.

When the family is seen as primary and there are strong boundaries between family and the rest of the world, a single adult may still have a role within the family, although his or her status may not be the same as that of the married siblings. Perhaps more problematic is the greater need of the single person to cross boundaries and participate in validating contexts outside the family, such as work and friendship networks.

•••

THIS WAS THE CASE for Anna Samperi, a 25-year-old woman of Italian heritage who came for therapy because she "thought she was losing her mind." She was anxious, not sleeping well, and couldn't concentrate at work. She had broken off with her boy friend of many years because of "his domineering ways and constant jealousy." "But this," she said, "is not really the problem. My family is the problem." Conflict between Anna and her mother had escalated to the point where her uncle had been called in, and he had hit her the previous evening. Anna was angry, but also confused. She was beginning to doubt her ability to succeed at all, even though she had recently been promoted at work and graduated college magna cum laude. She was thinking of taking a leave of absence from her job so she could pull herself together.

Anna's parents were born in a poor village in Calabria and emigrated to the United States in their youth. They met and married here and had four children, one of whom died at age five. Anna's father had died four years previously. Anna was the youngest of the remaining three children. The older generation, which included Anna's mother, maternal grandmother, uncle, and three aunts, had reacted to the strangeness of America by closing ranks and drawing a tight boundary around the family. This is not an uncommon reaction for first-generation Italian families (Rotunno & McGoldrick, 1982). They made a clear distinction between "us" and "the Americans." The Americans included all non-Samperis, and were regarded as dangerous, capable of putting foreign ideas into their children's heads. Again like many other Italian families, the family was close-knit, helping each other not only in times of trouble but also in daily life. Anna was the first to go to outside the family by calling a therapist.

Some of the Samperi values fit well with American mainstream culture: hard work, honesty, "doing the right thing," and education. In this last, the Samperi family differed from others of their generation: they believed in educating their daughters as well as their son. The family was proud of putting all three children through college.

In a consultation with the family, the idea of acceptable launching pathways for adult children was explored. It became clear there was only one: children can leave home through marriage. The two older children had done it "right," even though Gina, Anna's older sister, had given up a full scholarship to medical school in the process. When Anna broke up with her boyfriend, she gave up her only acceptable means to move out of the parental home. It also seemed as if the family could tolerate many of the differences Anna was embracing, such as upward mobility, as long marriage was on the horizon. Marriage would reaffirm her connection and role with the family. Without a marriage in sight, Anna's push for autonomy, e.g., setting her own curfew and choosing her own friends, had escalated the struggle so intensely that Anna had thrown down the gauntlet and threatened to leave home. This was the point where the uncle was enlisted to bring her into line.

In the family's view, a daughter living alone would bring great shame to the family and would be in danger living outside the protection of family. Autonomy and independence were the most dangerous ideas that the "Americans" were putting into the children's heads. For a first-generation Italian family, the value of the security and relatedness that a strong connection to the family provided outweighed individual needs or aspirations (Ragucci, 1981). Anna's view was influenced by the process of acculturation that occurs with each new generation. In many ways, she was more like her peers than her family. She was educated, earned a good living, and was ready for the next step she saw friends and coworkers taking: getting an apartment of her own. Because this action pushed beyond the acceptable family and cultural frame, the cost to Anna of choosing independence and singlehood could be great: a cut-off from her family.

In this family, marriage, as an anticipated step in young adulthood, signals many things and goes to the heart of the definition of family itself. Marriage is not the creation of a separate family but an extension of the multigenerational unit (Rotunno & McGoldrick, 1982). Anna's marriage would signal continuity with the family and, thereby, be an acceptable way to leave home. For many Italian families, adult status for females really comes only with the birth of the first child, presupposing marriage. Staying single might be acceptable in the context of the role of protected daughter. There is no role for the single autonomous adult, particularly female. While unmarried Italian men are given a wider latitude for venturing outside the family, their single state is still seen as a sort of a prolonged adolescent phase of sowing wild oats (Rotunno & McGoldrick, 1982).

When Anna broke up with her boy friend and decided to live on her own, both she and her family entered new territory, where there were no role models for the adaptation that was required to keep the family connected. Anna's goal was not to cut off or be cut off from her family, but to find more room to maneuver as an adult self within a traditional context. Some of her goals even matched her family's, as she eventually wanted to marry and have children. But as her experience diverged from her parents', and the anxiety about the difference increased, "doing the right thing" for an Italian girl — getting married — became the focal point of the negotiation between the generations.

Meaning of Marriage

While for some groups marriage is subsumed under the importance of the family, for others marriage in itself is an important rite of passage. In African-American families, for example, the importance of marriage and a strong family tradition is tied to their particular history and minority status and cannot be separated from a legacy of slavery and racism. After two centuries of being denied the legal right to marry, when slavery was abolished, black people married in large numbers, outpacing whites at the turn of the century (Staples & Johnson, 1993). The trend of high rates of marriage and the maintenance of a strong kinship system survived many generations, despite rampant racism. Only in the 1960s did the impact of urban and ghetto conditions began to seriously weaken the black family (Franklin, 1988). According to the 1992 census, the black community now has the largest percentage of single people of any racial group; yet, the emphasis on or desire for marriage has not changed. It is valued by the community (Staples, 1988) and congruent with the "mainstream model" marriage and family (Heiss, 1988). Like white men and women, black men and women continue to report greater life satisfaction in a married state than in non-married states (Zollar & Williams, 1987).

•••

BRIAN THOMAS, A SOFT-SPOKEN single African-American man, was extremely happy in his single life, but by age 32 he was beginning to feel pressure from his family to get married. He was not in therapy but was interviewed as part of our research for this book. He grew up in a large family, one of six children, and was raised primarily by his mother and maternal grandmother. His father, a hardworking religious man, died of a heart attack when Brian was eight.

Brian had his own apartment in a part of the city filled with young professionals; he enjoyed his work as an educator in a liberal private school. He had no trouble finding women who were "wonderful" to date and was always "going with someone." His principal joy in singlehood, however, was in "having things that were his." Growing up in a crowded apartment with little money to spare, he had few personal possessions and no personal space. He still took delight in coming home and seeing his things right where he'd left them — not all messed up or taken by a sibling. Brian had a large collection of records and tapes, and all kinds of books lined the walls. He had created a warm, hospitable space for himself.

Brian was close to his family and was a favorite uncle to his nieces and nephews, whom as he took to places all over the city. Relations with his mother, whom he cared about deeply, had become somewhat strained after his thirtieth birthday. "She doesn't really say anything, but gives me a look. I know what it means; it's suspicion and disapproval about why I'm not getting married." Brian joked that it would almost be easier if he were gay or a drug user; then there would be some explanation she could understand. "As it is, I have none, except my own selfish pleasure in having my own space, my own things, a life that is my own."

Brian feels he will have to get married soon. "For a black man like me not to marry would be letting down the race, and I couldn't live with the guilt of that." Brian's view is not only as an individual within a family-of-origin context. He is also a representative of achievement and stability within his larger cohort of American black men. Knowing that the loss of black men in America through death or incarceration is approximately one in four by his age (Staples & Johnson, 1993), Brian feels marriage as an obligation to his people. It therefore plays a larger role than in just defining him as a husband or father.

Indeed, it has been argued that the high incidence of singleness among African-Americans has nothing to do with eschewing marriage for a preference or pursuit of an alternative lifestyle, and all to do with social forces, such as racism and economic disadvantage, that have created structural barriers to marriage. One example of this is the severe imbalance between numbers of single women and single men, whose availability and desirability have been diminished by high rates of unemployment, exposure to violence, drugs, and other realities of ghetto life. As a black woman's educational and economic level increases, the pool of possible partners, who would match the expected norm of being older, better educated, and higher earning, diminishes. While for a man success increase his desirability as a marriage partner, for a woman it works the opposite. This obviously creates unique pressure on single people within the black community (Staples & Johnson, 1993).

•••

IN MANY JEWISH FAMILIES we find another example of how marriage has particular meaning that reflects history, religion, and minority status. For Allan Fried, a 38-year-old man from a Conservative Jewish background, the family assumption that he would marry was no different from the one that we would be a dentist like his father. He had, in fact, joined his father's practice once out of dental school; however, even though he was now approaching 40, he was still unmarried. Although Allan had been in individual therapy for some time, the issue of marital status and its meaning for his family came out in a family consultation, initiated by his mother, who was concerned about an escalating conflict between her husband and son. In some ways the conflict between Allan and his father was a typical "family business" conflict regarding how the next generation acquires full status and the older generation turns over the reins. Underlying the discussion regarding Allan's role in the practice was the unanswered question as to whether he would "ever settle down and become a family man." Would the other expectation of Allan's adulthood — marriage — be fulfilled?

The emphasis on and concern about getting married grow out of the central role that marriage as a prelude to making a family plays in Jewish life. This centrality reflects a cultural consciousness regarding the need to perpetuate the community that results from a blending of religious imperative ("be fruitful and multiply") and a history of persecution and diaspora. Marriage, as an institution, is valued as an important source of nurturance and support, which creates the structure for the connection to the next generation and the continuation of the group (Farber, Mindel, & Lazerwitz, 1988). Because of the elevated position of marriage and family, it has been argued that an individual's relationship to marriage and family will affect his or her self-esteem, with failure to fulfill the ideal of family stability leading to decreased self-worth (Brodbar-Nemzer, 1986). With this intense value on family, it easy to see that there is little role for a single person. It is often said among Jews, there is no such thing as being single, that there is only "not yet married."

When there is such a strong presumption of marriage, falling outside familial expectations may challenge the basic family script to such an extent that the single person may feel he or she has no place in the family anymore. For Gail, age 40, it was a watershed event when she attended a family wedding and relatives no longer came over to her and said (as is the tradition to say to an unmarried person), "This should only happen to you." She felt the family had given up on her, and her unmarried state had turned her into an outcast. Just as previously waiting for marriage had structured her family interactions and her perceptions about her fit with the family, now not being married determined the nature of those interactions.

Pathways to Adulthood

The role that marital status plays in the passage to adulthood is connected to the themes we discussed above, the definition of family and the meaning of marriage. We see this particularly when getting married is seen as the critical step toward taking one's place among the adults in the community, as in Italian families. When marriage becomes a major milestone, as in Jewish families, it inevitably structures the parent-child relationship as well. In the Jewish culture, preparing children for a successful marriage is part of the obligation of parents to children. Parents often spare nothing to make children desirable for marriage, whether pushing their sons toward "success" or in making their daughters attractive (Herz & Rosen, 1982).

Once children are married, parents shift their roles and enjoy the success of their children and eventual grandchildren. It is easy to imagine how the emphasis on making a marriage as the culmination of parental responsibility complicates the issue of achieving adult status. Allan, in our example above, was not making this passage to adulthood. His delay had put the father-son relationship in a stalemate. If Allan were to get married and then produce a grandchild, the relationship would evolve and the focus of the parents would shift from being good parents to being good grandparents.

Whether marriage is equated with adulthood is also affected by economic realities facing the group. Here class, race, and gender factor into family expectations. For example, while there is a high value on marriage and family within the black community, preparing a child for marriage has usually not been a primary, organizing concern, as it might be in certain ethnic groups or socioeconomic classes. Given the history of racism and oppression, this task is secondary to the need to be prepared to support oneself and be self-sufficient (Higgenbotham & Weber, 1995). Because of the barriers black men face in the job market, marriage and economic security have never been connected. Therefore, black women do not expect that marriage will remove the need to work. One study of upward mobility in women, as related to class and race, found that almost no black parents, middle- or working-class, saw marriage as a primary goal, while significantly more white parents, particularly working-class parents, did (Higgenbotham & Weber, 1995).

While establishing self-sufficiency is a value supported by the black community, giving back to the community by helping those behind you is equally valued (Boyd-Franklin, 1989). This potentially expands the roles for family members within the family regardless of marital status. For black families, this expectation grows out of the experience of being part of a extended family or kinship network that provided emotional and economic support needed to succeed. As a result of being part of a larger family network, where roles are less prescribed and one develops a sense of "social debt" (Boyd-Franklin, 1989), more role options are created for the single person. Although the upwardly mobile black woman may find herself with fewer marriage prospects within the black community, this does not necessarily diminish her role in the extended family. At times, however, the "career" of a single person may clash with this sense of family connectedness, particularly when the individual is in the position of giving and not getting or needing as much in return. Lorraine's story illustrates this dilemma.

•••

LORRAINE SAMPSON, a 48-year-old African-American woman, came for consultation around recent feelings of apathy and emptiness about her life. Usually she had a "zest for life," and took pride and pleasure in her work (she was a partner at a law firm), her family, and her friends. Lorraine had relationships with men off and on all her adult life. Currently she wasn't seeing anybody, but "men have never been the center of [her] life."

Lorraine came from South Carolina and was a middle child of four. Her family was well-known and respected in their town, having lived there for three generations. She had two sisters, both of whom married. Her brother had died in his twenties of a drug overdose. When Lorraine thought of her family, however, it included more than just her nuclear family, in keeping with the African-American definition of family, which may include several generations and aunts and uncles, real and fictive kin. She kept in contact with many of family members and visited regularly with them.

With her expanded notion of family came an enhanced sense of responsibility and interconnectedness. She had been benefited from this family sense as a young woman, when the "family" had sacrificed considerably to send her—the "studious one"—to college and law school. As soon as Lorraine got her first job, she began helping the next generation of children. First she sent money home to be used for education, and later she had nieces and nephews or cousins live with her while they attended school.

She had been "mothering" in this way for over twenty years, and now the younger generation was at the point where they could take over the mentorship of the next. Lorraine had been looking forward to using her money on deferred personal pleasure, when her sister, together with her two grandchildren, came north to live. Now again Lorraine felt she had to take Alva and the children under her wing, as they were strangers to the city. This was the beginning of her depression.

Lorraine, while single, had an integral place in the extended family network, as well as opportunities and obligations to be a close, involved active aunt and second mother to the younger generation. Childlessness or lack of legitimate role was not an issue for her in her singleness. In addition, her success was valued by the family. However, because she had no nuclear family and children of her own and she was self-reliant, the implied reciprocity in the mutual support system (Boyd-Franklin, 1989) was not enacted. Her desire to lead a more "selfish" single life put her at odds with her community. Her depression was related to the difficult task of finding the balance between fulfilling the family obligation and carving out a life of her own.

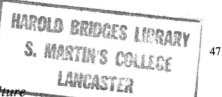
HAROLD BRIDGES LIBRARY
S. MARTIN'S COLLEGE
LANCASTER

Relationship with Dominant Culture

The fit of an ethnic or racial group with the host culture is an important ingredient in determining what traditions or values are adhered to, and which ones are tossed over or hidden in favor of the dominant culture. We have discussed some of this with respect to economic access and how a rise in class correlates with greater assimilation, at least for white ethnic groups. The process of immigration and assimilation, however, is an ongoing balancing act between giving up aspects of oneself to fit in, or pass, and holding onto aspects of self that are the connection to one's roots. While the length of time since immigration influences this struggle, in groups that are stigmatized in some way by the dominant culture the process can continue through the generations. The decision to marry or not and the choice of marriage partner, in or out of the group, can be defining moments in this struggle.

•••

FOR SUSAN YATASHI, age 30, the dilemma of whom to date as prelude to the next developmental step of marriage was an extension of the assimilation issues her family had been faced with since their immigration from Japan. As is typical for many immigrant families, those issues included sorting out which aspects of the culture of origin to hold onto so as not to lose family definition and a sense of connection to previous generations, as well as what aspects of the new, host culture to acquire to feel proficient or competent. Even talking to a therapist represented a struggle between the two cultures for Susan. To talk about her troubles violated her Japanese sensibility, which valued privacy and containment over self-disclosure (Shon & Ja, 1982). Yet, after being depressed for a number of months she sought treatment, at the urging of her "American" friends.

The depression began when her white Protestant boyfriend broke up with her. She couldn't talk with her parents about this because they had repeatedly advised her against dating non-Japanese men, reacting to the trend in the more assimilated generations of Japanese children, who marry out at a rate of 60% (Kitano, 1988). In other areas her family had been very helpful, valuing her ability to assimilate and to quickly learn language. Ignoring their advice, and only dating white American men, had been her vote to embrace and hopefully be accepted by the host culture. She felt that, if she could become part of the dominant culture, she might escape the inferior position of women in Japanese families. Even in her friendships with Japanese men, she experienced subtle messages to be more passive. In contrast, she felt more respected as an equal by her American boy friends, who appeared to value her career aspirations. She felt frustrated, however, after several relationships that were on the verge of "getting serious" broke up. Susan thought at least part of the reason was because she was Japanese and so the men's behavior unconsciously reflected the racism against Asians she witnessed in the wider culture. At the same time, she blamed herself for not fitting in or knowing the "rules" well enough to make the relationship work. Not only was Susan depressed at the breakup of this recent friendship, but she also felt hopelessly caught between two cultures.

Susan, a professional dancer, had immigrated with her parents and younger brother when she was ten and her brother was eight. Her father was an engineer and her mother had been a classical pianist who gave up her career to care for her family. The family came to the United States when the father was transferred by his company to a division in North America. While the loss of connection to the extended family in Japan was a major stress for the family, their adaptation to the move was aided by becoming part of a Japanese community associated with the father's work.

The parents, despite their own insular social life, had encouraged their children to fit in with the host culture. Her mother, for example, had suggested she use the name Susan rather that her Japanese name. Susan was also encouraged to achieve in school and develop a career. While educational achievement is a common value in many Asian families and represents a way children show respect and honor to their families (Shon & Ja, 1982), Susan felt the support also reflected a personal issue for her mother, who had given up a promising career and taken on a traditional role in the family. At the same time, the parents had been noticeably pleased with her brother's recent marriage to a Japanese woman. In this marriage he had brought honor to the family, which in the Japanese culture extends beyond the nuclear family to all the generations that have come before it (Shon & Ja, 1982).

The mixed messages of her parents no doubt stemmed from their own struggles to bridge the two cultures as well as changing mores. On reflection, Susan began to wonder if her anxiety about succeeding in relationships had to do with not knowing where she belonged. If she pursued Japanese men, would she be betraying not only her own assimilated values but also her mother's support of her purusit to be a fully developed woman? If she pursued non-Japanese men, she might always feel like an "other." For Susan, issues of culture, gender, and immigration converged in dating experience. With this kind of loading of anxiety, any relationship would sag under the weight. Understanding this multilayered context for the meaning of marriage and the ongoing influence of culture in her life was a way for Susan to decrease some of the intensity around her relationships and begin to address these issues in other areas of her life.

II

A LIFE CYCLE MODEL
FOR THE SINGLE ADULT

4

An Overview of
the Life Cycle

WHEN MARIA TURNED 38, her younger sister became pregnant. Within that same year, she managed to turn her long-term dating relationship into marriage. That marriage was short-lived, however, never making the transition from a loosely structured relationship to one with more prescribed roles. In retrospect, Maria guessed that the push for marriage had not come from the needs in the relationship, which had actually worked quite well, but from the anxiety generated by her sister's move to a new developmental stage, parenthood. Maria's sister was hitting a significant milestone that affected the life phase of all her family members and required a reorganization of roles. With the birth of the baby, Maria would be not only a sister and a daughter but an aunt as well. Her parents would become grandparents. Because there is always some ambiguity when roles change, anxiety about the change in this family became focused on Maria's unmarried state. Her dating relationship did not have markers to chart her growth. If she did not marry, how would she know she was "progressing"? Maria needed a rite of passage. Marriage seemed like a way to keep pace not only with the family but also with life.

That Maria would make a life choice prompted by changes in her sister's life represents to us the emotional interconnectedness of the life cycles of all family members. We cannot adequately understand the experience of one member without considering the developmental context of other members. That marriage seemed the only choice is indicative of the narrowness of our thinking, as part of this culture, about the correct way for our lives to unfold. In this section we will present a life cycle model for the single adult that expands the framework for what constitutes an authentic life and increases the options beyond the search for a relationship.

We have borrowed several key concepts in our life cycle schema from Carter and McGoldrick (1989) and other family theorists before them (Duvall, 1977; Solomon, 1973) who have helped to chart the family's passage through time. To these we have added our own modifications to highlight the developmental issues relevant to the single adult. Following this introduction to our theoretical framework, we will detail each phase of development, with particular attention to clinical implications of our formulations.

In trying to define commonalities in single people's experience, we also allow for the cultural, racial, and gender-related differences discussed in Chapter 3. The sociocultural context must always be a lens through which the life cycle discussion takes place. Sexual preference and identification as a gay or lesbian single adult also contribute to significant differences in the unfolding of the life cycle and the meaning one gives to being single. Recognizing this, we have included a separate chapter in the life cycle section to clarify the similarities and differences between heterosexual and gay/lesbian single people.

Because we are looking specifically at the impact of never marrying on adult development in the context of the family life cycle, we understand that we are magnifying this one aspect of a person's life as a salient organizing feature. This may feel overloaded at times, or even arbitrary. Certainly there are times or contexts where other salient aspects of one's life, such as race or sexual orientation, are more important. We also recognize that the developmental tasks we discuss will at times be similar to those of the single adult's married counterpart.

THE FAMILY LIFE CYCLE

The individual life cycle takes place in the context of the family life cycle. While we are focusing on one member and one generation of a family, that person can only be understood in the context of other family members' life cycle issues and the reverberations that then occur. It is the emotional interconnectedness of family members' lives in the present and with their past that gives meaning to their lives (Carter & McGoldrick, 1989). Without this awareness, it is easy to miss or not understand many of the influences that operate in people's lives. When we look at the life cycle of the single adult, we have to be cognizant of the impact of other family members' life stage issues, as in Maria's case, as well as how the family as a whole accommodates to the life choices of its members.

In families with grown/adult children, for example, the family has to negotiate a change in relationships that allows the physical exit or launching of the young adult and simultaneously makes room for his or her emotional reentry in an adult position. Young adults also must allow for a shift in parental involvement, with a refocusing of parental attention to other aspects of their lives. To weather these changes, the family structure as a whole must alter to accommodate the new roles and relationship patterns. Structures that are appropriate to one phase rarely work in another (Aylmer, 1989).

As we chart the developmental issues for the single adult, we will try to approach them from this multilayered perspective: the issues from the single person's vantage point, the response of family members to the single member at different stages, how other family members' developmental stages affect the way the single adult deals with not marrying, and how the family as a whole may need to restructure its definition of itself.

STAGES OF DEVELOPMENT

While the lives of many families do not fit neatly into a linear progression of life phases and periodic restructuring, the idea that there are predictable and definable stages of development in a family's life has been proposed by both family sociologists and family systems thinkers as a way to organize our thinking about families over time (Carter & McGoldrick, 1989; Duvall, 1977; Haley, 1973; Hill, 1971; Hill & Rodgers, 1964; Scherz, 1971). In most models, age and role, and their impact on membership and organization of the family, define those stages. To successfully move through a stage, there are emotional processes and developmental tasks to be completed in terms of renegotiating relationships and definition of self (Carter & McGoldrick, 1989).

Because of the cyclical nature of life, the next generation, the children, is usually used to define the emotional tasks of the family. Whether models start with the young adult as in Carter and McGoldrick's schema or with the newly married couple as in Duvall's, the next stages are defined by the entrances and exits of the children in the system, i.e., families with young children, families with adolescents, launching, etc. These changes in family composition create a ripple effect that precipitates a realignment in other family relationships. This realignment is also affected, as Carter and Mc-Goldrick emphasize in their framework, by the reciprocal tasks of other generations. Schematically, however, the birth and rearing of children, and how the family organizes around them, end up pushing and redefining the family through time (Combrinck-Graham, 1985).

Because the single, childless adult does not have the next generation to key his or her growth, a stage division that uses this cyclical pattern of family procreation to move the family through time is irrelevant. In our proposed life cycle schema, we follow the development of the single adult through the life span by targeting other developmental drivers that push the individual and the family through time. These "drivers" include one's relationship with work, finances, peer network, and family and culture. We have also looked to Bowen's concept of differentiation of self as an expression of adult development that best describes the individual process in the context of the system. The stages themselves are structured by biologic time, or age, as a key organizer of perceptions about oneself and one's fit with family and society. We recognize that these perceptions are constantly being shaped by societal expectations and available options.

Because the notion of stages, particularly based on age, implies a certain hierarchical progression, with one stage building on the others, we want to emphasize two points. First, it is important not to confuse the content of events in any particular stage with the process dimension of negotiating the life cycle (Falicov, 1988). This is most often where our clients get stuck. Events, like a marriage, have become developmental markers, but they can occur at any phase of the life cycle. The meaning of the event and the response to the timing of the event have more to do with the emotional processes that are occurring at the current phase and in the earlier phases than with the event itself. When everyone gets focused on the event, the developmental tasks usually get stalled.

Second, when stages are seen as building on the one another, and problems at one stage are thought to reflect unresolved developmental tasks at an earlier stage, we may find ourselves subscribing to an undesirably pessimistic view of change (Falicov, 1988). Rather than adopt this point of view, we assume that with each stage comes the potential for renegotiation of relationships, because everyone in the system is in a state of disequilibrium in some way. Issues like childlessness are also not resolved at one phase never to be considered again, but are revisited from the different perspective of later phases (Stein, 1981).

To be clinically relevant, any model must accommodate a wide latitude of experience, so as to not pathologize ethnic, racial, and gender differences (Falicov, 1988) or impose a rigid sense of right and wrong (Carter & McGoldrick, 1989). At the same time, we must acknowledge that the timing of biologically driven events, such as the birth of children, has shaped common societal expectations around when events in a family's life should occur. This contributes to a normative framework for nodal events in a family's life (Falicov, 1988). Marriage, partly due to its procreative function, is an event that in most cultures is assumed to take place in a particular part of the life cycle, the young adult phase. The expectation, prediction, and actual occurrence of marriage form a circularity, in that models of development reinforce our ideas about what we should be doing in life (Falicov, 1988). Even within cultural groups, there are norms that impose a standard, pushing the individual along the circle. When we work with single clients, who feel out of the norm with respect to their marital status, it is essential to address the culturally imposed expectation. Indeed, part of the clinical work at each developmental phase involves coming to terms with the normative expectations and expanding options beyond the prescribed choices.

TRANSITIONS, FAMILY DYSFUNCTION, AND FAMILY DEVELOPMENT

Within a stage model of the life cycle, what happens in the transition from one stage to the next is as important as what happens within each stage. Family therapists have generally distinguished the kind of change that occurs within stages as *first order* and the change between stages as *second order*. This is because moving from phase to phase often requires a new repertoire of response (Hoffman, 1989). Because of the greater requirements placed on the family to change and adapt during transitions, these are often the times of high stress. Transitions have been correlated with a disruption in the flow of the life cycle, leading to the appearance of symptoms (Carter & McGoldrick, 1989; Haley, 1973).

Problems can also arise when the family is poised for a change, and has a preconception about how that change should occur (based on familial or societal expectations), and then the change does not occur in the expected fashion. In one family with three unmarried children in their thirties, the parents joked about needing a support group for parents of unmarried adult children, as if this meant they were a "dysfunctional family." Their relationship with their children was frozen in time. Using a life cycle framework, the focus of therapy is to locate the developmental impasse, increase the flexibility and choices available to the system, and help the family reestablish a sense of movement in the natural progression of the life cycle (Carter & McGoldrick, 1989).

DIFFERENTIATION AS AN ASPECT OF LIFE CYCLE

While differentiation is not a life cycle concept per se, defining one's separateness and connection to one's family begins early in childhood and continues into adulthood. That process is demarcated by phases in the life cycle, as the meaning and tension in establishing self-boundaries, which allow both autonomy and intimacy, change. Combrinck-Graham (1985) has talked about the family as having times of being centripetal or focused inward and other times of being centrifugal or oriented outside the family. This suggests an oscillation between times of working on intimate connec-

TABLE 4.1

Stages of the Single Adult Life Cycle

LIFE CYCLE STAGE	EMOTIONAL PROCESS
Not yet married	1. Shifting the relationship with the family. Restructuring interaction with family from dependent to a independent orientation.
	2. Taking a more autonomous role with regard to the world outside the family in the areas of work and friendships.
The thirties: Entering the "Twilight Zone" of singlehood	1. Facing single status for the first time.
	2. Expanding life goals to include other possibilities in addition to marriage.
Midlife (forties to mid-fifties)	1. Addressing the fantasy of the Ideal American family (a) accepting the possibility of never marrying. (b) accepting the possibility of not having own biological children.
	2. Defining the meaning of work, current and future.
	3. Defining an authentic life for oneself that can be accomplished within single status.
	4. Establishing adult role for oneself within family of origin.
Later life (fifties to when physical health fails)	1. Consolidating decisions about work life.
	2. Enjoying fruits of one's labors and the benefits of singlehood.
	3. Acknowledging the future diminishment of physical ones.
	4. Facing increasing disability and death of loved ones.
Elderly (between failing health and death)	1. Confronting mortality.
	2. Accepting one's life as it has been lived.

(Variations on the life cycle model for the gay and lesbian single adult will be addressed in Chapter 10.)

tions and times of working more on oneself, the two faces of differentiation. How this occurs is affected by the patterns on interaction that have developed in response to nodal events and transition points over several generations. In Bowen's method of interviewing a family, he would ask about important life cycle issues in the past to try to make some sense of the present, implying the connection between certain stages of a family's life (Carter & McGoldrick, 1989).

In our work with the single adult, the idea and possibility of differentiation, as an aspect of development, come up anew at every phase of the life cycle. Increasing one's level of differentiation involves tracking the consequences of being different in previous generations at similar points of development, and then understanding how the patterns that developed in response to differentness influence present-day experience. It also involves understanding how major triangles get activated around certain issues at particular times in the life of the family.

Once a context for understanding the members of one's family is developed, reactivity and anxiety in relationships are decreased. The single adult can then work on changing her or his position in the nuclear family around the issue of not being married or not having children. This raises the possibility of forging new connections based on adult-to-adult interaction. Defining a self, having the courage and emotional freedom to make choices about it, and then communicating that to others are the products of understanding those issues that have shaped meaning in one's life.

THE SINGLE ADULT LIFE CYCLE

As discussed earlier, we have grouped developmental issues by chronological age. In doing so, we are cognizant of the considerable variation in the individual timing of negotiating these issues as well as the overlap of some issues from one stage to the next. Table 4.1 provides an outline of the stages and summarizes the key emotional processes.

5

Young Adulthood:
The "Not Married Yet" Phase

MOST PEOPLE SEE young adulthood as a time for consolidating personal identity and career goals. This is generally thought of as a transitional period, during which people are not necessarily seen as "single" but simply "not married yet." At the same time, since the cultural prerequisite for normal adulthood is marriage, there is a certain expectancy within the young adult and his/her family as well that marriage will occur. The young person's activities are observed with this unspoken expectation in the background.

There is a preliminary nature to this age period, which allows for some latitude in completing normative tasks. This latitude varies with the values of the young person's family. Family expectations interweave with cultural norms to dictate the degree of comfort the young adult will experience in this experimental period.

When, as in the 1950s and in some cultures still, the median age for marriage is in the late teens, expectations for focusing on marriage earlier in life will prevail (Coontz, 1992). The median age for marriage has risen by six years since 1950, and there certainly is more flexibility in expectations for young people in the 1990s than there was in the 1950s (Lang, 1991). Nevertheless, those young adults in their twenties who are primarily involved in developing their career paths and decisions about who they will be as individuals are still very much aware of the expectation of their family and society that they will marry.

When you consider that 90% of people in this country do marry and the majority of these marriages occur in the twenties, then young adults live with a veritable avalanche of people marrying around them (Lang, 1991). This was delightfully illustrated in *Four Weddings and a Funeral*, a 1994 film whose protagonist was virtually deluged with wedding invitations. He became so caught up in the mood of the moment that he decided to marry despite his clear lack of readiness for this step.

While single people in the young adult phase are not yet seen as "out of sync" with their peers, the fact that so many people are marrying puts real pressure on them. The ability of young people to withstand these pressures long enough to develop a sense of who they are and establish their life's goals depends on their own emotional development and the emotional system in their families, framed by their class, gender, and ethnicity.

The young adult period is filled with great anxiety. When people struggle with major issues, such as sorting out directions in life, worrying about the future, and struggling to change from dependent family relationships to independent ones, tremendous individual and family turmoil is not uncommon. There is a sense of uncertainty and urgency that may overwhelm the tenuous self of the young adult.

For many parents and children, uncertainties of this period are resolved by focusing on marriage. Since society uses marriage as a symbol of successful entrance into adulthood, many families see it as emblematic of the conclusion to the launching period. When this happens, the young adult experiences intense pressure to marry, which translates into putting more and more of his or her emotional energy into meeting potential partners.

Since young adulthood is usually seen as ranging from the launching period to the close of the twenties decade, anxiety about marriage typically rises as people near thirty. There is a sense that the preliminary nature of life is over; people should be moving on (Schwartzberg, 1991).

The culture also expects the young person to be considering marriage during his or her twenties. Most people are aware of these expectations, even if their families have not made them an issue. If they are actively involved in developing other aspects of their lives, however, they can usually gain some perspective on marriage.

When young adults have not resolved earlier life tasks and have focused on marriage as a panacea, they can become acutely distressed as they near thirty. These are the people who come into treatment feeling inadequate because they have not succeeded in marrying. As one 29-year-old divorced colleague said, "I went back into therapy so the therapist could get me married."

When, at *any* age, anxiety about getting married becomes life's focus, age-appropriate emotional tasks usually take a back seat. Not only does the experience of life contract into the goal of finding a mate, but life's difficulties become viewed through the lens of marital status. Loneliness, self-esteem problems, and depression are but a few of the emotional difficulties that people feel could be resolved if they could only find that special person to marry.

The therapist's task is to help the single person reevaluate his/her life

vision and expand it to include all of the emotional tasks of the particular
life stage. When people can shift their energy to the accomplishment of
these tasks, the intense anxiety about marital status will recede. This may
not be easy since, when anxiety about finding a mate is high, even looking
in another direction may be seen as delaying this pursuit. The young person's concerns should not be minimized or invalidated. At the same time
opportunities will arise to make connections between the difficulties the
young person is having in relationships and unresolved emotional issues. At
those points, he or she will be more willing to work on life cycle tasks.

The primary emotional tasks of the young adult period include: (1)
leaving home, (2) carving out a life path, and (3) developing a network of
emotional connections outside the family.

LEAVING HOME

The notion of "leaving home" is really a symbolic statement about moving
on in life. This includes shifting one's relationships both within the family
and in the adult world. Depending on the socioeconomic and ethnic background of the family, leaving home may mean literally moving out and
establishing one's own income, or it may mean establishing one's own territory in the parental home. "Leaving home" represents beginning to establish
a separate self from the family of origin.

Often young people misunderstand the meaning of this stage and try to
cut off from their families. Many terminate regular contacts or set up
residences as far from home as possible. Such cut-offs may signal a tenuous
emotional separation from the family. This affects the young person's ability to act in a mature fashion when close to the family. When people are
struggling with adulthood in work or romantic situations, they are loathe to
be reminded of their immaturity by being close to their family. The more
sensitive they are to the tenuousness of the separation, the more difficulty
they have being near their parents.

•••

THIS SENSITIVITY CAN be seen in the case of Lucy, age 26, who initially
came to see me (NS) for generalized anxiety symptoms. She had just completed a doctoral program in psychology, and while she could have found
work in her own city, moved 300 miles to be out from under her parents'
control. She had obtained a good job as a psychologist on the staff of a
large hospital and for the first time in her life was making a good salary.

Although her parents were not happy about the distance, they supported
Lucy's wish to be on her own. They were particularly worried about her
being alone in a strange city. Lucy was also worried about living alone;
however, at the same time she felt excited and challenged. She was experi-

menting with this newfound independence and was able to develop many friendships in her new environment.

When she found herself without plans for a weekend she experimented with finding ways to be comfortable alone. She often would make dinner for herself and then go to the movies or the theater by herself. She felt quite proud that she was able to be so successful at mastering her self-consciousness about being on her own.

When Lucy discussed one of her solitary escapades with her parents, her mother reacted with dismay at her being without company. Because of the tenuous nature of her feelings about these new accomplishments, Lucy reacted intensely to her mother's worry. She began suddenly to think there was something wrong with her for not having friends on a weekend.

In therapy she was able to look at how quickly she yielded her own valuation of herself when her parents expressed worry. Although holding onto her adult sense of self was the reason she left home, it was clear that she could not rely merely on distance to accomplish this goal.

As in Lucy's situation, in order for young adults to truly establish their separate identities, family relationships must be renegotiated (Aylmer, 1989). If these relationships are renegotiated in an atmosphere of uncertainty and turmoil, the anxiety of this period will rise.

"Leaving home" also implies making choices that previously would have been handled by parents. Attending to personal health, for example, is a small but critical piece of a person's functioning that would have been the responsibility of parents. In addition, relationships with the extended family are now in the province of the emerging adult.

An arena where family and young person typically get caught is personal finances. There is an understandable overlap of responsibility when young people move in and out of self-support, and a residual connection through tax returns and financial advice may persist even after the young person has established a stable income. This is particularly true with young women, who tend to count on their fathers to maintain control of financial planning. This can be a serious problem when the young person must resolve issues with this parent in order to move on.

•••

MARY, A 28-YEAR-OLD WOMAN, was desperate to find a husband and was unable to discuss any other issue in treatment for months. Her anxiety over being married was so high that her entire life had narrowed to this one goal.

Mary was the only child in a family where father was seen as aloof and critical and mother was self-effacing. Mary kept trying to get her father's attention. Mostly she behaved as an adolescent around him, either trying to provoke him or asking her mother to talk to him for her.

Although her father was either withdrawn or critical with her, when she brought home a date he would become alive and converse intensely with this man. Certainly part of Mary's desperation to find a husband was related to trying to connect with her father. Making this explicit was useful in helping Mary gain some perspective on her situation. She began to realize that she had to try to have her own relationship with her father.

Although Mary had an excellent job as a lawyer and was completely self-supporting, she typically used her father to help her with her taxes and financial investments. This was a very difficult experience for Mary, since her father ridiculed her judgment and her confusion about her finances. Mary could see how she accepted this because it was the only way she and her father connected. She saw the parallel between her actions with her father and her helpless interactions with men in general and realized that she had to change in both arenas.

Mary understood that she had to take an adult position with her father and that their financial arrangement ultimately had to shift. There was a long period between this awareness and her ability to change. She kept coming up against the feeling that, if she stopped going to him for financial management, she would have no contact with him at all.

Mary had to come to terms with the fact that there might be a different way of connecting to her father. If she could spend time with him in other activities, she might convince herself that this was a possibility. She reluctantly decided to start watching Sunday afternoon football with him.

Her willingness to spend time with her father drew puzzled but conspiratorial glances from her mother. This made her realize how much she had taken her mother's side in the interaction between her parents. She wondered whether her father was reacting to this. She began to see their interaction in a different light. Gradually, she gathered the courage to talk to him about his interest in football. When he told her his own father took him to games when he was young, she saw him as somewhat less formidable.

Ultimately, she was able to talk to him about her finances. When he scoffed at the notion of her taking more responsibility herself, she wondered whether this was his way of staying connected to her. Rather than being reactive, she pointed out her admiration for the way he managed money and said she needed to learn this skill herself. As a result of getting a better perspective on her role in the family system, she was able to gradually learn how to take an independent position with her father without cutting off from him. Not much later she made the connection between the unresolved issues in her family and her need to affirm herself through a relationship with a man.

"Leaving home," then, represents the ability of young adults to shift their relationships with their families in such a way that they act like mature people with their parents. The change in these relationships is complex and multidimensional — and it can take a very long time.

The young person's individuation from the larger system is an interpersonal process involving the family as a unit. Thus, the entire family experiences a metamorphosis involving reciprocal interdependent changes. Since changes in relationships require constant reorganization of the self, the shifting relationships in the family push the young adult to become increasingly more articulated as a person (Shapiro, 1988). Staying connected with the family while working through complicated emotional shifts allows the young person to truly "leave home."

At the same time, changes are occurring in all parts of the system. Parents have to change roles with each other and with other children, grandparents move on to another stage of life, and siblings must shift in relation to the separating young person. The hallmark of these transitional periods is tremendous anxiety and oscillations between separateness and connection. There are times, for example, when no one is absolutely sure how to act with each other or what their roles should be. If people have enough support and flexibility, they can take some of these changes in stride.

The young adult needs to be able to tolerate frustration, failure, separateness, and ambiguity. Changing interactions with one's parents also requires quite a bit of courage and willingness to take risks (Aylmer, 1989). The feeling of separateness from the family is quite tenuous and easily shaken. For this reason, many people develop a protective pseudo-independence and are actually reluctant to spend time with their parents (Schwartzberg, 1991). This is a normal part of this period and usually recedes when people can work through their uncertainties and develop a more solid vision of their life's goals. When the emotional resources that would help people work through the issues of young adulthood are not available, many either remain symbolically at home or resolve the anxiety and internal conflict through the acquisition of socially stereotyped roles. As a result, many focus on early marriage as a solution (Shapiro, 1988).

If family members are to successfully work through this period, they must be able to tolerate separation and independence while remaining connected, to tolerate differences within their membership and a range of lifestyles outside of the immediate family (Aylmer, 1989). One patient shared with me her instant horror when her 25-year-old son defiantly brought home a date who had her hair shaved off on one side and a ring through her nostril. After an uncomfortable silence, she offered the two of them coffee and cake, and shortly thereafter they relaxed and had a pleasant conversation. A sense of humor during the worst of these times can help enormously.

The confusion in roles, as well as the wish to see children happy and secure, often prevents parents from recognizing the importance of experimentation during this period. Driven by anxiety, they see marriage, rather than the young person's ability to develop a self-defined identity, as the symbol of the successful end to this period. Young adults need help in withstanding both internal and parental pressures long enough to be able to really "leave home."

CARVING OUT A LIFE PATH

The ability to carve out a path that places equal emphasis on the development of career goals and the capacity for intimacy is important for the healthy development of both men and women. Both sexes must find ways of resolving intimacy issues so that close relationships are possible. It is also necessary for both sexes to be self-supporting.

Since most theorists have done their research on men, career development and autonomy have been stressed as goals of the young adult period (Aylmer, 1989). Study of women's lives reveals that affiliation is equally important to adult development. Gilligan (1982), in fact, emphasizes that there is no one prescribed path of social experience for young adults but, rather, an ongoing reality of separation and attachment.

Although both autonomy and attachment are seen as important for adult development, in our society each gender is programmed to value one and minimize the other. Men early on begin to "try out" different career visions of themselves. "What do you want to be when you grow up?" continues to be more seriously asked of boys than of girls. Women who expect ultimately to be a wife and mother as a primary career and who do not give deep thought to a workplace career find themselves in difficult straits if marriage does not materialize. Furthermore, those women who are positioned to expect their financial status to come from a future husband are likely to experience mate selection as a highly overvalued and anxiety-producing process (Ehrenreich, 1983).

While women may unwittingly give over to men the task of earning a living, men are trained to leave the development and maintenance of intimacy in relationships to women. There has been very little research done on how these gender-related socialization differences play themselves out in the lives of single people. Peter Stein (1981), in his seminal work in this area, points out that retaining these areas of specificity can be debilitating for those who remain single throughout their lifetime. The women in his study who had never developed careers had severe financial problems, and the single men were socially isolated. It is critical for single young people to develop in themselves, if possible, skills of both sexes. Possession of both attributes will help them be either a more rounded marital partner or have a fuller life should they remain single.

Developing one's own unique career path is both gratifying and anxiety-filled. The questions are big ones: "What do I want?" "Can I get it?" "Do I have what it takes to succeed?" Young people need enough information to make choices and enough flexibility to experiment with those choices. The desire for some certainty coupled with the need to earn a living may drive a young person to settle decisions prematurely. It is important that they give themselves the opportunity to discover their interests — whether or not those interests are valued by their family. When their interests seem unacceptable or incomprehensible to their parents, young adults need to be able to tolerate this discontinuity. One of the therapeutic tasks of this period is to help them sort out which choices represent genuine personal interests and which are merely reactions against parental demands. Parents, on their part, need to detach their own personal expectations from their child's goals in order to be able to support the legitimate choices that are made.

Race, gender, and ethnicity greatly affect the career possibilities that are feasible. Some choices, because of discrimination in the workplace, will not be available — or will be available only with considerable struggle. Economic need may shorten or eliminate the opportunity for experimentation with different career options. The values of one's ethnic group also influence the vision of what choices are possible. Letitia, a 25-year-old Hispanic-American woman, provides an example of a young person caught in an ethnic and gender bind.

•••

LETITIA WAS A bookkeeper for a wholesale fruit firm, a job she had held for three years. She was quite depressed about her lack of a romantic life (she had not had a date in months) and because she felt she could be doing more with her life than being a bookkeeper.

She had graduated from a prestigious eastern college, which she had attended on full scholarship. Although she was bright and had scored in the top 10 percentile on her college entrance exams, Letitia barely made it through academically. She wasn't able to concentrate on her studies and felt alienated — like she didn't belong there. She did not affiliate with the small group of Hispanic students, but stayed more of a loner. Upon graduation, she had little confidence in her abilities and felt she could manage only as a bookkeeper.

Being the youngest of two and the only girl, Letitia struggled with feelings of guilt that she had it better than her older brother. He was married and held a factory job. Their father was the superintendent of their apartment building; their mother worked in a school cafeteria.

Puerto Rican families are traditionally patriarchal. The husband/father is the head of the family with the major responsibility of providing the living. The wife/mother's primary responsibility is the care of the home (Garcia-Preto, 1982). For Letitia, as a woman, to be the one with the opportunity for a higher status career outside the home was both exhilarating and anxiety-provoking. All family members experienced this conflict in role expectations. Her parents, for example, expected her to continue to do household chores when she was in college and after she graduated. Letitia responded by balking, becoming furious with them, and then walking out. As a result she became alienated from her family, as she had been with her classmates. She was unable to value the traditional Puerto Rican woman's role for herself, nor was she able to move to realize her career desires. She began to feel she belonged nowhere.

Looking at her difficulties as expectable and complex tensions between two value systems (Hispanic and American) helped Letitia gain some understanding. She was able to see her parents as people caught in the same bind she was, and began to feel more hopeful of a resolution that would not leave her stranded alone between two worlds. Bringing this issue to the surface was the first step in learning how to deal with her own and the family's feelings about her success.

Letitia chose to talk first to her brother about her feelings and was astonished to learn that he was proud of her. Equally surprising to her was his relief that she would be able to "take care of herself" well. As an Hispanic older brother, he had felt a sense of responsibility for her financial care if she wasn't able to find a job. For the first time Letitia saw the burden that accompanied the rights of the male position. She was able in time to find a real role for herself in her family that respected their values, which were also partially her own. Only then could she begin work on the use of her intelligence in a career.

The ability to have intimate relationships should grow out of the work of the young adult period. Complications with relationships are normal during this period of life and do not reflect the young person's ultimate ability to be intimate. There are advances and regressions as young adults emerge from an interdependent role in the family of origin to a more separate self. Since being intimate again requires interdependence, it will feel threatening to the emerging, insecure self, arousing intense anxiety (Kegan, 1982). Whether the young adult can tolerate this anxiety long enough to work through an intimate relationship depends on the degree of self he/she has acquired (Bowen, 1978). Since the degree of self depends on resolving issues with the family of origin, intimacy is inextricably tied to family role and relationships.

Many people, experiencing discomfort in close romantic relationships, either avoid them altogether by focusing on work or on peers or look to marriage as a way to avoid the challenge of dealing with self definition. It is important to normalize relationship problems at this age, emphasizing that they are a natural outgrowth of the development of the self. People work through these issues at different rates, depending on the unresolved emotional issues in the family. When young adults give themselves time to work out these issues, they will be able to distinguish between the wish to marry as an extension of self development and the need to marry as an avoidance of self development. People can work out these issues and still remain single. They need to be able to view their struggles and their single marital status as normal in order also to enjoy the benefits of singlehood at this time in life.

DEVELOPING A NETWORK OF EMOTIONAL CONNECTIONS OUTSIDE THE FAMILY

During the turbulent twenties, a large and caring peer support network provides crucial support. This is the first group of adults that can be relied on outside of the immediate family. The ability to shift the center of support from the family of origin to an outside peer group is a significant goal in this phase of life.

While a friendship network is extremely important for single people of all ages, it takes on different purposes during each era. For young adults, the peer group takes on the meaning of a supportive and uncritical surrogate family. If the unattached adult does not have meaningful friendships, the therapist must be alert to this problem and deal with it immediately.

For young adults the peer group balances a still tenuous separation from the family. Its support and validation strengthen the young person's ability to deal with frustrations with career choices, failures in romances, and struggles to be independent. These feelings are much more appropriately handled with peers than with family. Peers share a vision, a view of the world, that parents cannot experience. This can range from job market fluctuations to new expectations around sexual relationships. Peers can hear one's concerns and offer suggestions without being experienced as judgmental, controlling, or "out of touch."

The young person's peer system also provides an invaluable arena for experimentation with adult roles. When holiday rituals are shared with the surrogate peer family, for example, young people have the opportunity to add meaning to these traditions by making them their own. This can be quite useful when jobs or graduate school require moves to distant communities.

People come and go in any young adult peer group; consequently, having a large, flexible group of social contacts is advantageous. This does not mean that people should invest this circle of friends with any less importance. Peter Stein (1981) coined the term "patchwork intimacy" to capture the shifting but intense nature of these relationships. Normalizing the changes in friendships can be useful to people as they develop a comfortable, nurturing situation outside of the family.

Because friendships provide supports for people while they are struggling with the turbulence and upset of young adulthood, they help allow emotional room to experiment with life without coming to a premature closure through early marriage. Instead, young people can gain the necessary time to work through family relationships, which will enable them to develop a real capacity for intimacy. The therapist should recognize this need for peer support and confront any blocks to developing friendships. For those who do remain single into the next phase of life, this network will move along with them and help in the next set of emotional tasks.

6

The Thirties:
Entering the "Twilight Zone"
of Singlehood

FOR MANY, TURNING THIRTY is the signal that the preliminary stage of adult life is over. Not surprisingly, it is often experienced as a crisis. In his landmark research with men across several life stages, Dan Levinson found that at the age of thirty most of his subjects described feeling considerable turmoil and confusion. They all reported a reevaluation of their life goals, principally focused around work, and an intensifications of efforts to achieve them (Levinson, 1978). While researchers have found that women's aspirations at different stages are quite different from men's, in that their goals are principally focused around affiliation (Gilligan, 1982), entrance into the thirties is also a watershed for women.

Although in general men tend to be focused on professional goals and women on relationships, by their thirties the concerns of single people of both sexes spread to other aspect of their lives. Peter Stein (1981) reports studies done with single men and women indicating that when they approached thirty many became critical of patterns established in their twenties. Previously acceptable living arrangements, which may have been temporary quarters shared with same-sex roommates, became unacceptable. Occupational choices were reevaluated, new interests and activities developed, and friendship circles expanded. In our work we find that women become more keenly aware of lifestyle limitations of living on one salary. The vision of permanently staying in unfulfilling or low-paying jobs is a chilling prospect. Men, on the other hand, realize that a lack of spouse means that they must rely on themselves to foster emotional connections. Despite the media images of desirable eligible bachelors invited everywhere and endlessly carousing with women, frequently men struggle with loneliness and do not know how to reach out to people. The longer people remain single, therefore, the more they must cross gender lines in developing roles they assumed a spouse would do for them.

The changes required of single people to adapt to their single circumstances often increase their experience of being "out of sync" with married peers. The differences become further magnified when peers start having children. At this stage, the single adult generally reacts to this sense of abnormality by feeling increased urgency to have some evidence of moving on with life. Many women in their thirties, in fact, report feeling almost panicked about their singleness. It is understandable that this kind of intense reaction usually occurs sooner for women than for men due to the pressure of the biological clock and the social message that men choose to stay single while women do so involuntarily. While men's reactions may not be immediate and open, their unexpressed isolation and sense of differentness frequently lead to depression.

Many people react to the intensity of their discomfort by stepping up their efforts to find a mate. Despite the fact that this endeavor becomes wearisome and demoralizing, people feel compelled to pursue it when they feel they are growing older and nothing is being accomplished. It has been our experience that when single people can refocus on a broader range of adult developmental tasks, there is a sense of reconnecting with the important work of life and some of the anxiety of this period may diminish.

This chapter will address the developmental tasks that are important for the single adult to pursue in the thirties decade. These tasks by no means exclude the possibility of marriage, but neither do they focus primarily on the goal of finding a mate. Although this work often leads to a greater capacity for intimacy, it may not necessarily lead to marriage for a variety of reasons, often having nothing to do with the single adult. For example, some factors that affect the potential for marriage are related more to people's geographic area or the ratio of women to men in some age or ethnic groups than to their internal capacity for intimacy. This being the case, the therapist needs to help the single adult find other areas of self-esteem and fulfillment.

The role of the therapist is quite delicate here. Helping a person develop a full sense of self outside of the conventional benchmarks of a successful life could possibly be misconstrued as devaluing marriage as an institution or, worse, confirming the single person's fears that he or she is hopeless. It is important to validate the legitimacy of the wish to be married as well as to acknowledge the real difficulties of living single in a married world. The single person's concerns must not be trivialized.

It then becomes possible to help clients examine the ways in which being single influences their evaluation of their life. When they can redefine the problem not as their "inadequacies" and instead as the impossible position in which society places single people, a workable distance from their feelings of failure is created. When they are invited to reflect on the ways in which this position affects their lives, they may become aware of how much they participate in their own oppression (White & Epston, 1990).

Distancing from a static "hopeless" problem definition is important, since it frees up energy for growth. The developmental tasks that single people need to work on in this decade require stamina, the ability to develop perspective, and the sense that there are options in life.

In the thirties decade, single people need to work on articulating an adult self in the larger family system. They need to remain open to marriage, while at the same time starting to come to grips with the possibility of remaining single permanently. This means that there must be a consolidation of life skills, which includes establishing career paths, planning for the future financially, and deepening emotional or friendship networks.

ARTICULATION OF THE ADULT SELF IN THE FAMILY SYSTEM

While the process of asserting a mature self in the family of origin is, of course, necessary for everyone's development, it is of particular importance for single people, since it is necessary for them to establish a legitimate adult role in the family. Articulating a self within the family in the thirties age period, is somewhat different from doing so in the twenties, since there is often more anxiety for everyone around the single state. Often, other unresolved issues in the family shift to the back burner as marital status becomes more prominent. The single person typically responds to these increasing tensions with a rise in sensitivity. When this type of interaction begins to occur, people tend to withdraw from the family. Since articulating a self within the family is so important for the developing person, it is critical to address this issue directly. The single person will clearly need help in dealing with his or her own feelings about the single state before the larger issue of family interaction can be handled.

Although by no means an easy process, open, nonreactive discussion of singlehood needs to occur before further progress can be made in the single person's self-definition within the family. It may take considerable preparation before the single adult can address it in a productive manner. When this emotionally laden issue can be dealt with openly, it often is the doorway to the resolution of other significant problems in the family that have been ignored while the focus was on marriage prospects. One family that I (NS) worked with, the Levines, exemplifies how preoccupation with marital status forestalls dealing with other profoundly difficult issues in the family.

•••

HARRY AND NAOMI were a middle-aged Jewish couple who were devastated by their adult children's lack of marital prospects. Not only were they in pain because marriage was a prime value in their ethnic identity, but Naomi also felt pressured by other family changes. Her own mother was aged and had recently developed a serious illness. She had often expressed the wish to see great-grandchildren before she died; now this desire had become a deep lament. Naomi, who had become progressively more uncomfortable about her children's single status, was now acutely anxious about it. She ultimately believed that the children's failure to marry and produce grandchildren meant that she had failed her mother in some profound way. Her anxiety about this issue became so overwhelming that she regularly pressured her children to marry. As a result the children withdrew from her, causing her additional grief. If the children had been able to talk about this with their mother, rather than emotionally moving away, it might have brought the family relationships to a different level.

Finding meaningful ways to define adult status when marriage does not occur is challenging but critical to the emotional health of single people and their families. Several approaches can be useful. Of primary importance, however, is the task of learning how to become *proactive* rather than *reactive*. Rather than waiting to respond to the role assigned by the family, the single person *must* take charge of the communication of his or her role.

The process of carving out and communicating an adult position pertains to all areas of participation in family life, from having holiday rituals to helping out financially if someone seems to be struggling. When a family interaction invalidates the adulthood of the single person (and this will inevitably happen) the therapist's job is to help the client find ways to challenge the regressive messages in a calm but powerful way. Finally, it is helpful to keep reminding people that the process may go on over a significant period of time, with many backslides before the family recognizes the single child as an adult.

•••

JENNY, A 35-YEAR-OLD school teacher, demonstrates what can be accomplished over time if one remains proactive. She was the middle of three children in a middle-class Italian family. She lived with a roommate in an apartment near her parents' house. Her older brother was married and her younger sister, a 27-year-old accountant, was engaged and living in another city. Both parents had pressured Jenny to marry while she was in her twenties; lately, however, they had stopped discussing the topic. Nevertheless, whenever an invitation was received for a relative's wedding, there was usually an awkward silence.

Jenny had always struggled financially and, while having a roommate cut down costs, from time to time she had asked her parents for money. At these times her father would ask, "When are you going to find a husband to take care of you?" Usually a fight would ensue, resulting in Jenny's crying and demanding to be treated like an adult.

When this was discussed in therapy, Jenny complained that her parents treat her like a child, but at the same time acknowledged how she often both felt and acted a child when she was around them. She was also quite aware that, while her parents didn't openly talk about her getting married, the subject was always quietly lurking in the background. Their wish for her to marry was clearly connected to their perception of her as still a child who could not take care of herself or assume an adult role in the family. In the context of family relationships, in fact, she had done little to demonstrate this.

Challenging this perception soon became her goal in therapy. A plan was made where she would quietly explore ways to take on and demonstrate responsibility in the family. She began calling her brother and sister-in-law to make plans to take her nephew out to ballgames. She told them it was about time they had some free time and that she would like to get to know her nephew better. Although her parents resisted coming to her house for dinner, she showed up at their house from time to time with a dish she had cooked for them. On her parents' anniversary, she initiated plans with her brother and sister to take them out to dinner. Gradually, people in the family started to ask her more frequently to help out.

Enjoying her changed role in the family from one who needs help to one who helps, both she and her parents avoided the issue of marriage, although it continued to be an undercurrent of discomfort. Coming from a family that prized marrriage and family so highly, she felt sure she caused her family great humiliation in her failure to marry. Her own sense of vulnerability and loss related to not marrying also made it hard for her to expose her thoughts. She worried that revealing her own sadness would give her parents the message that she needing rescuing. Before she could open up the issue with her parents, Jenny clearly had to become more comfortable with her single status.

After some time, Jenny felt calm enough to have an open discussion with her parents about the issue of her not being married. She picked an evening when the three of them were alone. When they finished dinner, Jenny, quite frankly, asked both her parents if they ever wondered why she didn't marry. At first they were quite awkward and tried to minimize the issue. Jenny pushed them for their thoughts, making it clear she valued their input. By staying with the subject Jenny essentially gave them permission to talk about what had always been a sensitive subject. Finally, her mother opened up and talked about her worries that she was too overprotective when Jenny was a child. Her father thought maybe there was something wrong with her.

They were not able to talk about their disappointment on this occasion, but Jenny was able to bring up the subject on other nights. Ultimately, her father told her that the reason he got so upset when she needed money was because of his worry that she would not be able to take care of herself without a man. Jenny, for the first time, acknowledged his concern and told him that she, in fact, was also worried about her financial security. While she loved being a teacher and was unwilling to give up this profession, she realized she had to make extra money on the side so that she could do the things she wanted to do without asking him for help. She knew she had to make plans for her financial future. Her father was surprised that she had thought of these issues. Over the next few months the relationship between Jenny and her parents continued to change and she was able feel more like an adult daughter and less like a child.

Moving into an adult position in the family often takes a great deal of patience as well as the willingness to take on more responsibility. It also requires the ability to openly discuss the single status and accept the feelings that family members may have about this. This includes feelings that parents may have about the possibility of not having grandchildren, a subject that may also be quite painful for the single adult. At the same time, genuine discussion of feelings can ultimately enhance the relationship between parent and child.

FRIENDSHIPS AS AN EXPANSION OF FAMILY

While work in the family of origin is extremely important in this phase, it is also very useful for single people in the thirties to expand their notion of what constitutes family. As single people face the potential absence of a traditional nuclear family life, friendship networks can take on an added dimension, particularly if the division between family and friends becomes less rigid. When the quality of the relationships deepen and provide a significant "family like" structure with reciprocal expectations, friendships can also provide opportunities for the articulation of an adult self.

When friendships are valued along with family relationships as a source of connection and support, loyalty conflicts may arise. The single person may feel pressure to dismiss the needs of friends because they are not "family." Because of the unique position of the single person in the family and society, responsibility to friends must be negotiated so that the needs of close friends are significantly weighted alongside the needs of the kinship family.

While it is crucial to develop a solid friendship network in all stages of the life cycle, its meaning and importance shift from decade to decade. In the thirties it provides an important counterbalance to increased concerns about career and finding a mate. A community of friends also can provide a vision of a connected life that is different from the standard of married and family life. It is critical for the therapist to be aware of the nature and depth of the friendship network and work with the single person to develop it further if necessary.

COMING TO GRIPS WITH THE SINGLE STATE

Many single people live as if they were waiting for something to happen in their lives. This is particularly a problem in the thirties as people watch their married counterparts acquiring the trappings of a settled life. At the same time, making more substantial plans, like fixing up a home or taking more responsibility for financial planning, feels like giving up on marriage to many people.

The question of why people see these options as contradictory is important to consider. Making plans does not in any real way eliminate the possibility of marriage. Single people who were asked about this generally respond by saying that not planning for the future gives them the illusion that the single state is only temporary; soon they will marry and "real adult life" will begin.

In order for single people to feel they are moving on in life, they have to be able to give up the illusion that their adult life has not started. Coming to grips with the fact that they are, in fact, single allows people to make their present life as meaningful as possible and does not mean giving up the idea of marrying in the future. As people move into their late thirties and distress about never marrying is greater, there may be much more reluctance to embrace the immediate single state. To validate their current life, however, it is important to experience the sadness of a marriage not yet achieved in order to move on in life. Again, the therapist must be careful. People may not be able to separate accepting the single state from feeling a sense of hopelessness. It is important to continue clarifying that these two issues are not necessarily joined.

There are many emotional tasks to work on once people are able to deal realistically with their single status. For example, it is extremely important to help people—men and women—become serious about making a comfortable home for themselves. This does not necessarily mean that a great deal of money needs to be spent on a house or apartment; however, people must pay attention to how they live. A home, a stable living situation, symbolizes the separate and valued self.

When one is in a financial position to do so, the purchase of a home can be seen as a validation of adult status. The commitment of a home purchase is often experienced as difficult for the single person, as it is seen as permanent statement of status. This, of course, is not necessarily true—as many divorced couples can attest to. At the same time, it is experienced by many as a rite of passage, since it has important ritualistic significance in confirming a psychologicaly independent position for single people (Adams, 1981). When people can't afford to buy property, or when their ethnic or physical situations do not allow the possibility of independent living situations, symbolic ways can be found to develop and enhance a separate living situation.

•••

YOUNG SOON, A KOREAN-AMERICAN woman in her mid-thirties, was the youngest of seven children and the only single person in the family. Though she had a very successful career as a television set director she had never considered moving out of the parental home. Feeling a strong obligation to her widowed mother, Young Soon felt quite fulfilled. She was not concerned about her marital status, but did feel somewhat restricted in terms of her activities away from home. She also wanted to have some space where she could experience "alone time." Being single was somewhat atypical in her culture, and she was at a loss about how to manage some of her needs.

Lacking any role models in her culture, she decided that she could be creative about how to proceed. She took one room in the house and made it into a special place for herself. Being artistic, she was able to design the room as if it were a stage set of a Parisian boudoir. Here she felt she could establish her own identity. She was also able to speak to her siblings about needing their cooperation so she could on occasion go out on her own and stay away from home. The siblings agreed to regularly spend time at their mother's house, so she could have freedom to stay away a few days on her own.

In the Korean culture the autonomy of the individual is not stressed, as the needs of the individual are seen as secondary to those of the family (Shon & Ja, 1982). Young Soon was being responsive to what she saw as her role of caring for mother by not moving out of the house. Her challenge was to find a way to lead a more satisfying life as a single person without throwing to the side the other contexts — her family, her culture — that gave meaning to her life. Because being single pushes people to the margin, it is important for both therapist and client to make singlehood work within the other contexts that define the single person. At the same time there is an opportunity in difference that can allow for creativity, as Young Soon demonstrated.

Singlehood may offer a similar opportunity to expand gender roles that is not as readily available in marriage. If single women and men can be helped to experiment with different aspects of their selves, they can actually accelerate development in cross-gender skills, since there is no marital system to lock gender-specific tendencies into place.

Like Jenny, who had to come to grips with her financial situation in order to establish an adult identity, single women must deal with their careers in a serious way. If women have not taken their careers seriously because they expected to get married, the thirties decade is the time to change this position. Turning around the meaning of career and helping women to develop their self-esteem in this area are critical tasks of this period.

It is also extremely important to help women attend to their present and future financial situation. It is not uncommon but perhaps understandable that they tend to ignore this aspect of their lives. As long as women continue to make less than men society reinforces this neglect. If their economic resources are limited and they have focused on the idea that marriage is near, financial management might not have seemed necessary (Adams, 1981). Nevertheless, if even small amounts of resources are invested at this point, it will make a difference in later years. Financial planning is also helpful in creating the sense in women that they are not just "ladies in waiting" but substantial people in their own right.

For men in their thirties coming to grips with single status will mean not only developing a home for themselves, but also learning to deal with issues of vulnerability in relationships. Many men report having friends, but when these relationships are examined they appear to be quite superficial. That is not surprising, since the social conditioning of men works against the formation of intimate male-to-male relationships (Meth, 1990b). It is critical for men on their own at this age to learn how to deal with and get close to people.

•••

LARRY WAS A 36-year-old single man who came for treatment after failing the law boards. This was his second failure, and he reacted to it with a deep depression. Larry had decided to be a lawyer after having been a policeman for eight years, saying that he wanted to earn more money. His father was proud that his son would be a "professional man." Although his parents were very supportive of him, telling him he would do better next time, Larry could not get over his disappointment with himself for failing the boards.

Larry described a comfortable family relationship, many friendships, and frequent dates. He lived in his own apartment a few blocks away from his parents in a lower-middle-class section of the city. He was the oldest of three children, all men, in a second-generation Irish family. In his family, not only his father, but his grandfather and two uncles were policemen. He grew up with stories about the brave feats of the men in his family.

In the course of therapy, he was able to admit that he left the police force because he was afraid of being killed. His partner had been wounded while they were working together and ever since that time he had been terrified. He was so anxious to leave this line of work that he froze when he took his law boards.

Because he had never spoken of his fears, he had no context to normalize his feelings. While therapy provided the first framework to do this, he needed to talk with other members of his "police" family to not feel something was wrong with him. When he was finally able to talk to his father about his fears, he actually received a very positive response. His father gave him a glimpse of his own struggle with this issue and expressed his relief, rather than disappointment, when Larry left the police department. He had been concerned about his son.

The positive experience of talking with his father encouraged Larry to think more about his relationships. He realized that there was not one friend, male or female, whom he could talk to about his feelings. This was surprising because, when he had previously described his relationships, he had talked about them as being very close. It turned out that, although there were warm feelings between Larry and his friends, they spent most of their time drinking or watching sports and very little time talking to each other.

The feelings about the men in his family were similar, in that he felt warmly toward them but couldn't open up. They, in turn, could not open up to each other. His discussion with his father was probably the most open discussion he had had with him in his life. He understood that in order to be closer to people, he would have to be willing to talk about himself and run the risk of being rejected. Larry thought that he would probably get a negative reaction from some of his friends if he shared his feelings, but there were a few that he thought he could talk to. Much of the sessions after that were spent in preparing Larry to talk to his friends and to handle the problems he might encounter in doing so.

In order for men to deal with the lack of intimate relationships they must become aware of the importance of friendships in their lives. Since most men do not usually enter therapy with this as a problem, it must be established that this is indeed critical for their emotional well-being. The therapist must demonstrate that intimate connections do make a difference. At the same time, men can be helped to believe that it is possible for their friendships to be enriched without presenting a risk to their masculinity (Meth, 1990b).

Working on issues of intimacy is of primary importance to both men and women at this age. They are being bombarded by messages from the larger society that lack of marriage can be equated with problems in intimacy. This negative self-image is frequently enhanced by the anxiety and self-doubts associated with dating.

The therapist, however, walks a fine line when addressing issues of intimacy. It is critical not to mirror society's message of pathology. At the same time, if people do have problems in intimacy, they cannot be ignored. Evaluating these problems and tracking their connection to unresolved issues in the larger family system can be very useful. The process of working towards individuation in the family of origin enhances the adult's capacity to relate flexibly towards people who are close to him/her and can ultimately lead to greater potential for intimacy (Shapiro, 1988). It is important to emphasize that resolution of these issues may not necessarily lead to marriage and that marriage in itself is not proof of intimacy.

The anxiety people feel about their capacity to be close frequently emerges in the sexual arena. They often think something is wrong with them when they are not having the great unencumbered sex that the media leads us to believe single people enjoy. The reality is, however, that single people are no more comfortable or uncomfortable with their sexuality than married people are with theirs.

While sharing the anxieties most people in our culture have about sex, singles have the added burden of having to work out these issues outside the context of a long-term relationship. Anxieties about dating new people and anxieties about sex are often intermingled. One common result is to act out the anxiety about dating by having sex with a partner prematurely. This often leads to an escalation of concern about rejection and increased sexual tension.

When the specter of AIDS emerged in the 1980s, it made dating even more difficult. Fears of this disease hit the singles community particularly hard. Old sexual relationships were reexamined; new ones were approached with caution. Those who had partners tried to hold onto them for fear of potential infection from new ones. For many, the tendency toward self-blame when relationships failed was intensified. While many single people have adjusted their sexual behavior to be more selective and to include "safe sex," the impact of AIDS on dating continues to be felt.

CREATING NEW RULES

At the end of the thirties decade people tend to feel that the traditional options available to them through marriage and family are closing down. It is important to recognize that if marriage does occur later on, it will follow a different rhythm and answers different needs than a marriage in the twenties or even early thirties. At the same time, the immediate needs for companionship or desire for children can be addressed if people are willing to look outside the realm of gender, ethnic, and societal convention. The single person may decline to change the structure of the dream—a dream that says a relationship is only valuable when it leads to marriage or children can only be in your life if you are married. Evaluating the options lays the groundwork for the reconcilation process that must occur if the dream is not achieved at later stages.

Having a child without marriage is increasingly becoming an option. According to the Census Bureau, the number of children born to single middle-class women has more than doubled in the last decade (Lawson, 1993). There has also been an increase in adoptions, particularly foreign adoptions, by single people. Other countries are frequently more receptive to letting single people adopt their children and have higher age cut-offs for potential parents. As a result, it is becoming more common to find support groups, such as Single Parents by Choice, to help deal with the problems and share the joys. Although single men are also choosing to have their own children, their numbers are far fewer than women. Still, there are men who have taken this route (R. Diamond, personal communication, 1994).

Despite the growing number of single people having children, being a single parent is not easy and it should not be romanticized. Not only is it difficult to be at odds with societal expectations, but there is the need for greater financial stability and social resources when raising children on one's own. If support networks, friendship and family, have been developed and finances have been taken seriously leading up to this decision, the transition to parenthood will be easier.

For many single people, chosing to have a child outside the context of a relationship will not feel like an option or even seem desirable. Because the biological door for woman is begining to close, they must begin to confront the possiblity that not only may they never marry, but they may never have children. Avoiding this issue now will make the mourning process that occurs more fully in the forties more difficult. It is important to recognize that the issue of childlessness is never completely resolved, but has different significance over the course of the life cycle and in reaction to nodal events, such as the death of a parent. Susan Lang (1991) cites studies of never married older women who had few regrets about not marrying but continuing regrets about not having children, even in old age. Even in the thirties, when having one's own children is still a possiblity, those budding regrets need to be acknowledged so that alternative visions of life without children are considered and valued.

By the end of the thirties, the rules of relationships may also need to be expanded to accommodate intimate connections that are not necessarily marriage bound. If anxiety remains high and marriage is still the prime objective, relationships live or die in the first fifteen minutes as each person goes through his or her mental marriage check list. The result can be a more constricted social life than previously experienced in the twenties.

To continue to develop a meaningful vision of life it is extremely important for single people to emerge from their thirties without being ruled by the idea that time is running out. At the end of this stage in the life cycle some people are still desperately trying to get in "under the gun." This only increases their sense of desperation. When singles can be open to marriage but still entertain other options, turning forty becomes less daunting.

HAROLD BRIDGES LIBRARY
S. MARTIN'S COLLEGE
LANCASTER

7

The Forties to Mid-Fifties: Developing Alternative Scripts

THIS MIDLIFE PHASE is a crucial time for single people. It ushers in a very necessary period of taking stock, of reshaping and rethinking one's place in the world. Time is no longer the Ganges River, flowing forever, but a bag of sand that is slowly running out. A fortieth birthday, particularly for women, brings that emotional awareness to the center of one's being. While within the married nuclear family it is the developing younger generation that pushes along the tasks of the midlife generation, for the single adult it is the inexorability of time itself.

Because the emotional meaning and thus the impact of time are different for men and women at this phase, the emotional processes for the genders begin to diverge. In their forties single men and women live in markedly different social realities, with the emotional weight of closing options falling hardest on single women. Women have a procreative time limit; men don't. Women continue to feel social and personal pressure to "marry up" (taller, richer, older); men don't. Men continue to have the choice of bearing their own children down the road and have available a wide range of "acceptable" marital partners; women don't. Even so, men, too, usually have some kind of internal beeper that starts going off saying "It's time."

The fact of these differing options has tremendous implications for that crucial element in therapy called "joining" by Minuchin and "fit" by Richard Simon (in Carter & McGoldrick, 1989). Male therapists working with women need to be acutely aware of women's social reality; too often women's expressions of frustration or desperation about not finding a man are seen only as denial, resistance, or some such. For women therapists (especially single ones) working with single men at this phase, a common "fit" problem is not taking their emotional struggle seriously enough. Men appear to have the world at their disposal, and it is all too easy to minimize the intensity of their feelings — especially since men tend to minimize them as well.

The drift toward segregation between single and married people which began in previous decades as parents turned their energies to childrearing is usually firmly in place by the forties. There are powerful social, emotional, and practical reasons why segregation happens: for example, a single person's social life mainly takes place when married counterparts are hurrying home to deal with supper, homework, and putting children to bed. Married people, perceiving singles (particularly women) as a potential threat, may not readily incorporate them into their regular social life. Single people may often avoid contact with families, so as not to experience painful feelings of what they are missing. Vacations are in different social worlds: joining a family cottage at the shore is not usually a single person's ideal vacation plan.

This distancing may intensify thinking "of families as a standard from which we have deviated; *their lives are the reality, ours the imitation*, the variant, the makeshift" (Holland, 1992, p. 251, italics added). As one client put it: "I feel like the Little Match Girl with her nose pressed against the window watching everyone else on the inside eating and laughing." This segregation may contribute to the creation of some debilitating idealizations of what life on the other side is truly like, such that your single client becomes mired in longing and is unable to feel rooted in an authentic life of his/her own.

As we discussed in Chapter 3, class and ethnic variables may either mitigate or accentuate this segregation. Those cultures with a more embracing definition of family (e.g., American Black, Mediterranean, and Hispanic) will more easily include the single adult as a genuine family member, rather than as a guest (McGoldrick, Pearce, & Giordano, 1982). Single people are often called by family titles (such as aunt, uncle, goom-ba, cousin) and after a while the fact that there is no blood connection may even be forgotten. Other ethnic groups (e.g., WASP, Northern European) draw a firmer line between nuclear/extended and blood-related/nonblood-related, so that single people are made much more aware of their "not quite in" status.

As for class, the less money there is, the more likely a single person will continue to live with parents or other relatives. While this provides an unmarried person with automatic membership in familial daily life, it exacerbates issues around role definition and conflicts between family loyalty and personal freedom.

These themes — the differential gender impact of time and life's options, and the degree to which the single person is incorporated into or distanced from the lives of married family and friends — are the background for the playing out of the emotional issues of the midlife phase.

ADDRESSING THE "IDEAL"
FAMILY FANTASY

It's a rare person who doesn't respond to the template embedded within that says "You should be married by now." No matter how positive one's personal feelings about singlehood may be, there is usually a counterbalancing feeling that one's life is "off-track." It is almost impossible to avoid this self-appraisal, given the strong, unilateral messages in our society that marriage is the only sane goal for a mentally healthy adult (see Chapter 2). The fact that you didn't get there is felt to demand an explanation of some sort. Clients will already have explanations they've come up with: for women these explanations tend to be more deficit-based (e.g., some basic personality flaw) or blaming (e.g., my mother didn't provide a good role model). For men the explanations tend to revolve around problems with emotional connection (e.g., "I never found the right one," or "I'm afraid of commitment"). These statements may or may not be accurate personal appraisals. The question is: Why is an adequate explanation felt to be necessary? After all, the possession of basic personality flaws, poor role models, and fears of commitment could characterize a whole lot of married people as well. Only when either status can be equally casually questioned, as in "You're such a good-looking (bright, good, etc.) person — why did you ever get married?" will we know that singlehood has achieved societal authenticity.

We therapists need to listen carefully to these explanations, not reframe them away. They represent our clients' struggle with finding a place in a culture that hasn't made legitimate room for them. They are the meaning our clients are currently giving to their lives and the constructed reality they bring for therapeutic work.

Singlehood can take on all the qualities of other family skeletons, and clinical process should be designed to give them a good airing. If you can talk about it, you can start to dance with it.

Women's World: Watching Closing Doors

For women the heightened awareness and intensity of these closing door years may begin at mid-thirties or come in a rush on a fortieth birthday. Some women will have come to some resolution in their thirties; others may intensify their desperation as their forties unroll. Our experience is that feelings around marriage, and especially feelings around motherhood, will continue to recycle in lessening degrees of intensity throughout one's forties.

We need to allow room for the full expression of the feelings involved and to give permission for the exploration of the range of choices that are still available. They may not be easy choices, but they are, nevertheless, choices. For some women the intensity will primarily be centered around not being a wife; for others the core will be not having one's own children. We can be of great help by separating these two distinct experiences, wife and mother, to clarify clients' thinking about which are the experienced losses. Most women coming for therapy at this time, regardless of how articulate they may be, are experiencing such a massive assortment of feelings that they need considerable space to sort them out.

Everyone needs to be aware of and to address the choices that are available. If the pain is centered around not being a wife, then the focus should rest there. If a woman really wants to be married, she can always find *somebody*. Questions can shift from "Why am I such a failure?" to "How much am I willing to compromise?" and "What price am I willing to pay?"

•••

BARBARA, A 41-YEAR-OLD elementary school teacher, was briefly married in her early twenties. She came for consultation, mired in feelings of worthlessness, unlovability, and mild depression. Her "reality" was that not having found a husband publicly demonstrated her shame and failure as a woman, and prohibited her from enjoying her work, her family, and her friends. At the time she came, she was dragging herself to work and watching a lot of television at night. Her life was made doubly painful by having to watch all the "happy wives" at the end of each day as they picked up their children. She was considering switching to high school teaching, even though she loved elementary, to avoid this daily reminder of her loss.

An approach that attempted to move Barbara off her fixation on marriage and onto relishing what she did have would have devalued her "reality." The risk would have been Barbara's perception that even her therapist thought she was deficient, that a better person wouldn't be fixated at all. Framing the work of therapy needs to validate the client's notion of the solution: for Barbara that was getting a husband.

Barbara, like many women, was operating from the old school dance image of relationships; girls stand around looking nonchalant and wait for a boy to come over. Whoever doesn't get chosen is a publicly unwanted wallflower, trying to put a bright face on rejection. This view left Barbara passively waiting, obscuring the possibility that she herself could be the chooser.

Single people at this age are generally fairly comfortable with the notion of job hunting, job getting, and expecting a reasonable fit between their needs and the job itself. Work, after all, is a central foundation of the single person's world. This attitude and these skills can often be used directly to transform the enervating passivity of people like Barbara. Looking for a spouse can be viewed the same way as looking for a job; however, now the client gets to define the job description and do the interviewing. With this frame, the solution remains the same, but more interesting and enlivening questions present themselves: What *is* my job description? How *do* I want to look (e.g., advertise? interview men for a research project I concoct?)? *Where* do I want to look (in another state? another country?)? From this vantage point Barbara can again operate from within her own skin, using skills she knows she has, and take control over the choices available to her. She may not find a man she chooses to marry, but she will gain a deeper understanding of her priorities.

Whatever women's feelings about singlehood (pride, relief, yearning, or desperation), feelings about childlessness may intensify in the forties, particularly if the issue has not been addressed before. The option of having a child on one's own that we discussed in the previous chapter continues to be available and may seem more within the decision-making control of a single woman than finding a husband. The life of single parenthood may be a lot of work, but some clients will prefer this set of problems to the loss of not raising a child at all. These are real choices and should be treated as such in the therapy room. While marriage and *then* parenthood is still the "acceptable" life progression, therapy should not be implicitly structured as if this were so.

There has been a pervasive notion that women alone should not voluntarily choose to raise children. It's more socially acceptable if there was no choice: your husband abandoned you, or you tried hard to make the marriage work but couldn't. Not that long ago, a single colleague of mine (DJ) was fairly universally regarded (including by her own therapist) as irresponsibly neurotic for going ahead with a pregnancy, even though she had gathered a support network of family and friends and figured out how to earn a living and care for her baby.

Although society is changing, feelings run deep around this issue, reinforced by political views in which anything other than a household containing one husband and one wife is considered an "alternative lifestyle." There is also one's personal moral view about voluntary out-of-wedlock births. If you do not genuinely consider responsible childrearing an authentic choice for a single person, our recommendation is to refer your unmarried client elsewhere. Truncating the process of dealing with the potential loss of childrearing by overtly or covertly pathologizing an available choice will impede either the resolution of the mourning process or the process of conceiving or adopting a child.

The majority of single people will decide not to raise a child. For them this door will close. Mourning the loss of what will never be will be intense for some, minimal for others. It is only cultural myth that all women biologically and emotionally yearn for their own children. There are those who genuinely don't, and it's important not to impose a mourning task on them, implying that they are deficient in some basic way by not feeling this loss. For those to whom it *is* a loss, this sadness needs to be acknowledged as real. Experiencing the sadness helps clients to move ahead and deepen available relationships with children in the future, rather than avoid them because of the pain they dredge up.

Men's World: "Where Did Everybody Go?"

While approximately 40% of men before age forty are yet to marry, only about 6% remain never married in the decades following forty (based on 1993 poll data from the U.S. Census Bureau). Connecting with a viable social network of people who share the unmarried life becomes increasingly difficult for men. While opportunities for meaningful community are greater for men with an acknowledged gay orientation, others are most clearly "out of the mainstream" for their age. The acceptable life trajectory for an American man is as rigid as ever: get your work in place, then get married, then have children. To do otherwise smacks of irresponsibility, instability, selfishness, and/or doubts of sexual orientation in the societal eye. A study by Jacoby (1974) polling attitudes toward the never-married in the business world, for example, found that older single men were viewed as more unstable and likely to have personal problems that hindered their job performance. Never-married women at this age were viewed as assets who were more committed to their profession. Bernard (1982) found that, beginning in midlife years, the average never-married man drops significantly below his female single counterpart in socioeconomic variables (income, education, occupational prestige). What used to be regarded with some envy as a carefree single life in one's thirties—Club Med vacations and group summer homes—comes off as rather pitiable if continued into one's forties and fifties. Unmarried midlife men generally experience this abrupt shift in social attitude toward them in one form or another, and this may be reflected in their own sense of worth.

Those men who have more or less successfully negotiated the earlier task of establishing themselves in work continue to have a wide range of acceptable marital partners available, as well as time to father their own children. Men who have not been able to build a work life for themselves, for whatever reasons, may begin a critical drift at this phase. What is called "finding yourself" at thirty gets called "floundering" at forty. Without an achieved status and/or financial stability, they are not likely to view themselves or be viewed by most women as viable marriage partners.

Men's sense of identity and worth continues to be intimately linked to how and how much money they earn, and men tend to overvalue work as a self-definer while they undervalue character and human qualities. The attribution of "failure" may be an objective self assessment, or it may be a more personal construction.

●●●

JOE, AN ATTRACTIVE, personable, intelligent, very gentle 42-year-old never-married man, worked at a deli. He viewed this as a temporary job when he took it, but twenty years later he was still there. He'd risen to a management position, earned a reasonable salary, and had even purchased a brownstone in a distinctly family neighborhood. Joe's spoken desire was to get married and have his own family, but he felt unable to until he got on with his "real" life work—being a writer. "How can I be responsible for someone else when I haven't got on with who I am?" At the time, Joe was (not surprisingly with so much riding on it) blocked in his writing, and therefore, because of his viewpoint, stymied in moving in any direction.

While there are many issues here, the one we want to highlight is the enormous driving force behind the inner template of the "proper" sequence in which to live life. Single people need to begin consciously questioning its value and relevance for themselves. In Joe's mind (a societal mirror), until he was doing *his* work he lacked identity and therefore was not yet "present-able" for marriage. First you get a self (your work); then you get married. The closeness of the fit between self and work should be a regular part of the assessment inquiry. This is true for everybody, of course, but particu-larly so for men.

If men like Joe further lack the ability and/or opportunity for close friendships and family ties, they are highly likely to begin a sad move toward society's periphery. It is this age group (and older) who are most prone to poor physical and mental health (Bernard, 1982). Joe, for exam-ple, lived far enough away from his family of origin so that easy visiting was not possible. He had recently begun to feel like the odd man out at family gatherings (he was the only unmarried sibling) and was starting to avoid going home for the holidays. Neither did he invite family to visit him, though he had plenty of room—the idea had simply not occurred to him. While Joe had a few close friends, one was about to get married, and another was moving to a distant city. His network was inevitably dwindling as life worked its changes. He was also not integrated into his community, linked in any personal way to religious or neighborhood groups. Joe was in a bowling league, which he enjoyed, but conversation among the bowlers was at a minimum. Being a man, he was less trained in initiating friendships than his female counterparts, and more at the mercy of others to approach him to replace these recent losses.

Such single men typically do not initiate therapy, but they may come to it at the urging of a family member or a boss when substance abuse problems or depression interfere with work performance. It's important to locate the life cycle issues not only by chronological age but by where each person became "stuck"—in Joe's case on issues more characteristic of the thirties decade. The therapy should recognize and articulate the altered social reality of the older unmarried man. The consequences for men's mental and physical health if they continue to remain single are of concern. The bulk of the work will, of course, be in exploring the multigenerational themes and personal issues embedded in the choice to be single. For men, as for women, the therapeutic stance needs to include continued singlehood as an authentic, viable choice when made with clarity, self-knowledge, and awareness of the drawbacks as well as the advantages.

DEFINING THE MEANING OF WORK, CURRENT AND FUTURE

For single people, the workplace is usually the central anchor and organizing focus of daily life. As Holland puts it:

> Alone, without families . . . our jobs are our social and worldly reality, our connection to the wheels that move things forward, and a major source of nourishment. When the job feels worth spending the day's energy on, the evenings and weekends feel less restless; we need less payback from them, fewer ways to entertain ourselves. We need less input from our friends to reinforce our sense of self; we know who we are. (1992, p. 153)

We have tended to downplay or even denigrate the emotional importance of work and its connection to the soul in the therapy hour. This happens even in our heavily work-oriented culture, when we ourselves may be working long hours. After all, throwing oneself into work is often viewed as avoiding dealing with personal issues. For the single person, the connection of work life to personal meaning is essential, and we need to make room for deep exploration of this in therapy. Personal meaning comes in many forms—pride in earning one's living, giving to society, creating something enduring, power. The childless person has no progeny to carry on unfulfilled dreams, making their realization in this life more compelling. The single person's advantage is in more freedom to make changes in his/her work life, since the repercussions of change don't reverberate through an entire nuclear family.

Work is broader than just earning money. It is using skills and talents in a valued and valuable way in one's world, whether being paid or not. Clients who are obliged to stay in unrewarding jobs for economic reasons can and should consider additional "work" that is personally meaningful. A computer analyst began a program for food delivery to the homeless in the evenings; a telephone operator spent weekends working to track changes in aquatic life in a nearby pond.

A related issue of work's meaning is common to all who reach midlife. One hundred years ago the issue was resolved by early death; now increasing longevity provides us with the "midlife crisis." Work which may have been a good fit with one's needs and goals at age thirty may no longer be meaningful at age fifty. Perhaps a person wants to use different talents that had to remain dormant in the earlier necessity of earning a living. Now is the time to take a good, clear look at one's work and how it relates to personal goals. The opportunity for a second "life plan" is still available. One can either solidify or reshape the personal meaning of one's current profession or begin the thinking and visualizing that precedes planning another life work. This process of contemplating change and reshaping meaning is particularly important for the single person, given the centrality of work to her/his life. In this the single person is at a distinct advantage over married counterparts. Unburdened by financial obligations for schooling and continued parenting, the single person at this age can reap the benefits of the increased freedom and autonomy of the single life to responsibly risk changes that may be unavailable to those heading nuclear families.

DEFINING AN AUTHENTIC LIFE
AS A SINGLE ADULT

Authentic means not feeling that one's life is an imitation, that "real" life is being lived by those married and/or with children. Most people in their forties have been or are married and most have children by this time. Some people will have an easier time with the notion of marching to a different drummer than others; some will value the freedom and autonomy of singlehood and some will not. Seeing one's life as authentic does not necessarily mean giving up the idea of being married — it means giving up waiting to be married for real life to begin. Lina, for example, looked at her single status as a badge of feminist pride in her thirties and felt vitally engaged in building her career. By the time she was in mid-forties, however, and her friends were married with young children, she regarded her singlehood as a "stupid failure." She indulged in endless fantasies of her life as it might have been and should be (i.e., married). The issue of defining authenticity is a life theme that continually recycles. What makes this issue more poignant in midlife, however, is that we are programmed to believe we should have "already gotten there" by then. Wherever "there" is, we define ourselves as deficient if we seem to be somewhere else.

Reforging the Love = Marriage Connection

A client told a story of an evening when she and two good friends got together with the intention of going out to a singles event. They talked, they laughed, they ate, they were having a good time with each other. It was very cold outside, yet they all reluctantly agreed they "should" go out and try to meet someone. This is what a mentally healthy woman is supposed to do. Then they began to figure the odds: they started with 10 million people in the New York area, but, after listing certain basic criteria (male, unmarried, ages 35–55, no serious mental problems or drug addictions, employed in a respectable job, heterosexual, interested in commitment), decided that the chance that one of these now numbering 2,000 men would be at the 92nd Street Y tonight was remote. They heaved a sigh of relief and settled in for an evening together.

Why did these women need to justify to themselves their clear preference for their own company that evening? The women interviewed in Anderson, Stewart, and Dimidjian's (1994) project seem to have resolved any ambivalence they might have had about this issue: "Of all the women, only a few were willing to go out of their way . . . risk time, money, and feelings that might range from boredom to humiliation to seek a relationship" (p. 200). While many midlife single people may have reached this point, in our experience a sizable number have not.

The old emotional template—that "real" love and intimacy can only be found with a mate—needs to be reforged. The reality is that at midlife intimacy is primarily linked to long-term friends and family, people who have a shared history together. And, despite the messages of the media to the contrary, sexual passions are usually secondary in importance to the desire for companionship. Love is another story, but as one woman in *Flying Solo* put it: "It's so much fun being in love . . . but that isn't always a corollary to being married" (Anderson et al., 1994, p. 196). By the forties, the notion that the intimacy and love that count can be found only in marriage needs to be jettisoned. Holland, in *One's Company*, expresses it admirably:

> We need to stay open to the simple possibilities of loving. We were told in youth that the whole point and purpose of love, the only possible excuse for it, was to set up a traditional household that becomes a working part of the social machine. Just maybe, though, love comes in other shapes usable by us, the non-traditional unfamilied legions. (1992, p. 252)

Once the love = marriage equation becomes dismantled, the single person can begin to give true and *equal* value to other shapes of loving.

This dismantling is necessary for viewing what Anderson et al. call "encapsulated intimacies" as valuable and authentic in themselves, not as "make-do" substitutes for the real thing. These "encapsulated intimacies" can take an infinite variety of shapes: romantic liaisons with someone at a great geographical distance, opposite-sex friendships without sexual desire, shorter or longer term relationships where marriage is not a possibility (including affairs), and friendships.

We must be watchful as therapists to encourage this developing shift. It's easy to automatically mirror our own cultural images — particularly so for therapists not yet at midlife — and implicitly treat the "natural" progression of any relationship that "counts" as leading toward marriage. Questions like "Where is this relationship going?" or "Is this what you *really* want?" may be taken by clients to mean that anything short of marriage is not a good goal. In addition, the impact of marriage on daily life for a financially viable midlife person is great; there may be more to lose than will be gained in quality of life. Of course, therapists need to operate within their own values and principles. Those who believe that sexuality outside marriage is morally wrong will find working on this issue with single people difficult for both client and therapist.

Connecting with Future Generations

Some people feel the need to seek a wider meaning for their lives as age fifty approaches. Pride taken in prior accomplishments may lose importance as a personal motivator. For others the continued pleasure and satisfactions in what they've done, what they have, and where they've been will be enough.

Others will want to broaden their perspective, to see themselves as part of a larger picture. One aspect of this is being able to experience oneself as a part of the ongoing historical flow. For people with children, placing oneself in an ongoing line of generations past *and* future is biologically given. For those without children, this historical linkage will need to be created. The advantage the single person has over married counterparts is that he/she can choose his/her connections to the future.

For those with special talents, skills, or knowledge, the important core of historical connection may be through their body of work. The first step in linking oneself to history is acknowledging one's debt to the past — all those people whose influence has contributed to one's present accomplishments. This means getting in touch with mentors in the past and directly expressing one's appreciation. Connecting to the future may be meaningfully done simply through leaving tangible work or more personally experienced by actively mentoring younger people in one's field.

Others may want to be connected to the future through young people outside their work arena. This may involve deepening relationships that tend to be underdeveloped in our society as a whole and in certain ethnic groups in particular (e.g., uncle, godmother, cousin). In other cases, relationships already closely developed may need to be modified.

•••

JACQUES, A 53-YEAR-OLD never-married man, had been extremely close and important as a brother to his divorced younger sister and as an uncle to her now 18-year-old daughter. His contribution had been in helping them out financially, and serving as a "Dutch uncle"—disciplining, talking sense into, and generally trying to control his always rather rebellious niece. At the time of consultation, Jacques was feeling so burdened, helpless, and unappreciated in his efforts that he was considering cutting off contact with them, even though he cared for them enormously and believed he should be helping.

Jacques had the responsibility of parenthood but few of the joys. Working with him to modify the way in which he was helping so as to greatly increase simple pleasurable time together and to decline pressures to lecture and control was enough to reestablish his valued brother/uncle connection as an enjoyable, meaningful relationship.

When deepening underdeveloped connections, people need to be aware of what "emotional job openings" are available and what ones will be resisted.

•••

ONE OLDER WOMAN, ROSE, sought to reconnect with her now grown niece and nephew by resuming her former "teaching" role with them. She gave them admonitions on proper diet, on how to deal with bosses, on personal growth issues about which she was concerned. Not only did they already have parents who were still giving advice on how to live better, but they were of an age where this kind of advice was annoying, if not downright intrusive. They would have welcomed Rose's involvement in other ways, but became negative and avoidant when she continued her mentoring approach.

Others, unlike Rose, will be able to view companionship and shared interests as personally meaningful ways to be connected. For those like Rose to whom teaching or passing on knowledge is their medium of connection, it may be necessary to seek mentorships outside the family circle.

Developing a Relationship to the Larger Community: Life Beyond Self

In an informal survey done as part of our singles project we inquired about what special activities people would like to become more involved with. The largest interest of all (79%) was in connecting with community projects (special travel packages, 73%, restaurant guides for singles, 73%, continuing education, 69%, cultural programs, 69%, and counseling services, 41%). The average age of the respondents was 38, so this group represented a goodly proportion of those either moving toward or already in midlife years. The strength of this interest may reflect both a need to counterbalance the marginalization of single life from the larger society and a shifting need to connect to community in broader ways than personal achievement.

Unmarried childless people have the widest possible latitude in being able to define and act on the ways in which they will connect. Choices made are not going to have the reverberations that being part of a nuclear family often bring. Questions like "You're going out *again* tonight?" or "You're going to a *Buddhist* retreat???" and the issues behind them don't arise and don't have to be negotiated.

In earlier years connection to the community may have primarily been spurred, and therefore limited, by motives to meet a mate. As people come to terms with their single status, their community connections are defined more by personal meaning. Too often, community involvement is looked upon simply as a hobby, a spare time activity, or something to stave off loneliness. For many single people, however, it is *the* way to keep a healthy balance between doing for self and doing for others. Parents at midlife are generally still embedded in responsibilities toward their children; "doing for" and "giving back" are daily life routines. For single people not involved in care-taking, a life focused on individual gratification may come to feel empty.

The "midlife crisis" often precedes this shift in defining what makes one's life meaningful—less emphasis on ego and personal achievement and more on spiritual, social, political, or religious contributions. Mental health theory tends to focus on the clarification and assertion of individual needs, and it is easy for both therapists and clients to overlook the emotional importance of living a good balance between giving and receiving.

Maintaining and Deepening Friendships

For the single childless person, friends *are* family. You have a shared history; you don't have to introduce yourself; friends remember how you were when you were younger. It is a real loss in the lives of many married people that friendships tend to be overlooked and underdeveloped. At every phase of the life cycle, we will continue to underscore the importance of valuing and maintaining friendships.

Taking Responsibility for One's Financial Future

While assuming financial responsibility for oneself can seem like a good idea in the thirties, it is a necessity in forties and fifites. Because people at midlife in the 1990s were brought up in an age where women were trained to believe that "men took care of all that" this task is too often postponed. As Anderson et al. in *Flying Solo* put it:

> Whole categories of life-maintenance tasks were staked out as the province of the American husband. We were raised to believe we were *not supposed to know these things*. . . . We were not supposed to have to balance our checkbooks or do our own taxes. We were not supposed to have to figure out how to save enough money to live comfortably in retirement. We were raised to expect we would be taken care of, that our husbands would willingly manage all these unsavory little details. (1994, p. 258)

The emotional baggage that accompanies assuming these responsibilities is decidedly different for men and women. While men may have anxiety about the *way* they are doing it, they generally have no doubt that they *should* be doing it. Responsibly managing their money and planning for the future only enhances their personal value in their own and in women's eyes. A man in his fifties continually bouncing checks is rarely regarded as "cute." Because men are educated to believe that the acquisition and management of money are part of their very identity, a man at midlife who does not do so should be confronted. It may indicate that he does not take his life seriously, more so than the same attitude in a woman would.

For women, on the other hand, the act of taking on these responsibilities may have the subconscious emotional meaning of *giving up the idea of ever being married*. Women at many stages of the life cycle may avoid a commitment to securing their own home base, for example, because they feel they must leave themselves maximally available for building a home around a man's needs. As we discussed in the previous chapter, from a purely logical point of view, going ahead with securing a home and planning for the future doesn't decrease one's marriageability. It may in fact increase it. Some women, though, will need to work through this issue before they can begin confronting the steps and the anxieties involved in overall financial planning.

In these times of increased longevity, decreased social security, and spiraling nursing home costs, planning for one's future is a key factor in later life satisfaction for all of us. Parents may feel they are buffered from poverty by the belief that their children will keep them from it. The single person has no such buffer, and money worries weigh heavily (see Chapter 18 in Anderson et al., 1994). Overcoming one's emotional baggage, one's anxieties, and one's fears enough to begin using money for future security is one of the most important of the specific tasks of midlife.

ESTABLISHING AN ADULT ROLE FOR ONESELF WITHIN ONGOING FAMILY LIFE

This is another of life's themes that continues to recycle for everyone until death. Resolutions and shifts made in one span of life need to be reworked in the next. As we change, so do our parents, even after their death. The issues common to us all are presented in Chapters 11 and 12 of *Reweaving the Family Tapestry* (Herz Brown, 1991). Our focus here will be on variations commonly encountered by the single, childless person. Midlife intensifies emotionality around the "loss" of the American ideal family dream not only for children (particularly daughters), but for parents as well. They, too, have proceeded with the notion that they will have in-laws and through them grandchildren. Through the years of the thirties, parents still have "expectations." The onset of children's middle age, however, usually brings its own kind of "giving up"—or intensification of pressure—for parents, too.

With Parents

This conversation was overheard at a wedding: a 48-year-old guest, an established Washington lawyer, arrived breathless and just on time. His mother had been anxiously biting her nails waiting for him. "Bernie," she said, "I'm so glad you're here. *Do you have to go to the bathroom???"*

If Bernie were married, presumably his wife would be in charge of this piece of mothering, and his own mother would be free to establish a different relationship. The "giving away" of children at marriage ritualizes the termination of certain modes of parenting: fathers can hand over financial responsibility, and mothers other forms of protection and nurturing. In the absence of this ritual to move relationships to a different level, parents and/ or children may stay stuck in earlier patterns of relating. Bernie's mother's perception that he still needs someone to supervise his bathroom-going is far from acknowledging his adult status. The issue for Bernie is whether *he* can feel like an adult even if his mother may never recognize it.

The ideal emotional process for the "child" is to work on decreasing reactivity, on opening oneself up to listen and give legitimacy to parents' feelings about one's singlehood and childlessness. The more a "child" expresses heated feelings about parents' inability to accept his/her single status, the more it is a measure of inability to confer his/her own legitimacy on a life without a mate and children. Parents are likely to have strong feelings about a "child alone in the world." Furthermore, if there are no other children, or those children are also childless, the loss of the experience of grandchildren and the end of the family line is usually keenly felt.

The other half of the emotional process is for sons and daughters to be able to express to their parents their own thoughts about being single — without blaming, apologizing, attacking or defending. There may be areas of agreement: a daughter may also be worried about being alone, especially as she moves toward later life; a son may also feel he has failed at accepting the responsibilities of being a man.

Many people, parents and children alike, close off this entire area of communication because of its toxicity. The emotional distance this creates, as well as the "as-if" sham quality of relating that can be engendered if it is closed off, may be emotionally quite damaging for all family members.

The amount of toxicity around being single or childless varies enormously among different ethnic groups and different families within the same ethnic group. There may be little or no intensity in families that place high value on independence and achievement, who have no history of genocide, and who already have grandchildren to carry on the family name and traditions. Others will have much greater anxiety around children whose singlehood heralds a more distinct break with family belief systems and traditions.

Opening up and giving legitimacy not only to one's own feelings but also to one's parents' feelings is difficult work and usually takes place over a period of months or years. Sometimes it is possible to arrive at complete understanding; sometimes it is not. Establishing an adult role may mean giving up the desire for unconditional love and accepting the legitimacy of parental disappointment.

With Extended Family

Feelings tend to be less intense with the rest of the family members, and so emotional work may often be more easily accomplished. Sometimes it is simply a matter of suggesting to clients that it is time for them to change their position; they may be able to do it with only moderate amounts of anxiety. The specific tasks we are suggesting are to: (1) develop a nonperipheral, nondeficit based role in family life, (2) develop a separate relationship with children in the extended family, and (3) host significant celebrations oneself.

Certain habitual routines may tend to reinforce a "not-quite-adult" family position. The experience of always being a guest and never a host is one. Shifts don't have to be monumental or tradition-cracking (e.g., taking on casts of hundreds for Thanksgiving); they can be small (e.g., inviting three or four family members for Sunday dinner). Hosting these occasions also serves as a sort of inner gravity shift: "I have a home too, not just a waystation, and this is it." Men, in particular, need to be encouraged to be a host, as often they may not feel able to entertain without a woman.

Never being alone with younger children is another habit that should be questioned. Counting on parents to step in and take over when children begin to misbehave, whine, or argue has definite advantages. It also puts limits on what the relationships will be and blocks a single person's own growth into an adult who can deal with these behaviors somehow or other on his/her own.

We also believe that developing real, nonperipheral relationships between single clients and married family and friends brings many emotional rewards. It can counteract the drift toward segregation between single and married worlds mentioned earlier, cut into the "grass is greener" fantasies that inevitably sprout, help both married and single siblings/friends stay closely connected, and clarify for the single person the advantages and disadvantages inherent in both states.

$$\searrow \cdots 8$$

The Fifties to Failing Health:
Putting It All Together

WHILE THE ISSUES of this later life phase are triggered by chronological age (reaching "the big five-oh"), we see the subsequent developmental tasks and their emotional processes as more dependent on the state of one's health than on chronological age. The later life phase contains pre-retirement planning and retirement itself; it extends through the post-retirement years until failing health pushes the individual into the elderly phase. In our schema, then, the later life period may extend over thirty years or more, depending on how long good health continues. The emotional processes represent an inner duality: one aspect is a felt need to slow down and savor life; the other is a sense of urgency about setting priorities to make life meaningful in the time that is left (Bergquist, Greenberg, & Klaum, 1993). The specific tasks suggested below reflect this duality.

Single people who have resolved earlier emotional issues in an inwardly peaceable way are ideally situated at this time to reap the fruits of the single status: freedom and autonomy. While married counterparts may continue to carry heavy financial and/or emotional responsibilities toward their children, or may just be starting to recoup savings after school and wedding expenses, single people have the use of their disposable income for the furtherance of personal satisfactions. Unencumbered by the chores and unwritten emotional contracts of married life, single people can devote more time and energy to shaping personally meaningful work. They have more freedom to pull up stakes and move into new figurative or literal areas.

A significant number of their cohort have become divorced or widowed, particularly women, and are coping with this loss and the newness of an independent single life. Only 49% of women after age 50 are now married, and of these 21% are living alone (Walters et al., 1988). The single person has navigated singlehood already, and therefore is a step ahead of many in her/his age group. The increase in the number of single women also means that being a woman without a spouse is numerically less "deviant"; the gravity of the numbers shifts to equalize. For unmarried men, the reverse is true. At these ages, 81% of men are married. The single childless man continues to be "out of step" with his counterparts (Walters et al., 1988).

Some single people move into later life with considerable financial resources; some have few. We asked one 72-year-old never-married woman interviewed for our singles project what advice she would give to younger people who remain single. Without hesitation she responded, "Tell them to earn as much money as they can!" Since socioeconomic status has often been found to be positively correlated with life satisfaction for never-married adults (Cockrum, 1983), this advice is apt.

People who live alone tend to be inveterate advance planners. There has been no one else in the household to count on with unexpected emergencies. One might expect, then, that single clients would actively plan for economic security in old age earlier than married counterparts.

Besides long-range financial planning, the other area that moves from the wings to center stage at this phase is physical health. The old saw, "As long as you have your health, you have everything," takes on new meaning as age sixty approaches. The ability to live independently and to use one's freedom and autonomy hinges on continued good health. Average life expectancy now is such that many people can expect to live well into their eighties—about twenty years past traditional retirement age. The quality of life during this twenty-year period is as dependent on health as it is on money.

If people have been accustomed to longevity and good health in their forebears, they will approach old age with that vision in mind. Others, whose parents might have died at earlier ages or suffered lengthy illnesses and debilitation before death, will have grimmer images in mind. Calling these "images" implies an articulated consciousness that guides people's planning for later life; however, this usually isn't the case. For most, the notion of how and when they will die is an unarticulated underground channel with the power to enormously influence planning for later years. One therapist, for example, was completely frustrated in trying to change a client's continued spending. Questions about saving for the future fell on deaf ears. Only after some multigenerational theme exploration did it emerge that this client's image was of dying in her sixties from cancer—just like her mother. Saving to provide for herself in old age was, in her subconscious vision, totally unnecessary.

These three areas—money, physical health, and the visions of old age provided by familial experience — form the framework within which the enjoyments and satisfactions of this phase will be lived out.

CONSOLIDATING DECISIONS ABOUT WORK LIFE

We see this process as a culmination of the thinking begun in midlife. Spending one's last ten or fifteen years just sitting it out until retirement is depressingly unpalatable. It is important to exercise as much choice as possible to ensure that one's work is personally meaningful. For single people it is crucial, as work life is usually a central axis of self-definition.

Deriving Satisfactions from Current Work and/or Initiating Second Life Plan

Getting satisfaction from one's work is important across all ages, and initiating second (or third or fourth) life plans can be done at any time. We are highlighting this task in the later life phase because of the "last chance" feeling that creeps in; emotional intensity around using one's talents meaningfully tends to increase as one hears that inner voice, "If I don't do it now, I never will."

For some, economic necessity, lack of opportunity for promotion or change, and financial constraints such as need for a future pension or a current health insurance plan mean continuing in the same position. Single women now in their seventies, who entered the work world in the late 1930s and early 1940s, encountered considerably more restrictions on the kinds of jobs available to them throughout their work life than women only now at the beginning of later life. Those older women interviewed by Simon "emphasized three themes in their work life: (1) How badly they had been paid, (2) How few were the choices of occupation open to them when they were young, and (3) How central to their identity working for pay has proved to be" (1987, p. 112).

Many people who are not able to consider changing jobs will be able to keep emotional hold of personal meaning and pride in their work:

washing floors, doing laundry, vacuuming, ironing . . . that is hard, dirty stuff. No glory there. But that scrubbing and bending kept me whole, kept me close to Jesus, kept me useful. The pay was pitiful, let me tell you. But I was able to keep my mind on the important things.

And I did something else, too, all those years I was a housemaid. I knew I had a talent for reaching children with my example. Even white, rich children. They saw how much I respected myself for doing a good job. They saw what

hard work looked like. We had a lot of talks. . . . I might have been no more
than a maid, but I was a proud one and a fine one. (Simon, 1987, p. 125)

Those who have lost sight of this pride and meaning need to recapture it
for themselves and hold it within them each day. This is true for everybody,
but truer for the single person who has no spouse or children whose work
success can be felt as also one's own.

Others have the freedom to make major shifts. Women and other minority groups arriving more recently to the work world have taken advantage
of a wider range of careers and correspondingly higher salaries. While
inevitably bumping into the "glass ceilings" beyond which they would not
be promoted, a new cadre of professionals is arriving at later life with much
more disposable income and therefore more options for second life plans
than their predecessors. Many of the women interviewed for *Flying Solo*
(Anderson et al., 1994), for example, shifted from a demanding corporate
environment to more autonomous, "slower track" work in later life. In our
experience, this process is rarely as emotionally seamless as it might appear
at first glance, however.

Nancy, an exceedingly intelligent, hardworking single woman, came for
consultation when she was offered a junior partnership, the prelude to a
full partnership, in her public relations firm. She told her bosses she wanted
to think it over, and the place she chose to do so was in therapy. She framed
her dilemma as "Why am I so depressed now that I've gotten to where I
wanted to be?"

Nancy had a number of answers already in place: it could be a fear of
making commitments ("After all I never married"); it could be not having
a man in her life; it could be "fear of success"; it could be her relationships
with her father and brother.

While these areas, particularly her position in her family of origin were
of concern, it took some exploration before Nancy could articulate not only
that there were problematic issues for her in the firm but also that her
feelings about these *really counted*. These were ethical issues, and problems
regarding what to do with her feelings: the non-partners were treated as
"peons with no rights," and she was hard put to keep dealing courteously
with clients who treated her arrogantly and whom she did not respect.

Nancy's blinders had kept her from seeing that she had a *right* to leave a
firm that had basically been very good to her—as she had been for it.
Anderson et al. (1994) have noted that while this sterile, bottom-line orientation of business is problematic for men as well as women, men seem to
take it more in stride. Perhaps this is so. We suspect that any major lack

of fit between one's moral standards, one's self-respect, and one's work environment erodes men and women equally. Men may just complain less because of less facility in articulating these feelings or because of a belief that complaining seems unmanly.

In either case, the first emotional hurdle may be realizing that one *does* have a right to leave. The anxieties about how to leave, what to leave to, and how to make it financially in the transition, while big ones, are also more tangible. They can be grasped and shaped; they are no longer clouded by an inchoate belief that "something is wrong with me."

White men enjoy the fullest opportunities to choose careers and gain access to the "top floors." This blessing may bring a serious drawback in later life, however. Men who have not arrived where they want to be professionally tend to blame it solely on their own limitations, rather than lack of opportunity. White men are also the ones in those managerial positions that are highly vulnerable to corporate "downsizing." This group of men can be more prone to anger or depression at this life phase; unless these feelings are worked through, their ability to assess viable changes will be limited.

While the single person's choice to leave a financially secure position does not trigger the ripples of anxiety or possible resistance in spouses or children that married people often encounter, the downside is that the person alone knows there is no buffer available. There is no other paycheck, and so images of future poverty may be more intense, regardless of how unrealistic those fears may be.

ACKNOWLEDGING FUTURE DIMINISHMENT OF PHYSICAL CAPACITY

While those with spouses are certainly aware of the likelihood that one of them will be alone in later years, we've yet to meet the mate who is doing any practical planning at this phase for life without the other, except, of course, when divorce or death is imminent. When a spouse is still healthy, planning ten, fifteen, or twenty years down the road for life alone is just not emotionally timely. For single people, however, life alone is here, and diminished financial and physical capacity may feel just around the corner.

Planning for Retirement

The specter of poverty in older years is a fearful one, and for some older people it is a coming reality. Simon (1987) reported that 55% of women over age 65 had an annual income of less than $6,000, compared to 26% of men. This was in 1983, when the median income for married people 65 years and over was $11,718. Although most people don't need a lot of money to enjoy life, contentment is difficult to achieve if life feels financially precarious, as this comment from one of Simon's subjects shows:

> When I reached age 50, I took a hard look at my savings and at my income and at my projected piddling pension. I imagined myself at age seventy, scrounging around for bus fare, just to get to church on Sunday.
>
> It occurred to me then that living on my own works swell when I am healthy and bringing in a living wage. But what would happen to me if my oh-so-independent body decided to become old, all of a sudden? And how would I manage on the few dollars I figured would be mine in retirement?
>
> Everything pointed toward me making a change. (p. 151)

Planning for retirement involves securing a home base that feels financially and physically viable. It may also mean joining forces with someone else to pool resources. For some single people this may catalyze another upsurge in intensity about finding a mate. The motivation this time around, however, is apt to be anxiety at the thought of being alone in later years, rather than out of need to prove one's marriageability or desire for romantic love. For others, planning involves keeping or finding a roommate. Many single people therefore search their families and friendship networks for someone who can offer both compatibility and solvency. Of Simon's sample of 50 never-married women, only four elected to continue living independently until death. The majority preferred to trade privacy and autonomy for companionship, assured solvency, and mutual care.

The experience of singlehood may allow for a broader vision about what constitutes a satisfactory living arrangement in later life than the experience of marriage does. Having lived so long without a mate opens one's eyes to other viable ways of shared living. For Simon's (1987) women, the most satisfaction was expressed by those living later years independently or with friends. Those who combined forces with family, mainly with siblings, gave mixed reviews.

These issues are equally pertinent to men alone during the later life phase. Unfortunately, their stories are as yet largely untold, at least in academic literature. Rubenstein (1986) found in interviewing eleven never-married men living alone in later life that only two were actively connected to social circles. Both of these men had girlfriends. The rest (82%) were either what he called "socialized isolates" (had some acquaintanceships) or "outsiders" (social contact was cursory).

The whole concept of being *able* to plan one's retirement date has begun to seriously erode in American society over the past decade and shows every sign of continued erosion. The unwritten social contract between most workers and the boss, that one provided lesser paid labor in return for employment security until retirement, has crumbled. Companies are now openly laying off their senior (more highly paid) workers in order to bring on less expensive younger people. A poll of involuntarily retired workers conducted by the AARP (*AARP Bulletin*, 1994) reports that "What we are seeing is the emergence of a new class of permanently unemployed or underemployed middle aged (i.e., fifty years and over) workers." While we have no good data available, our impression is that older white men are those most affected by early, involuntary layoffs. These men have the greatest access to senior, highpaying positions in the first place and are those least likely to be able to challenge a layoff on grounds of racial or gender discrimination. At the same time, Congress is openly talking about setting the age at which Social Security benefits begin at 70 years (instead of the current age 65). This includes the all-important Medicare coverage for health care.

These cold, hard trends affect all those in later life, in either the actuality or the fear of being laid off. People living alone are most seriously affected. Work is a central axis around which emotional life is organized. There is no other paycheck coming in as a buffer. There are no health insurance coverage benefits at exactly the time when people start needing them most. Without having some degree of control over one's earnings, or at least the faith that one can count on stability, planning may very quickly become worry. Creating mutually satisfying joint living arrangements may be one of the most important specific tasks for those who will have limited money.

Those single people who have lived their lives with their parents or other family members, usually out of economic or caretaking necessity, are generally in a more predictable situation. They may have had less independence and freedom in earlier years, but they also do not usually have to envision dislocation at this time. Mortgages on parental homes are paid off, and pooling money with other family members has already been a regular routine.

As therapists we need to overcome our squeamishness about inquiring about money. We can relatively easily ask about the most personal aspects of our clients' life, including sexuality, but shy away from getting details of their economic situation (including expectations of future inheritance). There are times when, even though we may be aware in a general way of someone's finances, we ignore their impact on daily life. One client provided a brisk reminder by interrupting to announce, "My relationship with my brother is useless to work on when I'm worried about paying the rent tomorrow!"

Preparing a Will and Communicating its Contents/Whereabouts to Others

Making one's will is not just a responsible duty; it's a profound emotional process. The process set in motion by decisions about what possessions you have that are of value to you, and who will also value them after your death, can be intense. How do you wish to live on, and through which people, institutions, or causes? The act of looking around their home and imagining what will happen to their possessions after their death can change clients' entire perspective. What things are not important, things that they could easily stand to have someone crate up for Goodwill? What things are prized, such that they want them to continue to have a valued life with someone else in the future?

Looking at possessions in this way can serve to reattach people to the meanings of what they have and what they have accomplished, if these attachments have faded. People can connect emotionally to their past, as they remember the time and setting when they acquired particular possessions. Equally important, the process opens a bridge to future generations, as people consider how they want their "things" to carry on for them. Who would value that teacup and saucer your mother brought with her from Germany eighty years ago? What of your own would you want to have become part of the family heritage? Decisions about money are weighty too, but in our experience giving away money does not carry the same visceral charge and possibilities for opening up new dimensions in feeling and relationships that giving away possessions does. It is our things that hold our memories.

Communicating the whereabouts of one's will usually brings a peace of mind — a responsibility completed and the knowledge that one's wishes will not be lost and forgotten after death. Communicating the contents of one's will is another matter entirely; complex and complicated issues may be set in motion. In an informal poll of lawyers of our acquaintance, *all* of them said they recommend against specific disclosure of the contents of a will to heirs, except between spouses.

Clearly a decision to tell people what is in your will needs to be thoroughly and judiciously weighed. The idea that you shouldn't tell seems to be an unquestioned principle by most people, however, not just lawyers. We are suggesting that the possibility at least be questioned, and the ramifications of disclosure be explored. Below are a few examples of early disclosure that served to enrich the meaning and relationships of all involved.

•••

FRANK, A 60-YEAR-OLD never-married only child, now retired, had always taken an interest in family history. He'd saved all the many letters, mementos, and heirlooms passed on to him from his parents. He himself was an eighth-generation American, and being the end of his particular family branch was a keenly felt sadness to him. He had always been distant from his rather large extended family. His parents were the only ones still living in Vermont; the rest had long ago moved west. So he had not grown up with any of his cousins. He had also never disclosed his gay orientation to any family member, thus closing off a large part of his life from them.

Frank had gotten a couple of letters from a cousin in Nebraska, saying she was putting together a family history and asking for any information he could give. He'd always answered briefly and politely, and provided her with a few anecdotes.

Frank had always intended to will his family's heritage to her, but now he decided it would feel better if he knew her first. He arranged what turned out to be one of several trips to her home, and came to know his extended family and their stories for the first time. The most personally important story he heard was of a much beloved great-uncle who had lived his long life together with his "friend." The discovery of another family member who was not only gay but much loved and closely integrated into family life was pivotal for Frank.

• • •

LUCY HAD ALWAYS had an affectionate relationship with her nieces. They'd gone together to plays and museums and to her house at the beach. Now they were in their late twenties, and Lucy decided to make full disclosure of their inheritance from her. She felt they should know, so as to be able to make informed judgments about life and career choices now.

She was advised not to do this by other family members, on the grounds that it would make them lazy, but she went ahead anyway. Her telling signaled to them for the first time how deeply she cared about them. They had always known she was fond of them; now they came to see her as more like their "other mother," not just as their fun aunt. It moved their relationship to a deeper level.

• • •

AN ELEMENTARY SCHOOL TEACHER for many years, Carrie had always believed that good books were essential in helping young people dream for future goals. Her very small town library's children's section consisted of a handful of cast-offs. She estimated that she could afford to buy ten books a year and still meet her expenses, and approached the town mayor with her plan. She would select the books and give them to the library.

The network that developed, when parents and young people began to come to her with their ideas, eventually extended wide and deep. She also was able to see "her corner" grow in her lifetime.

The writing of a will is often a very perfunctory affair when one is still in good health. It is difficult to confront in such a direct way the certainty of one's death. We are including it in this life phase, and suggesting it be done in an extremely thoughtful way, because of the many enriching possibilities that can appear while there *is* still time.

Taking Care of Oneself Physically and Emotionally

A doctor relates that he tells all his patients in their fifties that the care they take of themselves now will determine the quality of their life in older years. The body has started to signal that it's slowing down. People get tired more quickly, may need a brief nap during the day, can't stay up as late at night, can't drink or smoke without really feeling it. Being kind to one's body in physical ways and kind to oneself in emotional ways are the concrete acts that herald a necessary later-life attitude shift: a continued affection for, rather than an angry or adversarial relationship with, a body that can't be automatically counted on anymore.

American culture provides precious little emotional or practical help with this; even traffic lights are timed for those who can move quickly. Images of beauty do not include wrinkles, spare tires, untoned muscles, and liver spots. Those men and women alike whose physical beauty has been a key aspect of who they are and the degree of social power they have enjoyed will, of course, find aging more difficult. For them this specific task, having affection for a body that's "betraying you," will be complex. It includes an entire redefinition of self.

We are placing the issue of the expression of sexuality in later life here, in the context of changing one's relationship to one's body, although it could equally be placed in the section on love. Schnarch (1992) has differentiated between what he calls "genital prime" and "sexual prime." He states that "the most important sexual exploration occurs in later life" (p. 88). Sexuality needs to be detached from genital performance and sexual arousal from the beauty of one's body and moved into a sexual and sensual intercourse that involves true personal intimacy between partners. This involves broadening sexual intimacy, exploring new sensualities, and bringing more of oneself into sexual experience. This is what he views as "sexual prime." Those who do not make this shift will be in an increasingly adversarial relationship to their body, rejecting this part of self and life.

FACING INCREASING DISABILITY
AND DEATH OF LOVED ONES

Mourning Losses

One's peers in older years begin to die not from accidental causes but from heart attacks and cancer—deaths that seem to be built into a genetic stopwatch. Increasing familiarity with others' disability provides experience and practical information on ways to seek services and cope when one's own time comes, but the death of long-loved friends and family creates a vacuum that cannot really be filled by new connections. Longtime friends and family are the repository of shared history and memory. One of the women Simon interviewed commented:

> Once you get past 70, you have to somehow come to terms with the fact that most of the people you have shared your life with are dropping like flies. You have to squeeze the best out of every minute of an evening with a buddy, 'cause he may be gone within the year. You have to seize every opportunity to show someone how deeply you care, as that may be your last chance to do so. (1987, p. 167)

This awareness of impending loss can lead to a deep savoring of the time together. However, because of the very profundity of the relationships, the loss is deep. Many older people talk about these losses of family and friends with stoicism, making it easy to underestimate the impact of their loss.

Estimates of how many never-married people have lived their lives with parents are sketchy (Rubenstein, 1986). While some theorists (Schaie & Willis, 1986) regard singlehood as an advantage because the death of a spouse does not need to be endured, this view underestimates the impact of the death of parents on those who have lived their lives with them. Rubenstein's group of men had been very close to their families (50% had lived with parents until their death), and clearly most had never succeeded in creating such close connections again. Married people continue to have close connections and daily routine to anchor them at the time of parents' death. Many unmarried people do not.

An additional unforeseen loss may be dealt those single people who have continued to live in the parental home throughout their lives, usually taking care of their elderly parents until their death. In situations where savings are meager and their home is all they have, parents may leave the family home to all their children equally in their desire to *be* equal and leave something to all. When the children have plenty of money themselves, the remedy of buying each other out or forgoing one's inheritance altogether is available. When money is tight, however, siblings may insist on the sale of the house because they need their share.

•••

EAMON, WHO HAD LIVED in the same stable working-class neighborhood with his mother for 65 years, did not have the money to buy his four siblings shares of the house following his mother's death. Bitter conflict erupted among the four about what should be done.

Eamon, a very gentle person, abstained. In the end the vote was three to one in favor of selling now and getting the money. Eamon went to live with his older sister in the suburbs, far from his neighborhood pub, all his friends, and access to Red Sox games. This loss of all he had known and loved was a devastating one; Eamon never regained his ability to experience joy in life.

Realigning Relationships to Maintain Network

We again underscore the importance of the single person's network of connections: to friends, to family, and to community. Those whose meaningful connections revolve around causes, ideas, special talents, or religious life are somewhat buffered to weather losses, as institutions continue even if the people change. Those whose connections are primarily personal will be hardest hit by the loss of friends and family. Meeting new people, while diverting and valuable, will never replace these losses; there can never be the long-term history and memory of life together with a new acquaintance. By realignment, we are suggesting deepening or modifying relationships that have been there through the years and have the potential for greater closeness.

Those who have lived alone for some time appear to deal with these losses better than those more recently divorced or widowed. Essex and Nam (1987) found that never-married older women (and older married women) reported fewer feelings of loneliness and isolation than did the formerly married. Whether this is true for men as well awaits research. The data regarding the poor health of older single men suggest that they find aloneness very hard to deal with.

While all groups of women studied had frequent contact with both family and friends, findings have been consistent in noting that contact with friends is more important than contact with family in lessening feelings of loneliness. Investigators have suggested that "friendships are more emotionally satisfying than family relationships because the latter involve a more formal obligation rather than the mutuality more often found in friendships" (Essex & Nam, 1987, p. 94). Other studies have shown that self-reported loneliness actually declines (at least for women) as people get older (Rubenstein & Shaver, 1982).

These results (at least for women) clearly challenge the prevalent notion that single older adults are alone and isolated. While cultural myth creates its images, unmarried older women (defined in studies as either age 55 and over or as 65 and over) appear in actuality to be deriving a great deal of enjoyment from their lives.

Dealing with Generational Issues as Parents Age

As one's parents approach more certain awareness that their days are surely numbered, there is often an intense upheaval of unfinished emotional business that might have remained dormant over the years. Those who have done the emotional work suggested at the earlier phases (establishing adult status with parents) will have a more solid grounding for encountering these parental agendas than those who have not. For the single person in particular, parental concerns may center around anxiety about a son or daughter who will be left alone and "uncared for" (i.e., no spouse).

•••

MARY'S ADOPTIVE FATHER had recently passed away, and her adoptive mother had begun a campaign that was infuriating Mary, as well as deeply confusing her. She was not only giving Mary's name to matchmakers in her Jewish circle but also actively engaging with agencies and an investigative service to trace Mary's biological parents and any biological siblings. Mary herself had broached doing this twenty years earlier when she was in her thirties, but she had encountered such fear and resistance that she had never wholeheartedly pursued it.

Now, at age 55, Mary had other emotional issues on her mind. She did not want to make room for those attached to her biological mother as well. In any case, she did not want her mother to be in charge of the search, if one was to be made. And finally, while she wouldn't mind meeting a man, doing it through her mother's matchmaking was definitely not her way.

Mary initially read her mother's actions as evidence that her mother "still" did not respect her competence, the fullness of her current life, and the reasons why she chose not to remarry. Feeling hurt and angry, she engaged in many hot arguments while trying to stop her mother's crusade. Reframing her mother's actions as her way of trying to provide family for Mary after her death brought Mary's reactivity down enough for her to be begin to talk more deeply and directly about the ways they needed love from the other.

In other cases parental reactivity may center around continued feelings of having failed as a parent (because of having an unmarried child), of bitterness at not having grandchildren, or of fears that, because the daughter/son did not follow parents' path, he/she does not respect their life as they lived it.

Areas of reactivity for the single "child" may equally center around the anxiety of being alone or the sadness of not having their own children. Men may feel that they have not adequately "proved" themselves. Another big issue is common to both single and married: wanting to gain assurances of love and respect and parental approval for their lives as they have lived them, while there is still time.

These deep concerns may be dealt with tenderly, bitterly, angrily, or by closing off and emotionally distancing. They may be dealt with directly or indirectly, through battles in other arenas, such as fights over politics, or who gets great-grandmother's teacup. Emotional intensity can be very high, making therapeutic work difficult.

The difference at this phase of life, compared to the years when everybody was younger, is that the power dimension of the parent-child relationship has usually either equalized or shifted to reverse as parents age. A parent's increasing infirmity also increases his or her need to count on children for current or future care, and this need confers power to children in relation to the parent.

In doing family-of-origin work with clients at this phase of life, it is essential to inquire about the current power balance (state of needs). Since in general people stick with habitual patterns of relating until something pushes them out of them, parents are often aware of their increased need (and lessened influence) long before children are. Since it is usually the "child" who comes for therapy, it is the "child's" vision we hear. A son/daughter who continues to view the aged parents as all-powerful needs to be challenged in this view. Work on differentiation issues may well involve bringing to awareness the reality that one's parents' needs for approval and concern are now equal to or greater than one's own. Resistance to this realization is usually high, since it means confronting one's parents' coming death and one's own "orphanhood."

Opening up Sibling Relationships

Sibling positions are often frozen in time at the point they were when each child left home. Rarely do siblings actively work on shifting their relationships once they reach adulthood. Daughters may continue to be more in touch with the emotional life of the family than sons. The "responsible one" continues being responsible in relation to a "carefree" younger sibling. The shift in care-giving patterns when parents become infirm generally puts strain on underdeveloped and outmoded sibling bonds and positions (Jacob, 1991).

Spoken or unspoken pressure to take over the care of aged parents is often felt most keenly by, or is directly put on, single people (especially daughters). This is more pronounced if married siblings are still involved in active childrearing themselves. In Simon's (1987) study, ten of the fifty never-married women terminated fulltime work earlier than they wished in order to care for their mothers. The troublesome issue for them was not so much the caregiving itself but the "presumption that women . . . in particular single women . . . *should* bear the weight of long-term care.

> If I saw any men in our family retiring to care for their mothers, I might not mind the early retirement I was obligated to take. Not one voice was raised to question: "But what about Nancy's life??" . . . instead, my brothers and sisters hid behind marriage and children. I had no official bodies to hide behind. (Simon, 1987, p. 147)

It is our sense that single persons' time, men's as well as women's, is regarded as more expendable than married persons'. Therefore, while single men may not be directly asked to take over caring for elderly parents, the unspoken pressure is there. Furthermore, single people may partially agree with this assessment; Nancy herself apparently did not raise her voice in support of her time and life.

A major portion of the family-of-origin work at this time will often involve a greater proportion of work with siblings, in contrast to earlier phases when parent-child issues are usually most relevant. Since the very content of one's life is at stake, emotionality can be very high and the potential for conflict to get triangled through third-party authorities, such as parents, social agencies, courts, and therapists, is great.

The economic reality is that few Americans can afford either nursing home costs or a home health aide. For example, an agency-backed live-in aide costs approximately $1,500 per week in the New York metropolitan area. Providing most of the care within the family system is the only feasible option for the vast majority of people.

The resolution of these issues may involve very difficult therapeutic work. Sibling bonds may be weak, siblings may have no experience in joint decision-making, and reactivity and emotionality can be intense. Even the best of therapists may not be able to help siblings resolve these issues well. The stakes are high in the way these very intense issues are dealt with, however, because the outcome will determine the way in which, or even whether, the family holds together following the last parent's death (Jacob, 1991).

ENJOYING THE FRUITS OF ONE'S LABOR

Ideally enjoyment and good use of the freedom and autonomy that are the prime benefits of singlehood have been part of one's life all along, not just blessings of later life. We include this facet of emotional life here, however, because of the crucial importance, as one's healthy years are limited, of being able to view what one has done with pride, to savor it, and to feel emotionally free for further enjoyment.

Deriving Esteem Built on One's Accomplishments

While the bulk of one's life has already been lived by later life, it is by no means over. For most people what follows after the fifties will not be all that different from what went before. The varied lives that could have been lived — a wild life photographer, a spouse and parent, a film producer — are now almost certainly closed. Emotional upheaval in midlife involves a clarification of personal goals that encompasses the possibility of still achieving major life shifts. The emotional process of later life, while encompassing the possibility of further shifts, devolves more on acceptance of the life that has already been. The specific task is to look objectively at one's accomplishments, one's contributions, one's struggles, one's failures, and one's regrets, and take from that a solid core of self-esteem. Some people never lose sight of what centers their life, as in the example of the housemaid whose words were quoted earlier. But others do. They may become mired in self-pity or bitterness at the roads not taken. Therapeutic work on family-of-origin issues, as well as attention to the other routes suggested, may be helpful in broadening their vision.

In these days of increasing longevity and increasing costs, many people continue working at least part-time well into much later years. Those who do actually retire, however, and have no daily job to serve as an external anchor for self-definition need to establish other moorings. The man or woman living alone tends to "worry more. People in families can talk it over, and get a bit of reassurance or a derisive horselaugh, and then forget about it. People alone can sit in a room worrying till their ulcers bleed and their hair falls out, and no one's there to stop them" (Holland, 1992, p. 223).

In this job of building a solid core of esteem, those living alone are more affected by their habitual judgmental proclivities than those who are married. Someone who is naturally tolerant and accepting of self will not have the problems with developing healthy self-pride that someone who is more critical or harddriving will. Then, too, the avenues of diversion available to those who are married, such as picking a fight, focusing on children's problems, or just playing Scrabble, are not readily at hand.

The research of Simon (1987) and Essex and Nam (1987) suggests that unmarried women (the research samples did not include men) do well at achieving this self-esteem. The findings that unmarried women's emotional and physical health is better, on average, than married women's also support this notion. These same findings suggest that unmarried men do not do well here, although again there are few specific data available.

Use of Freedom and Autonomy in Meaningful, Pleasurable Ways

The ability to view pleasure as a necessary part of life varies enormously from person to person and from culture to culture (McGoldrick et al., 1982). In the Brazilian ethos, for example, a "real" Brazilian is someone with great gusto for life and its sensual and social pleasures. The hardworking, hard-driving people of São Paulo, while possibly having more material possessions, are seen as too "European" to embody a "true" Brazilian.

The amount of money available also obviously influences greatly the extent to which the single person can use his/her personal freedom. Still there are always ways, as shown in this example.

•••

A NEVER-MARRIED WOMAN in her late fifties, Betty had worked and would continue to work all her life in a factory in a rather dreary city in the northern part of England. She lived with her now elderly mother.

While in her late thirties, her dreams of marriage and children faded. In her mid-forties she found another dream: a vacation in France. The farthest anyone in her family had traveled was a week in Brighton, so for ten years she collected brochures, talked to anyone she could find who knew anything about France, and saved her money. By her late fifties, she was ready.

She picked her place, bought her motor scooter, and arranged for a friend to stay with her mother. It was a bold and happy adventure, a three-week stay that gave her life meaning and herself pride in her accomplishment for many, many years — before, during, and after the trip itself.

For others, the hurdles to benefiting from one's autonomy will be characterological.

•••

CHRISTINE, A STILL ELEGANT WOMAN in her mid-sixties, now retired, came for consultation seeking relief from her "apathy about everything."

Raised in a rather stern, duty-bound Episcopalian family, she had broken out of the traces only once in her late twenties in the form of a disastrous marriage to an Italian artist. Since then she had finished her schooling and worked her way up the ranks, eventually becoming director of a social agency. As a single person, who presumably had no other life that "counted," Christine was the sibling who took primary care of her mother during her final two-year illness. Now her mother had died, and Christine had "inherited" the supervision of her mildly retarded brother.

It took some sessions before Christine hesitantly and obliquely mentioned a major happening: her childhood sweetheart, now a widower living in Oregon, had contacted her. He had never forgotten her, had always loved her, and wanted her to come west to visit and see if they could make a life together. Christine, too, had warm feelings for him. Her cool demeanor relaxed into a girlish joy when she spoke of him.

Then she related with tears in her eyes that she had written him back to say she couldn't come. She was responsible for her brother and couldn't uproot him from his apartment and the day program he loved.

Christine's family-of-origin messages prohibited her from even considering the available alternatives, from seeing that duty and responsibility do not always have to be shouldered personally, but can be delegated to responsible others. For her, family-of-origin work was important in allowing her to give herself "permission" for personal enjoyment. She had been raised to believe that using autonomy in this way would be selfish, and that enjoyment was something you "earned" after a hard day's work.

It turned out to be surprisingly easy to hand the overall supervision of her younger brother to her older brother. He came from the same traditions, after all, and had been feeling guilty about not doing his share. Christine did go west.

We therapists, trained to regard family and love (i.e., romantic/sexual) relationships as the stuff of therapy, may overlook the need to shift to the use of personal freedom in "selfish" ways as a central issue of clinical work. But this enjoyment is a main benefit of singlehood, and needs to be given its due value.

Elderly Phase:
Between Failing Health and Death

AS THERAPISTS WE SEE proportionately few elderly people. Surveys show that the older age group (those over seventy) represents only 6% of people served by community mental health centers, with an additional 2% seen by private therapists (Roybal, 1988). When the elderly are served by professionals, their mental health needs are met primarily by physicians, visiting nurses, home health aides, or social workers at neighborhood senior centers. Mobility is one factor; economics is another. Many clinics and therapists do not accept Medicare since the allowance for mental health care is so low, and many older people cannot afford to pay for therapy or bridge the gap between Medicare and clinic fees.

At any given time, less than 8% of the older generation are in nursing homes (Silverstein & Hyman, 1982); most are at home. Those over 80 years of age are the fastest growing segment of our population, and many are still in relatively good physical health. Those who are now elderly grew up when psychotherapy was a stigmatized process and are not likely to consult a mental health professional in times of trouble. However, those now in their sixties were raised in a different climate. Chances are that significantly more elderly clients will seek counseling in the future. We need to make ourselves more familiar with their strengths, their needs, and their developmental issues.

Carlsen (1991), in her excellent sourcebook for those working with older people, suggests that the first crucial step for clinicians is overcoming the stereotypes of "ageism":

> Ageism places the elderly in the category of "them." Here are people seen first as old, people who have many of their unique qualities and assets negated, demeaned, or ignored through the sightings of age. (p. 97)

She points out that ageist beliefs lead us to parent older clients, turning them into people who are less than competent in making choices for their own lives and contributing to the solutions of family problems. Birren (1983) called for clinicians to become more informed about the "bread and butter" issues — money, health insurance, and health care — which form the context of life for older people. He also urged us to recognize that older people will "increasingly demand options for working or retiring, options for volunteering, and options for personal growth" (p. 299). They will no longer be willing to remain "the invisible generation."

When do we move from being a person in later life to being "elderly"? There is no consensus in the literature; most studies choose some chronological age (some as young as age sixty-five). We have conceptualized previous life stages and transition points, as well as the related issues and emotional processes, as set in motion at a turning point, a chronological marker. We see the elderly phase, in contrast, as triggered by the onset of health decline serious enough to alter one's mobility and/or ability to communicate with others. With this decline the possibility of living one's life as it has been lived is removed. Polls and research all confirm that older people regard the state of their health as by far the single most important factor in their life and its satisfaction (Schaie & Willis, 1986).

Some people may enter the elderly phase issues in their sixties or seventies, while others will never be elderly. Those who die suddenly, as from heart attack, while in relatively good health never personally experience this transition from independent living to elderly. Their life cycle ends with the age-related issues of their phase at the time of death. Those who do live with increasing disability move into one last phase of transition and development.

Little attention has been paid to middle-aged adult development until relatively recently (e.g., see Carter & McGoldrick, 1989, Levison, 1978, and Herz Brown, 1991); still less has been devoted to conceptualizing the elderly phase as a time of new emotional development. Many existing theories tend (1) to emphasize either gradual societal disengagement, as people prepare inwardly for death, (2) to regard successful aging as maintaining the attitudes and activities of later life for as long as possible (i.e., no new developmental issues), or (3) to see the final phase of life as a continuation of the predilections of a lifetime (Schaie & Willis, 1986). This latter attitude may well mean expressing a lifelong tendency in a new way (e.g., someone with an adventurous spirit returning to live in an ancestral village in Ireland), but it does not include the notion of new developmental tasks.

Erikson (1982; Erikson, Erikson, & Kivnick, 1986) and Carlsen (1991) present alternative theories that emphasize the opportunity for emotional and developmental evolution in elderly years. Erikson (1982) labeled this last stage of life as "Integrity vs. Despair." Old age is not viewed as a "new childishness" but as an attempt to "recapitulate developmental potentials." Successful resolution of this developmental struggle for integrity results in wisdom, a world view that is not achievable in earlier years. Both Carlsen and Erikson et al. highlight the importance for the older person of maintaining a "vital investment" in life—the continuity and expansion of as many habits and connections as possible given decreased mobility.

The developmental tasks of this phase are to confront one's own mortality and to accept one's life as it has been lived.

CONFRONTING MORTALITY

Confronting mortality has been part of the developmental emotional process since one's late thirties or forties. Then it was the realization that one's biological clock was running, and some options were nearing their end (particularly for women). Along with this came the realization that it was time to frame a meaningful life if it had not already been done. After one's fifties issues shifted to include practical planning for retirement years and efforts to fulfill unrealized dreams or pleasures. Now, in the elderly phase, confronting mortality means confronting death itself.

Taking Responsibility for Making
Final Living Arrangements

Many single people will have made arrangements long before disability hits (see Chapter 8), as they tend to plan well in advance for the years when they will need care. A significant percentage do continue to live alone. Keith (1989) reports that 49% of single women and 19% of single men over the age of 75 are living by themselves, and that those with the highest income are the ones most likely to live alone. Sixty-seven percent of men and 20% of women over age 75 are still living with their spouses (Schaie & Willis, 1986).

Economics is the single most important determinant of living arrangements, and financial realities for too large a percentage of American elderly are grim (Keith, 1989). She reports that 15% of elderly women and 8.7% of elderly men are living below the poverty line. Of the groups who have been disadvantaged economically throughout their lives (minorities), the poverty rate is significantly higher (i.e., 35% of black women, and 26% of black men). In *Minority Aging*, Manuel points out that blacks and other minorities are less likely to be receiving pensions due to greater difficulties in obtaining jobs with pensions and less likelihood of continuous enough employment to become vested. Thus, minorities tend to have little beyond Social Security in older years.

Mindel and Wright (1982), surveying type of living arrangement and its effect on morale, found that the elderly living with a spouse had the highest morale and those living with children the lowest, with those living alone in between. Of Simon's (1987) group of never-married women, those who owned their own home expressed strong commitment to staying there until their death:

> Do you think I spent twenty years paying for this place only to wander off near the end like a stray dog? Susan (a sister) and I plan to stay here . . . until the Grim Reaper appears for each of us. We have considered our options. If we get stuck in wheelchairs, the visiting nurses will help us out, or we'll ask neighbors to fix our meals. . . . I see no reason we cannot navigate old age as skillfully as we steered the rest of our course. (p. 157)

Those who chose a retirement home expressed the same clear satisfaction with their living arrangements: companionship, activities, and the security of knowing nursing care was there if needed. Both homeowners and those in retirement homes clearly indicated their intention to stay until their death. The group of renters felt the least secure, due to yearly rent increases that gave them little predictability over future finances. Most renters were actively looking at senior residences or considering moving in with someone who owned a home.

The issue of childlessness appears to be insignificant in determining happiness, satisfaction, or loneliness in the elderly (Keith, 1989). Lang (1991) notes that 20% of seniors do not have living children and another 10% are estranged from them: "This means that almost one third of seniors today live without any contact or help from children" (p. 242). There is extensive evidence to suggest that children provide 70–80% of parents' social, health, and emotional needs (Krout, 1986); yet, in the few studies done, the absence of children in old age has not been associated with lower life satisfaction. Studies on loneliness, such as those by Brown (1981), Conner et al. (1979), Essex and Nam (1987), and Peplau et al. (1982), suggest that contact with friends is much more important than contact with children in reducing feelings of isolation.

Differential suicide rates among the elderly raise a disturbing finding, one with wide-ranging implications for mental health practitioners. Schaie and Willis (1986) report that white men over the age of 70 are three times more likely to kill themselves than white women, black men, or black women (the comparison groups studied). In fact, older white men have the highest suicide rate of any group throughout the life cycle. The authors state that theorists explain this on the basis of "social power theory"; white men are used to having power, and its loss therefore seems devastating. This group is most vulnerable to social isolation as well. Having more income at their disposal, they are better able to finance living alone; also, they have less experience in putting together friendship networks.

The single person may have distinct advantages over the widowed at this phase. A lifetime of self-sufficiency makes planning ahead for the years when one will be alone and need care a continuation of a natural way of living life, rather than a newly acquired ability following the death of a spouse. The single person also has greater freedom in deciding where and how he/she will live: a single person who opts for spending his/her last years (and money) in the south of France with a friend may be admired and applauded. A parent who did so might well be considered "unnatural"—selfish and uncaring of the children, squandering the family money and indifferent to their needs. Finally, friendship networks tend to be developed both more deeply and more widely for single people (especially women), leaving them less vulnerable to the major losses potentially sustainable in a long-term marriage (death of a spouse and children moving away).

The other aspect of final living arrangements—contacting needed services (e.g., Meals on Wheels) and asking friends, family, and neighbors for assistance—provides a trigger for personal growth. The single person's coping style is based in self-sufficiency; any yearnings to be taken care of have had to be kept tamped down. Now emotional room must be made for allowing others to help. Of practical necessity, a previous inner balance must shift. People need to put themselves in a new and different relationship to those around them. Some will be able to accept help easily, some grudgingly, some barely at all. The extent to which an elderly person can validate those offering aid is a measure of the extent to which they have moved to incorporate a previously submerged or denied part of themselves into a personal unity—their ability to experience dependence and accept help.

Maintaining Personal and Community Ties

The loss of mobility with serious disability severely affects all elderly. The research findings of Essex and Nam (1987) suggest that the repercussions are felt most strongly by never-married people (only women were included in their study). Declining health was significantly associated with greater feelings of loneliness *only* for the unmarried group. While frequency of personal contact with others remained the same as before, the type of contact varied. Those in poor health saw their friends less frequently, and their family members and neighbors more frequently. These data underscore the profundity of the bond of friendships that single people develop and the importance of their maintenance throughout life.

Those who have had meaningful investment in the larger community have a buffer against the loss of friends. Long-term association with a church, synagogue, or other house of worship serves to provide continuity in one's caretaking network. Being able to count on visitors during a hospitalization and knowing that word will spread through the congregation of any illness give a further sense of security. Volunteer drivers usually make sure the elderly can physically get to services. Community groups (political groups, civic groups, social causes) will also try to enable elderly members to continue to attend and contribute.

Many elderly people decide who would value their possessions after death (see Chapter 8) and then pass them on before death. This is an important way to maintain emotional links: of person to person and of the present to the future. The elderly are much less squeamish about the reality of their approaching death than are younger people, who may refuse gifts with protestations that death is a long way off. When a gift is offered with clear knowledge and the recipient refuses, this is unfortunate for the elderly. It closes off an opportunity for deepening that relationship.

ACCEPTING ONE'S LIFE AS IT HAS BEEN LIVED

In Erikson's (1950) words this means "the acceptance of one's one and only life cycle as something that had to be and that, by necessity, permitted of no substitutions: it thus means a new, a different love of one's parents. . . . [It is the knowledge that] an individual life is the accidental coincidence of but one life cycle with but one segment of history . . . " (p. 268). In his conception, those who are not able to get beyond a narrow view, who only see that time is now too short for them to try alternative lives, are more vulnerable to feelings of despair. This acceptance is by no means passive resignation but an active reevaluation of the tapestry of one's life. This developmental task is vital when one is aware that death is the "next step," when it is clear that there *are* no alternative lives possible (unless one believes in reincarnation). It is then that this broad vision (wisdom) becomes emotionally timely.

Perhaps those with children have less emotional need to achieve this acceptance of the limitations of their own life. "Alternative lives" can be and often are experienced vicariously through one's children, so there may be less inner experience of a historical end in sight. This remains a question for speculation.

Seeing One's Life Story in Meaningful Context: Familial and Historical

The process of seeking meaning beyond one's own personal achievements began at midlife, was deepened through later life, and now culminates during the elderly phase. Placing oneself within a familial context means appreciating which multigenerational themes and/or issues one's own life has represented in the ongoing family saga. Which of the many family dreams and struggles have been worked out, one way or another, through one's own particular journey? For the single person the themes might center around the unique family meanings attached to marriage (e.g., security? happiness? responsibility? entrapment?) and the family meanings attached to personal autonomy and achievement (e.g., highly prized? selfish?). For example, in her life, Lorraine (see Chapter 3) clearly furthered the family's strong drive towards bettering their position through education and achievement. She most probably would not have been able to go as far as she did with a husband, and certainly not with children. With children of her own, she would not have been able to bring "up" the extended younger generation as she did. Her efforts would have been more concentrated on her nuclear family. Lorraine picked up one motif of the family's themes and lived her life carrying it onward. Those who continue to place their lives within the narrow frame of individual self and ego, who perhaps view their own saga as a personal failure or their singlehood as a demonstration of their unlovability or of social deviance, need to work on achieving this broader vision.

We also live out our lives within a particular time in history. Simon (1987) noted that the older women in her group had a very strong sense of generational solidarity. They were "acutely aware of the placement of their biographies" within an historical chronology (p. 176). Identifying with an entire generation in its shared experience and struggles provides a breadth far beyond those smaller and more divisive categories (e.g., "single" or "successful") more characteristic of self-definition in one's earlier years.

Communicating with Others to Further the Process

While placing one's personal biography in the broader context of family and social history could be done alone with one's own thoughts, it is more easily done in communication and connection to others. One way to connect is by writing. For instance, a letter from an elderly widowed man living alone in Florida was printed in a local newspaper. He had been a basketball coach at the local high school fifty years earlier and had moved away and lost touch. He wrote a brief account of the team's life in the 1940s and closed with an invitation for anybody who was involved with the team then or now to write to him.

Another is to talk with someone from one's own generation: Two elderly women, one in a wheelchair, got acquainted at a local concert. They struck up a conversation and began sharing stories about being school children years ago when teachers could be very harsh. They talked about what was said, what they did in return, and laughed at their girlhood fears. They took pride that their generation had changed things, that children couldn't be hit or publicly shamed anymore.

These anecdotes illustrate ways of connecting to one's history and to the future through placing one's life in a broader context. The women had not personally devoted their time to school reform but they emotionally shared in the progress of their generation as a whole. The former basketball coach seemed to be trying to do the same, by finding someone to enhance his attachment to the ongoing history of the basketball team.

Another is to talk to one's family: Lorraine, mentioned above, was already something of a family legend. She might well, in her elderly years, want to reduce her "legend" status (it is lonely on a pedestal) by talking to her siblings and the younger generation. She might tell them about what she had regretted as well as what she achieved, how others had helped her before, and how she felt the family no longer had to push so hard to find its place—this family dream had been accomplished.

The experience of knowing that one's end is near pushes emotional development toward broader perspectives. It is this long view, coupled with an ability to comprehend life's gives and takes, that we call wisdom. As our culture ages, and there are proportionately more older people than younger, perhaps we will come to give this wisdom more respect than we now do.

10

Single and Gay:
Issues and Opportunities

THE BEST WAY TO INTRODUCE a discussion of this group of single people is to present its inherent paradox, since technically there can be no defining category as homosexual singles. Because singleness can only be defined in opposition to marriage, and legal marriage between homosexuals is not available in our society, then the corresponding "singles" classification loses its significance. The fact that the society in which we live does not provide legal sanctions for homosexual unions places us firmly on the road towards understanding the context in which homosexual people live out their lives.

The implications of not having full legal rights are numerous. For starters, it implies not only that this group of people is in a fringe or marginal relationship to the larger society, but also that they may not receive full protection under the statutes of our society. This chapter will examine the implications of living in this marginal relationship to the larger society and also being unattached. We will be using the category homosexual singles to refer to people who are not participating in a relationship that is seen as a committed by both partners.

Some of the issues that gay and lesbians experience when single are similar to the issues outlined in previous chapters, in that they too feel loneliness and often desire nothing more than to connect to partners. However, because of the homophobia/heterosexism present in the larger society, gays and lesbians encounter a different set of problems when dealing with a single life.

Single status, for example, presents increasing problems for heterosexual people as they grow older. Not only do they have to deal with the challenges of single life, but they also have to confront their growing marginality as a member of society. For these people marriage would automatically remove them from the marginal status.

The unattached gay and lesbian people we worked with and interviewed for this book believed they would always be marginalized by the larger society. We asked them to look at their perceptions of some of the satisfactions and the difficulties of their lives. For the most part they saw their gratifications as coming from feeling connected to others in deep and meaningful ways. They wanted to be able to be themselves, work and have friendships. They wanted to be able to feel good about having a homosexual identity and to share this identity with others. While the goals were noteworthy in their very normality, the pitfalls these people experienced were often huge. Developing themselves as complete and fulfilled people on their own, and at the same time finding the support to survive and thrive in the midst of a generally hostile society, often became the major focus of their lives.

We have been struck by the vibrancy and creativity with which gay and lesbian people confronted these challenges. We have also heard many tales of frustration. Out of these stories we have tried to formulate the issues single homosexual people need to confront and resolve throughout their lives. Starting with the context in which gay and lesbian people develop, we will look at how their environment affects their lives. We will then examine specific aspects of life cycle tasks for single homosexuals.

THE SETTING

According to Dalheimer and Feigal (1991), twenty million Americans are gay or lesbian. Although surveys identifying numbers of homosexual people vary widely due to hesitation in disclosing sexual orientation, Lamda places the figure at roughly 10% of the population (Joe Narvis, personal communication, 1994). These people are not generally reflected by the media, since the number of books, movies, and television shows reflecting the homosexual culture is small. Even in our own field of family therapy, few books are available to reflect the joys, problems, and complexities of homosexual family life—and certainly not single life.

This absence of normal media attention creates an overall sense of invisibility. When there is a societal focus on homosexuality, it is almost always negative. This negative attention can range from mild to extreme, often resulting in destructive forms of anti-gay hysteria. An example of this was the intense reaction to the New York City school board's inclusion of the book *Heather Has Two Mommies* in the 1992 school curriculum. The extremely negative response to a book that attempted to normalize same-sex parenting revealed the deep feelings of fear and hostility in our culture towards the homosexual population. This reaction has not infrequently taken the form of open hostility and violence.

"Where are the safeguards in our society?" one might legitimately ask. "Isn't this a country where all constituencies have the right to be protected under law?" Unfortunately, this basic right has often been blatantly disregarded when it comes to the homosexual population.

Not only have the institutions of our society not protected the homosexual population, but in many instances they have been oppressive (Simpson, 1976). Religious institutions cannot be depended upon to provide support for their gay and lesbian members; many, in fact, take the position that homosexuality is a sin. The legal system cannot provide protection either, since only eight states in this country guarantee full legal rights for homosexuals. This, of course, does not include the right to marry (Joe Narvis, personal communication, 1994).

It is difficult to comprehend that, despite these infractions of civil rights, the present atmosphere is more supportive of gay and lesbian lifestyles than in earlier periods in history. When being a known homosexual meant that you might get arrested or lose your job, it was very difficult to feel safe or comfortable.

One's ease in accepting a homosexual identity and sharing it with others is very much affected by the point in history at which this identity becomes evident. The more oppressive the time in history, the more difficult it is to be open about one's sexual identity. The ability to express a gay identity is particularly important for gay and lesbian singles, since developing a viable social life depends on being able to identify and connect with others.

HISTORY

Coming out as a homosexual in the post World War II years would have been an extremely frightening thing to do. A reactionary trend saw all people not espousing "family values" and the American way as outsiders and thereby highly suspicious (see Chapter 2). Communism was perceived as a monumental threat and somehow homosexuality was included in the general hysteria (Adam, 1987). In March 1950 the State Department identified homosexuals as "security risks." As a result, applicants for government jobs who admitted their homosexuality were turned down and many of those already holding jobs were dismissed. The repression was so intense, that it actually took the form of rounding up gays and lesbians in bars and regularly arresting them (Adam, 1987).

Needing to make emotional connections with other single people, gays and lesbians placed themselves in risky positions. As a consequence, people frequenting gay bars developed elaborate family-like groups to both provide support for their members and protection from strangers who might be undercover police (Dunne, 1993). Out of this intense repression and persecution, homophile movements began. The Mattachine Society, an organization of gay men, and The Daughters of Bilitis, an organization of lesbians, developed in the 1950s (Adam, 1987). Although starting out in a mutual attempt to deal with the suppression of the post World War II era, the groups ultimately went their separate ways due to the different concerns of men and women. Gay men, having more financial independence than women, wanted to address general issues involving gay rights. Lesbians, on the other hand, needed to address fundamental problems facing all women, such as violence and equal opportunities in employment. As a result, the lesbian societies eventually joined forces with the Women's Movement. Although initially welcomed wholeheartedly, lesbians ultimately encountered ambivalence from the leaders of this movement (Adam, 1987), due in some part to the straight women's reluctance to surrender heterosexual privilege.

The homosexual societies presented opportunities not only to coalesce political power, but also to socialize and develop a sense of community. Single people entering these groups participated in an arena where they could be known and accepted.

Though these organizations were historically and politically significant, most homosexual people did not belong to them. They shared their sexual preference with only a select few. Single gays and lesbians had few places to meet and get to know others, which resulted in circumscribed social contacts. It was not uncommon for gays to date across social groups. Thus, a young man from a midwestern farm might easily become involved with a college professor through the bar scene (Dunne, 1993). Women did not tend to frequent bars and met other lesbians in private homes and through introductions (Carl, 1990). Many were either isolated or stuck in unfulfilling heterosexual marriages.

Societal changes in the 1960s and 1970s reflected people's disillusionment with the status quo. The civil rights movement opened the way for all disenfranchised groups to assert their power (Coontz, 1992). As a result, coming out became significantly less toxic than in previous years.

For both gays and lesbians, the Stonewall riots in New York's Greenwich Village in 1969 marked the turning point in the gay rights movement. No longer would homosexuals passively expect or demand their civil rights. There was now a movement to join and be proud of when one became aware of a homosexual identity (Adam, 1987). This new assertive position heralded more and more confrontations with the Establishment. One significant and highly successful confrontation involved the psychiatric community. Homosexuality had been seen as a disease by psychiatrists and listed in the DSM-II as one of the "perversions." How could people feel good about coming out when it automatically implied they were pathological?

The gay rights groups realized that this was a critical issue to confront. After a long and bitter struggle in which the psychiatric profession was literally polarized, the issue reached a climax in 1973. Despite resistance from the conservative membership, the council of the American Psychiatric Association ultimately accepted the deletion of homosexuality from the diagnostic manual (Adam, 1987).

The effects of this vote were profound in some ways but less than earth shattering in others. Since many traditional psychotherapists continued to hold onto the belief that homosexuality was an abnormal condition, their therapy reflected this assumption. As a result, gay and lesbian patients had to be perceptive and vigilant in choosing sympathetic therapists. This was often experienced as a burden by people who were already suffering from emotional problems. Nevertheless, the continuing pathologizing of homosexuality by some therapists did not diminish the empowerment that was experienced by gay rights groups when they changed the collective mind of the American Psychiatric Association. Finally homosexuality did not have to be quite such a secret. Single gays and lesbians could be more open in their search for friends and lovers. Moreover, it was now possible to envision and develop communities where homosexuals could support each other and feel less isolated than before.

With the advent of AIDS, in the mid 1980s, the gains made by the gay rights movement became vulnerable. Not only did the Christian Right exploit this new crisis, but since very little was known about the transmission of the disease, the public panicked. Again there was a societal backlash against homosexuals. The gay community itself was besieged by anxiety and losses as a result of this crisis (Adam, 1987). Many men knew scores of people in their network who were either ill or dying. For unattached homosexual men AIDS was devastating. It not only dictated changes in relationship patterns but increased tensions tremendously around dating. For young men struggling with their identity, it marked a renewal of the hesitancy to embrace a gay lifestyle.

The homosexual community as a whole responded to the AIDS crisis in a mature and responsible way. Despite the terrible losses suffered, some important changes gradually began to happen. The gay and lesbian population, which had previously gone their separate ways, coalesced in an effort to deal with the enormity of this problem (Carl, 1990). Paradoxically, the crisis also served to make homosexuality visible to the general public. Despite the initial backlash, plays and movies about the disease and the heartbreak it engendered served to stimulate new understanding and empathy for this community in the American public.

There were many positive changes in attitudes toward the homosexual community in the ensuing years. More legislation was passed in the 1980s protecting gay rights. Openly gay and lesbian individuals ran for office and won (Adam, 1987). The continued growth and cohesion of the gay and lesbian communities became a vital support to homosexual people.

Despite the many advances since the 1950s there is still a long distance to go before homosexuals feel safe and protected in our society. This was exemplified by the American public's negative reaction to President Clinton's 1993 attempt to assure homosexual people be given full rights in the military. The "Don't ask, don't tell, don't pursue" compromise was a tremendous disappointment to most gay rights groups. The controversy that was unleashed by Clinton's directive highlights the fact that repressive elements in this society make expressing oneself as a homosexual dangerous. As a result, people find that they can "be themselves" in some situations and not in others. Some spend most of their time living a lie.

Having a secret identity can have problematic consequences. The more people feel they must keep their identity hidden, the more they feel it is wrong or bad to be who they are (Clark, 1977). The consequences of this process can be far-reaching. Jo-Ann Krestan points out:

> When gay people are, in any way, cut-off from the rest of society, they are vulnerable to the kinds of difficulties which often plague closed systems. Some of these difficulties include relationship problems, chemical dependency and depression. (1988, p. 118)

This observation has unfortunately been validated by the high incidence of alcoholism in the homosexual population (McDonald & Steinhorn, 1990).

IMPACT ON SINGLES

The impact of living in a homophobic society falls particularly hard on unattached people. Single gay and lesbian clients must find settings where their identities can be expressed. The fact that they need to be recognized as homosexuals to establish friendships and community places them continually in the vortex of the political climate of the day. How open the society is to homosexuals determines where they can go to meet others, how they can display affection and with whom they can connect.

For example, in times of great political oppression, people could only be assured that those who frequented certain bars were gay. This placed many single people frequently in bar scenes. The combination of the normal anxiety attached to meeting people, the stress of having a secret identity, and the constant presence of alcohol increased the tendency for many to abuse alcohol (Adam, 1987).

When gays did meet. there were additional difficulties. People were both struggling with their identities themselves and meeting others who were also at varying levels of self-acceptance. This affected whether or not they could publicly date and with whom they could interact. As a result, added pressure was placed on the dating process, which was already fraught with normal acceptance-rejection anxiety. Difficulties in disclosing a homosexual identity has implications for finding role models people can emulate and identify with in their dating patterns. Growing up in heterosexual communities, they had only their parents, siblings, and heterosexual peers to observe. There was no way to learn about homosexual dating patterns, romance, and ways to explore their sexuality. The sense of invisibility this situation engenders is enhanced by societal heterosexism. When everyone is automatically seen as heterosexual, single gay people are continually either turning aside attempts to introduce them to members of the opposite sex or being seen as pathological because they are not yet married.

Living in a society that makes them feel either invisible or profoundly different affects homosexual people's self-esteem and emotional development. It is necessary for therapists working with gays and lesbians to take these issues into account when making an evaluation or a treatment plan. It is also vital that they be aware of the impact of societal homophobia on the therapeutic discourse. This is particularly true when there is a lack of congruence between the sexual orientation of the therapist and the patient. It is therefore critical for heterosexual therapists to be alert to internalized homophobic reactions as well as the potential for gaps in information about the needs and realities of homosexual people.

THE LIFESPAN OF THE HOMOSEXUAL SINGLE

Responding to the need for a model for viewing normal adult development of the single homosexual person, we have developed a life cycle that describes important emotional transitions. This life cycle is always being influenced by the historical moment in which the individual lives, gender factors, special characteristics operating in the family of origin, and the different stages of the emergence of the homosexual identity. How these factors interact will ultimately affect how people work out their life course. We have taken them all into consideration in thinking about the life cycle of the single homosexual client.

Because the discovery, acceptance, and shift to a homosexual self-portrait may happen in childhood, in adolescence, in early adulthood, or even very late in life (Berzon, 1988), a linear life cycle model may not fit the experience of the single homosexual person. We believe that it is more appropriate to define critical emotional tasks that may be accomplished at different points in a person's life span. We mean these to be thought of more as guideposts than as rigid rules.

These tasks include:

1. The development and the unfolding of a homosexual identity
2. The development of gender identity in the absence of prescribed roles
3. The development of a "family of choice"
4. The assertion of a homosexual identity within the family of origin
5. The development of a fulfilled life when the "prince or princess" doesn't appear
6. Realistic planning for old age

The Development and Unfolding of a Homosexual Identity

Acceptance of and positive feelings about a gay or lesbian identity are critical to the self-esteem of the homosexual client. Because people grow up in a heterosexual family and in a heterosexual world, fully accepting this identity may take some time. Vivian Cass (1979) has conceptualized a series of stages people go through in the process of working this out. It is important to remember that these stages are fluid and do not necessarily follow a linear progression. People can feel quite comfortable about having accepted and expressed themselves in most areas of their lives, for example, and them get thrown off when moving to a new town or meeting new people. It is nonetheless useful to keep these stages in mind when assessing single homosexual clients, in order to put their struggles into an understandable context.

Cass offers *identity confusion* as a first stage, in which the person begins to become aware of homosexual thoughts and feelings. Still, the person attempts to maintain a self-image that is heterosexual and develops strategies to avoid acknowledging the homosexual fantasies. There may be tremendous anxiety at this point, since the person is frightened by the entrance of these unwanted thoughts. When this is occurring, it is important for the therapist to connect the anxiety with these thoughts and try to understand the personal meaning of homosexuality to the client. This involves assessing family and cultural issues as well as the patient's belief systems about homosexuality. Investigating these issues is useful in ultimately dealing with and working through the anxiety.

The second stage, *identity comparison*, occurs when the person accepts the possibility that he or she may be homosexual. As he/she begins to look at the implications of this fact, he/she may have a variety of responses—

from feeling alienated from others to trying to disassociate from anything homosexual. When the client is in this stage, it is helpful to explore these responses. While accepting the clients's feelings, the therapist may suggest alternative reactions and introduce positive images of homosexuality.

Cass then presents a third stage, *identity tolerance*, in which the person comes to accept the probability that he or she is a homosexual and begins to recognize the sexual and emotional needs that go with this. With this acceptance the person is freed to pursue social, emotional, and sexual needs. The turmoil and confusion recede. When people finally begin to experiment with romantic connections, it is not uncommon to see "push-pull" relationships in which people approach and back off from each other. This results from people's fears of the implications of a relationship with a person of the same sex. The therapist should normalize this process and encourage people to continue their experimentation.

A fourth stage, *identity acceptance,* occurs when the person accepts rather than tolerates a homosexual self-image and increases his/her contact with the gay and lesbian culture. This can be a liberating experience, since it may mean a gradual shift from living an isolated existence to feeling part of a community. At this point the therapist will encourage the exploration of homosexual communities and new relationship systems.

Stage five, *identity pride*, occurs when the person feels good about and becomes immersed in the homosexual culture. At this point relationships become more solid, as people are no longer fearful of being involved with others of the same sex. Finally, stage six, *identity synthesis*, occurs when the person no longer has a need to dichotomize homosexuals and heterosexuals and can integrate aspects of his or her gay or lesbian identity with all other aspects of self (Cass, 1979).

The unfolding of the homosexual identity is crucial, whenever in life it happens. The therapist's attention to this life task and assistance in this process cannot be underestimated. A good deal of this assistance involves normalizing the struggles, experimentation, and regressions that are all part of exploring life without family role models.

For example, because homosexual people grow up in heterosexual families, the typical adolescent exploration does not occur. Children who are afraid to admit or share their homosexual desires don't find others with whom to experiment. Lacking family role models and like-minded peers, gay and lesbian adolescents may be quite isolated. As a result, they may engage in experimental sexual encounters whenever they do become aware of a homosexual identity. When they do come out as homosexuals, whether at 21 or 51, they need to go through a reenactment of the missing practice period (Carl, 1990). People then tend to "fall in love" and move in together without realizing that this is somewhat experimental. When such relationships break up, they may easily become disillusioned. The therapist can help to normalize this process, explaining that this is all part of the trial-and-error process of identity exploration. It is also important to emphasize that coming out can be a lifetime process and situations in which discomfort about homosexuality recurs will be encountered from time to time.

The Development of Gender Identity in the Absence of Prescribed Roles

Numerous factors, including biology, psychological identity formation, and expected stereotypical role behavior, contribute to gender identity. Nevertheless, according to the research of Robert Stoller (1964), gender identity is irreversibly established by the age of three.

Growing up in heterosexual households, homosexual people develop a set of gender expectations for themselves that are culturally traditional. As a result, the expectations most gay men have for themselves are initially similar to those of most heterosexual men. They expect themselves to be strong, self-sufficient, and effective. Many emotions, particularly fear and sadness, are defined as weak. They are, as most men, taught to believe that they should be able to perform sexually without any help and regardless of their feelings or the circumstances (Meth & Passick, 1990a). Individuality and autonomous thinking are seen as signs of healthy adulthood (Gilligan, 1982). Unfortunately, since men in this culture are reared to be intensely "homophobic" (Meth, 1990b), gay men inherit and internalize this attitude with the assumption of traditional male values.

Women, on the other hand, define themselves in the context of human relationships and value their ability to care. According to Jean Baker Miller (1976), "women stay with, build on, and develop in the context of attachment and affiliation with others (p. 83)"; their sense of selfhood is organized around being able to make and maintain affiliations. As a result, when women remain unattached throughout their life cycle, this is often experienced as a lack.

Women may also be conflicted about competition and success. This stems from society's notions of femininity and women's concerns about being different and risking rejection (Gilligan, 1982). Early conflicts about success, of course, affect career choices and the ability to be competitive in the work area.

Although there have been important changes in the last thirty years, the pull for people to define themselves through traditional gender roles is powerful. Much has been written about how gender roles affect family dynamics (Walters et al., 1988), but very little has been understood about how these roles affect the behavior and expectations of single people, particularly gays and lesbians. In our experience the areas where gender expectations affect single people most are dating, sexual experimentation, and expectations for fulfillment in work.

As indicated earlier, dating usually provokes intense anxiety for men as well as women. Heterosexual people frequently fall back on familiar gender roles to lower this anxiety. For homosexual people, there are no such clear guideposts. Since a public and well-defined script does not exist for same-sex courtship, they initially draw on gender-related heterosexual models.

In a study of lesbian and gay dating patterns (Klinkenberg & Rose, 1994), gay men reported more often than lesbians that they sought physical attractiveness in mates. In the early phases of a relationship they are also more likely to stress the sexual aspects of a relationship over the emotional ones. Lesbians described having experiences where deep emotional feelings were shared on first dates; as a result, first dates became quite intense.

Sexual scripts are also confusing, since people may not automatically know how to behave with partners of the same sex. People are not often comfortable talking about this with one another. Therapists must be alert to this issue and encourage patients who are dating to talk directly about sexual issues (Pat Colucci, personal communication, 1994).

The lack of gender-prescribed roles can have positive as well as negative consequences for gay and lesbian people. Released from rigid gender roles, homosexual people may experiment in meeting new people. Klinkenberg and Rose (1994) pointed out, in fact, that within the context of these gender-related assumptions, the homosexual dating patterns did allow for much more role flexibility.

The special needs of single gays and lesbians necessitate alteration of rigid gender prescriptions. The AIDS crisis revealed the potential for these changes to occur, with men acting as sensitive, loving caregivers to other men, and gays and lesbians working together to battle this scourge. Yet flexibility in gender roles needs to happen in everyday life, so that people can find the work and companionship they need.

Many of the single gay men we interviewed said that when they tried to meet a partner for a committed relationship, they met only men consistent with the stereotypes—interested only in brief sexual encounters. Paradoxically, the results of an extensive survey reported by the *Advocate* magazine contradict this assumption. In this survey, to which 10,000 gay men responded, 80% said that, if given a choice between being able to have sex without love or love without sex, they would choose love without sex (Lever, 1994). Although there are many possible implications of this study, the wish to have a romantic relationship stands out as a significant life goal. Of course, sexual fulfillment often enhances intimacy rather than interfering with it. It is important to note, however, when sex is being used as a substitute for other forms of intimacy in a relationship.

Lesbians, for their part, have moved away from strictly female roles. They have learned to value assertive behavior and explore issues of power within their own and the larger women's community. They have become more interested in sex as part of personal fulfillment and in general abandoned the position that the only allowed "female" expression of sexuality would celebrate gentleness, egalitarianism and other warm and loving but not necessarily orgasmic aspects of sex (Nichols, 1989). The therapist's role here is to challenge rigidly conceived ideas when they are clearly interfering with the lesbian or gay person's life. In providing an atmosphere where notions of masculinity and femininity can be potentially expanded, the therapist enhances the feeling of having options in one's life.

Asserting a Homosexual Identity in the Family of Origin

The overarching concern for the single gay or lesbian client is the search for community. Many are fearful of expressing their homosexuality to their family for fear of being cut off from a vital source of support. Others have fantasies that expressing their true identities will make for more intimate relationships. Many people either remain hidden and disconnected from family or divulge this identity without comprehending its impact on the family. Sometimes this information is even expressed in an emotional moment as a way of making a point. The distress following these extreme solutions can evolve into serious problems for the homosexual adult and his or her family.

Strained relationships or cut-offs from family can have a major impact on the single person's life, since emotional supports are vital. When people try to fill this void by increasing the intensity of the effort to find a mate, they very often neglect other aspects of their lives. This can result in frustration or a sense of emptiness.

When a homosexual identity can be revealed to the family in a planful and compassionate way, the process, however tumultuous, can become an important milestone in everyone's emotional development. The therapist's coaching of a gay or lesbian client in this area can be pivotal to the ultimate success of this process. It is essential for the client to feel good about his/her identity before beginning the work. In preparation for the coaching process, the therapist and client should be aware of how different family dynamics will influence the response to a disclosure of homosexuality. This is essential in helping the client prepare for potential reactions. The client's ability to understand, tolerate and be nonreactive to the family's response is part of the work of differentiation (Herz Brown, 1991).

Both the homosexual single person and the family live under the cloak of a homophobic/heterosexist society. As previously noted, this influences the time it takes for homosexual people to accept their identity. It also affects the family's reaction to disclosure, as well as the time it takes them to accept and embrace the sexual preference of their child.

Carol Griffin and Marian and Arthur Wirth, authors of a book which resulted from their joint experiences with other parents of homosexual children, talked about shock and disbelief as a typical initial response. The pain these parents felt resulted partly from their own homophobia and partly from feeling responsible for their children's choice. Regardless of their initial reactions, most were genuinely concerned about their children's future (Griffin, Wirth, & Wirth, 1986).

Whether parents can accept their gay or lesbian child depends on what homosexuality means to the nuclear and the larger family system, the degree of flexibility of that system, and the degree to which the ethnic or cultural system accepts homosexuality.

The disclosure of homosexuality immediately brings the issue of sex into the forefront. How people react to this disclosure depends very much on how the family deals with sex in general. Since sexuality is such an emotionally laden and misunderstood area in American society, many people grow up in families where any discussion of sex is filled with high anxiety (Rosenheck, 1992). The introduction of homosexual sex, with its stereotypical erotic images of bar-hopping, increases anxiety. Larger themes from families of origin will also affect parental responses to disclosure. Unresolved issues from previous generations, which elevate marriage or raise the ante for children, may intensify the family's response to the disclosure of homosexuality. When homosexuality is seen as precluding children, then strong negative reactions can be predicted. Understanding this will help clients not only withstand an intense reaction but also develop compassion for their family.

The degree of comfort a family has with accepting difference within its "ranks" also affects the ability to accept a gay or lesbian offspring. The emotional forces within the system, developed through generations, can lead either to flexibility or to rigid fusion. The way the family deals with differences determines how it will tolerate individual member's challenging the family norms (Carter & McGoldrick Orfanidis, 1976).

Since homosexuality brings along with it a discontinuity with the family as well as the society, the disclosure might be expected to produce emotional upheaval in more rigid family systems. Although an emotional crisis can probably be predicted, the homosexual person may have a difficult time managing his or her reactions. The client's reaction often mirrors the family style, for instance, "If they don't want me, then I don't want them." It may take some time for the therapist to work with this reaction, so that ultimately the gay or lesbian person can reenter the family in a productive manner. It helps if the client has low expectations and is patient about seeing the results of his or her efforts.

The family's ability to accept the homosexual child is also influenced by how involved family members are in their ethnic or religious subculture and how tolerant the culture is towards homosexuality. Black lesbians, for example, relate tremendous difficulty in expressing their sexual orientation in their community, where homosexuality is often a taboo subject. At the same time it is of tremendous importance for black people to stay connected to their culture to satisfy racially related support needs (McDonald & Steinhorn, 1990). Consequently, many gay and lesbian blacks wind up not coming out for fear of being excluded from their community.

Puerto Rican people find themselves in a culture that is openly hostile to homosexuality. Gay men, in particular, find it difficult to deal with the notion that the entire culture values strong heterosexual stereotypes, in which men are expected to be "macho" and to derive status by exerting power over women (McDonald & Steinhorn, 1990). Fearing the repercussions of revelation, Puerto Rican gays often try to hide their identity or remove themselves from the family.

If these aspects of family functioning are understood and anticipated, the client will be more effective in asserting a homosexual identity in a productive way. This is where coaching comes into play. Carter and McGoldrick describe this process as follows:

> The effort of family therapy with one person is to help this person to define his own individual beliefs and life goals apart from the family's presumption of shared positions, policy, and goals. The measure of emotional maturity is thus that an individual is able to think, plan, know and follow his own beliefs and self directed life course, rather than having to react to the cues of those close to him. (Carter & McGoldrick Orfanidis, 1976, p. 197)

If people are genuinely attempting to be authentic, they must be willing to express themselves with the understanding that they will not always be accepted. This is particularly important for homosexual people, since disclosure to the family may initially bring disapproval. At the same time, divulging their true selves may counteract the internalization of society's homophobic messages, as well as opening up the possibility of building authentic personal relationships with family members (Krestan, 1988).

The timing of disclosure should come from the client rather than a lover or close friend. The therapist or coach needs to work with the client to determine how ready he or she is to think clearly about the family situation. It is critical to keep in mind these steps: (1) planning for the disclosure, (2) the family's reaction, and (3) dealing with the family's reaction to the disclosure (Carter & McGoldrick Orfanidis, 1976).

When people understand how family systems operate in general, it often helps them look at their own families in a more dispassionate way. This involves learning about the family's history and how patterns of interacting developed. Getting to know individual members personally also helps, since it serves to dispel preconceived ideas of who these people really are and why they may react the way they do.

Underlying this sometimes tedious planning process is the attempt to help the client become less reactive to possible negative reactions. If the gay or lesbian client can remain calm and stay connected as much as possible during any crisis that occurs as a result of the disclosure, there is a much better chance that emotions will calm down quickly (Carter & McGoldrick Orfanidis, 1976). When negative responses are anticipated, people can run through alternative methods of response. Sometimes, for example, it can be useful to write practice letters to members of the family who might have the strongest negative reaction. If these letters are reviewed in the therapy session, there is a chance that the accompanying emotions can be dealt with before the actual event.

When the client is ready for disclosure, he or she might start with the family member who is expected to have the most positive reaction. Everything, including the choice of words that are used, needs to be planned in order to avoid a toxic reaction (Krestan, 1988). Dealing with the reactions to disclosure is no small undertaking. It important for the client to understand that shock, grief, and mourning may occur after the disclosure. With fused or rigid family systems, in fact, fallout from the disclosure may well be the focus of therapy for years. While helping clients work through their family's reactions may be experienced as excessively time-consuming, it can also be extremely useful. The process of trying to understand, have patience with, and deal with these reactions not only is important for the eventual goal of asserting an identity in the family, but also contributes to the client's development of a mature self.

The family's reaction has to be understood in relation to its own multi-generational history. It also changes over time. Just as the gay or lesbian person had to go through a process to accept his or her identity, the family will pass through several stages on the way to acceptance.

The intensity of the fallout from the disclosure of homosexuality does not necessarily mean that there will be a cut-off in the future. Many studies reveal that, despite the initial reaction, most families come to some resolution with their homosexual children (Weston, 1991). In fact, a study by Cramer and Roach (1988), which followed gay men after coming out to their families, found that most relationships improved after an initial period of post-disclosure turmoil. One interesting finding of the study was that many relationships reached a state that was more satisfying than the period prior to disclosure (Cramer & Roach, 1988). This is not surprising when you consider that keeping a secret lessens intimacy. However painful, the process of opening up may lead to better relationships.

The Development of a Family of Choice

No matter how excellent the family-of-origin relationships have become, the sense of differentness that homosexual people experience necessitates a broadening of the kinship system to include more people similar to themselves. The feeling of isolation and marginality that develops as a result of being a minority in one's very own family can be debilitating. Involvement with others in meaningful ways not only contributes to pride in one's own identity but also provides support while experimenting with different options in life. Meaningful networks or "families of choice" may include deep friendships or biological family; whether or not blood relatives are included, these networks need to be acknowledged as *real* family systems. Kath Weston (1991), who has researched these family systems, emphasizes this point, and goes on to say that families do not need to be defined as either "straight" or gay, since even that division implies a value judgment.

Participation in a chosen family does not mean one has broken ties with the family of origin. Resolving relationships with the family of origin and asserting one's homosexual identity within that family are vitally important. However, the entire notion of "family" needs to be broadened. There are many people, in fact, who consider the family of origin and chosen family as parts of the same larger unit. The issue becomes: can people be involved with loving family units that positively mirror them and where there are reciprocal commitments and responsibilities? For single people families of choice represent opportunities for inclusion and love outside of a committed dyadic relationship. These families don't have to be complex or large to be experienced as deep and supportive. Weston (1991) describes many different types of families, from small groups who meet regularly for dinner to large complex units. It is only necessary that these units provide nurturance, support, and the feeling of belonging. It is important for therapists to encourage single homosexual people to participate in the development and involvement with these families and consistently to validate their importance and legitimacy.

When the Prince or Princess Never Comes: Fulfillment as a Single Adult

Most people, homosexual and heterosexual, expect to connect with a special person in their lives. As one older lesbian client we interviewed put it, "You're brought up with that idea. It's hard to let it go." She herself maintained that dream until the age of 60, when she finally decided she did not need to hold onto it anymore. Interviewing and working with gay and lesbian single people from their early twenties to their late sixties, we have found that most people want to be connected. Many people see a long-term commitment as the only way their lives would be fulfilled.

In their series, "Love Stories in the age of AIDS," the *Village Voice* introduced Careen and Maria, two women who met while one was in prison. The fact that one was potentially very ill did not affect their happiness in what they described as a "repelling time" (Schoofs, 1994). The tremendous importance placed on the redemptive and therapeutic powers of a dyadic love relationship, even in these painful circumstances, highlights the media's elevation of "coupledom" to a sublime position. It is not surprising that single people — "gay" and "straight" — feel a constant underlying pressure to find the right person.

The intensity of this focus has been evident to us in working with both heterosexual and homosexual single people. As Douglas Carl puts it, "Attitudes have changed in the last several decades, but most of us still aspire to finding the one *right* relationship that will help make our lives fulfilling" (1990, p. 45). When this does not occur, people get the sense that life is passing them by and nothing is happening.

It is important to distinguish here between the normal wish for a loving relationship and the pressure to find one so that one's life can feel fulfilled. When people can find a sense of personal fulfillment within themselves, the pressure to find this in a relationship often diminishes. In this respect, there are many similarities between heterosexual and homosexual single people. The differences often are seen in the choices made for a fulfilling life and the options people felt they had in pursuing their goals. We therefore looked at areas single homosexual people reported as giving them a deep sense of personal fulfillment.

One recurring theme was that people felt their professions brought meaning to their lives. The work arena became a focal point for their lives, as it often is for single heterosexuals. What distinguished homosexuals was that they felt their choices were limited due to their homosexuality. Although the restrictions were by no means seen as severe as in earlier times, the perception of limitations continued to affect people's job choices. As a result, they often delayed making career choices or remained hidden at work. Those who felt successful, however, deeply valued their work experiences. One single man told us that he was fearful of working in the financial area, since he thought that people would be more conservative and therefore would not accept his homosexuality. He did ultimately move into this field in his thirties and was gratified by his success. He felt his frustrations in relationships were offset by his fulfillment at work.

Many people reported having a deep commitment to the community spirit of gay and lesbian activism. These activities not only were experienced as deeply rewarding in themselves, but also provided automatic community supports for the volunteers. Some people tried to help others in areas where they had been frustrated in their own lives. One man, who had a particularly difficult time coming out to his family, ran "coming out" groups in a gay and lesbian center. He found this to be so gratifying, in fact, that he changed his profession to social work, where he found he could more consistently use his skills in working with people.

A particularly rewarding area for people was volunteering to work with gay and lesbian youth. The Hetrick Martin Institute in New York City, for example, provides therapy and peer group experiences for young people. Many homosexual adults volunteered to work in the youth centers associated with this institute and to serve as positive role models. The satisfaction people experienced in this work was related to their having opportunities to mentor the next generation.

The sense of helping the next generation develop seemed to be an area which was very often missing in the lives of homosexual people, and something many people craved. Some people formed special relationships with their siblings' or friends' children. Although in the past very few single gay and lesbian people have seriously considered the possibility of having their own children, in the last ten years this has certainly changed. Lesbians have begun to have children as couples or as single women; in fact this phenomenon has been referred to as the "Lesbian Baby Boom" (Martin, 1993).

The decision to have children as a single gay or lesbian person has complications of its own. The task of resolving homosexual identity, along with issues involved in raising a child alone, can feel daunting. Often gay and lesbian people find their own young adulthood so filled with issues of identity formation that they don't have the time or inclination to think about having their own children. As one 30-year-old lesbian exclaimed when asked about children, "Children! I can't think about children now — first I have to figure out who I am!"

As people age and issues of identity formation and profession are clarified, some do think about having their own children. Women in their late thirties and forties, in particular, start thinking about this issue. Despite the potential problems some men and many women find contemplation of having children critical to their development. In fact, now that reproductive advances and less restrictive foreign adoptions have made having a child a real possibility for lesbians, a developmental crisis may occur if the possibility is not considered. When single lesbians do decide to be mothers, they have found tremendous gratification from this choice. Many lesbian mothers have developed communities to provide support and education for each other.

When women do confront this issue seriously, they can then put it aside, whatever the ultimate decision. For example, one woman told about coming out after living for ten years in a heterosexual relationship. When she finally left her husband, she realized that what she truly regretted was not having had the experience of parenting a child. Because she was already in her forties, she decided that it would make sense for her to become a foster mother to an older child. She did make arrangements to bring a 10-year-old girl home, but ultimately had so many difficulties with this child that she realized the situation was untenable. She was deeply saddened when this opportunity did not work out but grateful that she had made the attempt. After this experience she found that parenting was no longer such a compelling issue. It is, we think, critical for people to think about this issue seriously and, if they decide not to have children, to deal with this loss.

Although it is not as common as among lesbians, some gay men also wish to have children of their own (Spordone, 1993). One 30-year-old homosexual man I (NS) interviewed, for example, decided to become a sperm donor for a lesbian couple he knew. When a child was conceived he chose to take an active, if limited, role in the child's life. When complications developed, he worked them through, and ultimately he felt no regrets about his decision.

Because of the homophobic reactions of society, many gay men lack the confidence to pursue this idea beyond an initial thought. Consequently, it is particularly important for the therapist to support this option, while helping the client examine possibilities of operationalizing his wish. While there is very little research in the area of gay fathering, the studies that have been done report initial positive results. Scallon (1982), who compared gay and heterosexual fathers, noted no differences in child-rearing practices in these two groups. What he did find was that gay fathers assessed themselves more positively in their paternal role than heterosexual fathers did and appeared to demonstrate greater capacity for nurturance. In his 1993 study, Al Spordone found that the experience of fathering helped to lower his subjects' internalized homophobia.

Complicated as fathering may seem for a single gay man, we believe that whenever a man is interested he needs to seriously consider this as an option. Considering all options and deciding to pursue some and not others may be painful. At the same time, it will give the client the sense that he has made real choices in his life and is not merely the victim of circumstances.

The therapist working with single homosexual adults must help them find the courage to focus on what they need to do to find fulfillment in their own lives. The more people can feel they are living their lives in the fullest sense, the less they will focus on a relationship to accomplish this goal.

Planning for Later Life

Gay and lesbian single people must make plans for themselves as they get older. This includes financial planning as well as plans for emotional support. In working with people in their late forties, fifties, and sixties, therapists need to bring up these issues. The research on the isolation of aging gays and lesbians points to the critical importance of working through coming out issues and networking earlier in life. Working with people in early maturity involves helping them maintain and manage support systems that are in existence and developing connections in the community when there are none.

Because of the oppressive nature of society when our present older population came of age, many were not able to do the necessary work of networking. As a result, there is a tremendous degree of isolation in the aging homosexual population. There are now over four million homosexual people over 60, many of whom are living alone and isolated (Kochman, 1994). According to the research done by A. J. Lucco (1987), aging homosexual people are much more likely to be living alone than the general elderly population. Loneliness was frequently reported as a serious problem among Lucco's respondents, since few reported close kin relationships. Many gay and lesbian people in later life report that they have little or no relationship to their biological family; yet, they are less likely to join organized senior citizens activities than the general population (Hammersmith, 1987). This may be due to the potential for discrimination as well as the discomfort many have with feeling different from the general population at the typical senior citizen center.

When homosexual senior citizens were asked whether they would participate in activities or join retirement communities if these communities were primarily composed of homosexual members, over 60% said they would (Lucco, 1987). This means that people at middle age need to investigate such living arrangements. Although there are now agencies, like the S.A.G.E. Foundation in New York City, that provide socialization and services for homosexual senior citizens, few live-in residences presently exist.

To prevent the isolation of single gay or lesbian senior citizens, therapists need to be alert to problems people have in maintaining emotional ties as they grow older. Coaching people to resolve relationships with their families of origin, and encouraging them to develop "families of choice" are two means of preventing future problems. Richard Friend (1987) suggests finding ways to explore cross-generational interaction, so that older homosexual people can connect with younger ones.

Financial security is another area that is of primary importance. When single people have limited resources, they tend not to plan for their financial future. It is important to emphasize, however, that even small financial supports can make a difference in later years. When these issues are confronted directly, living arrangements can be planned for to make life meaningful in old age.

III

CLINICAL APPLICATIONS

11

The Twenties:
Bob's Story

A VERY ATTRACTIVE, well dressed young man came to see me (NS) for help with what he thought of as depression and low self-esteem. Despite his self-confident demeanor and his warm, engaging manner, he saw himself as quite lonely and unable to bring himself to make friends.

He had recently broken up with a women whom he had planned to marry. After graduating from college, he and this woman traveled from their home town in Georgia to New York City so both could start their careers. Gail, his girl friend, had hopes of being an actress and Bob, my client, wanted to be a commercial artist. Bob actually became quite successful as an artist and was making a very good living. In fact, in the three years since he had come to New York he had risen from a freelance artist to the assistant director of the Art Department of a widely read magazine. In his free time he had done his own painting, for which he had already received some recognition. At the age of 26, Bob was considered one of the rising young artists in New York City. The contrast between this attractive, successful young man and the vision he had of himself was startling!

Bob told me that he wasn't quite comfortable reaching out to people, tending to make few but lasting friendships. In a new environment it would take him a very long time to make a circle of friends. As a result, he had a tendency to rely on his female companions to develop friendship networks.

In New York City Bob found himself isolated and expected his girl friend to make the social contacts for both of them. When he and Gail broke up, therefore, he felt terribly alone, and without the resources to make friends on his own. He considered returning to his home town, but ultimately dismissed this thought since it meant leaving his contacts in the art world. Turning to new women for support, he soon realized this, too, was an

unworkable solution. As a result of his placing so many emotional expectations on new relationships, the women he met tended to withdraw from
him.

Bob's decision to enter therapy at this point emerged from the increasing
frustration he was feeling about his life. He was also starting to be aware
that he was expecting too much from women. He wondered why he himself
wasn't able to tap his own resources to negotiate his social life.

The intensity of Bob's focus on finding a permanent relationship rather
than developing friendships suggested that there were issues in his family
that contributed to the sense of urgency. Since it is critical for a single
person of his age to be able to establish a community of friends, it was
important to track issues in his family that may have contributed to his
belief that he could not do so.

Bob told me that he is the oldest of two sons in a Caucasian Protestant
family. His brother Joel, two years younger, works as a school teacher.
Joel lives in the family home but is out most of the time with friends and
job related commitments.

Bob's father, Al, 53, and is a salesperson for a large computer company.
Although he has many friends and is seen by the community as a friendly,
outgoing person, he has been chronically depressed for many years and has
always used Bob as a confidant. Al is seen as the warm one in the family.
His wife, Sonia, Bob's mother, is cold and distant. She has no tolerance for
what she describes as Al's weepy, dependent ways. Consequently, Al has
spent many hours with Bob expressing his pain, mostly about his wife's
coldness. As a child, Bob complained about her when his father did, but at
the same time he secretly longed to be close to her.

Sonia has a Ph.D. in art history and works as an assistant curator in a
museum. She is the middle child and only daughter in a family of high
achievers. Her father is described as a warm but passive man, her mother
as cold, hypercritical, and emotionally distant. Sonia's mother lost her own
mother at birth, a loss which significantly affected the entire family.

Al is the younger of two sons in a family where both parents abused
alcohol. Al's mother was unavailable a good deal of his life because of her
drinking. His father spent long days at work and then usually drank until
late in the night. Al did not have a drinking problem and often considered
himself the caretaker for the whole family. He was quite ambivalent about
this position: on the one hand, he felt he had an important role in his
family; on the other, he felt that his brother usually got more attention
from his parents than he did.

Looking at Bob's family from a three-generational perspective, we see
that issues of loss and addictions pervade the system. Such systems usually
have problems at times of launching, since separations are experienced with

HAROLD BRIDGES LIBRARY
S. MARTIN'S COLLEGE
LANCASTER

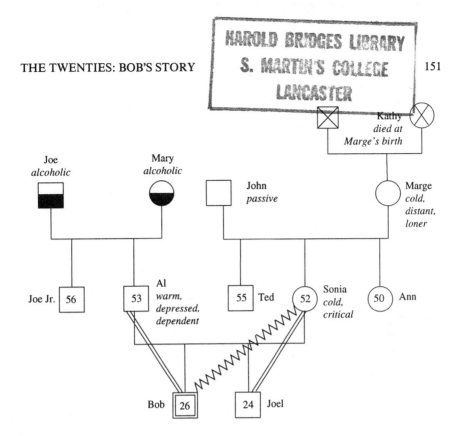

FIGURE 11.1   Bob Smith's Genogram

great anxiety (Herz Brown, 1991). Viewing the family in this context, Bob could see past the individual nuclear system to issues that were passed on from generation to generation. He saw that the ability to make friends was not a neutral issue in his family. Not only were friendships a source of tension between his parents, but his mother's family had a long history of isolation from peers.

For a single person, understanding one's role in one's family is only the first step. It is also critical to look at the meaning of marital status in the family, as well as in the milieu in which the family operates. In Bob's family, attachment issues are significant. There are no single adults on either side of Bob's family, and both parents expected their sons to marry — despite their disillusionment about their own marriage. Conflicts around attachments play an important role in parents' marriage. Father highly values closeness and sees mother's withdrawal as causing his depressions. Many times he told Bob that, "without a loving wife, a man's life is incomplete." Mother, on the other hand, values self-reliance and regularly berates father for his dependence. Given their British Protestant family background, it is not surprising that issues of attachment and self-reliance play themselves out as such important themes (McGill & Pierce, 1982).

Bob spent the first few months of therapy understanding the importance of these themes in his family. By asking uncles and aunts about their version of family events he was able to get some objectivity about his parents as people (Carter & McGoldrick Orfanidis, 1976). For example, he learned from mother's older brother, Ted, just how much education was valued. Ted said that his parents, Bob's grandparents, expected Sonia to marry a highly educated man, but she was attracted to Al's warmth instead. Although the parents gave their approval to the marriage, there was always some hint of disappointment in their attitude. Bob was surprised to learn that there was a point in mother's life when she valued the warmth of an attachment over her parents' expectations. He wondered whether mother's anger with Al was really anger with herself for not living up to the family's expectations. He also learned that she had been timid and shy as a young woman. Bob began to wonder whether what he saw as coolness in his mother was, at least in part, shyness.

Bob learned from his father's sister that his father had been seen as quite competent earlier in his life and was considered a top salesman in the firm in which he worked. Bob was struck by the similarity between his father's worldly success and dependency at home and his own successes at work and dependency on women.

Surprisingly, Bob's discussions with various relatives provoked no response from his parents. He thought this was typical of his family since very little information passed from sibling to sibling. In this way the parental sibling system was similar to his own—he and his brother barely spoke.

The more Bob learned about his parents' early motivations in life, the more he gained objectivity about them as people. This became ultimately critical in helping him get some objectivity about his own struggles in life. Tracking themes and emotional processes in his family, Bob saw how the role he played in his family, that of father's confidant, maintained the equilibrium of the family. He also began to understand how his role with his father affected the way he saw his mother—he was so allied with his father that he was only seeing his mother through his father's eyes. Not only did this alienate him from his mother, but he spent so much time propping up his father that he was unable to focus on his own needs.

Although mother was seen as negative and critical, she upheld the moral values of the family. Mother's contempt of father's need for friendships was translated into a contempt for friendships in general. In a misguided attempt to connect to his mother, Bob was attempting to emulate her by devaluing friendships. When he realized that what he thought of as an inability to reach out to people was really an inhibition due to his identification with his mother, Bob felt elated. He realized that this identification was also contributing to his isolation from his brother. Believing that he had to present a model of self-sufficiency, he acted cool and detached with Joel, who apparently emulated Bob but kept his distance.

Finally, Bob realized that his parents' relationship to their own parents and grandparents affected their belief systems about themselves as individuals and as parents. Perhaps they were acting automatically according to a belief system that did not really work for them. He decided that these belief systems were irrelevant to him; he had the right to establish beliefs for himself.

Becoming aware of how family themes affected him was extremely helpful to Bob. However, in order to make real changes for himself he had to shift his role in his family. This is the difficult part of any coaching work. One's ability to shift one's position in the family and thereby change the traditions and rules of the system depends on the rigidity of the system and the strength of the individual (Herz Brown, 1991). Bob's actual strength was a good deal greater than he initially experienced. He had begun to develop a better perspective toward his parents and was eager to deal with them directly.

In order to ensure that he would be able to approach his family with clarity, Bob followed up on the previous work by confronting in imagery all of his unresolved issues with his parents. He wrote practice letters in which he poured out all his emotions and fears about acting differently with them. We went over these letters in therapy until he was able to maintain his perspective (Carter & McGoldrick Orfanidis, 1976). He kept searching for a sense of who he was in relationship to his parents – not their *child* but their *son*. This process, though tedious and at times frustrating, actually helped to lower his anxiety.

Interestingly enough, with an increased understanding of how his family system worked, Bob developed empathy towards his mother. He then became aware of how deeply he missed having a real relationship with her. He realized that part of what he thought was expected of him as a grown man was to deny his need for his mother. Denying this need was in fact contributing to his difficulties.

Finally, Bob was ready to take the plunge! He planned to visit his parents and attempt to extract himself from the parental triangle. Since it was right before Valentine's Day, Bob did a highly unusual thing for him. He sent his mother a Valentine's Day card signed "Love, Bob." His mother called immediately to tell him she loved the card and she was looking forward to seeing him. He was a bit puzzled about why he had never done anything like this before but delighted that once he changed his role, even through a very small act of sending a Valentine's Day card, his mother was able to respond differently.

Bob was amazed to realize that he had the power to change his relationships with his family. This whole process so empowered him that he continued preparation for his visit home with a good deal more confidence than before.

The last part of helping Bob prepare for his return was actually going over with him how to remove himself from the parental triangle. Specifically, he tried to find a way to no longer be his father's confidant whenever father complained about his mother. Having learned about systems, he knew that there would be tremendous resistance to this shift and that he had to plan for every possible eventuality (Carter & McGoldrick Orfanidis, 1976). Bob was very clear that he no longer wanted to be in this position and would be willing to deal with any amount of discomfort to remove himself from his typical role in the nuclear family.

Planning for the visit included thinking about the typical scenario that would occur when he returned home. Mother would at first be very happy to see him, but then immediately retreat to the den. This left Al and Joel with Bob. Joel would typically leave Bob and Al together and go out with his friends. This would begin an evening in which Al would express his depression and complain to Bob about Sonia.

Bob thought he could counter this process by acting differently when Al complained. Instead of trying to be as helpful as he had been in the past and listening endlessly to complaints about mother's flaws, he would simply act confused and have absolutely no answers for Dad. Under no circumstances was he to listen to criticisms of his mother, saying instead that he knew Dad could handle things.

Bob knew that despite the relative simplicity of this response, it would nonetheless be quite difficult. He suddenly realized that he did derive some pleasure and a tremendous sense of power in being so important to Dad. Nevertheless, he understood that it was too high a price to pay and was willing to give up this position in order to change his role in the family. He knew Al would be frustrated at this change in the interaction, but Bob felt he could deal with this. He did have very warm feelings for his father and felt he could project those without getting caught in the same old pattern.

Bob thought that the relationship with his mother would be more difficult to change. He decided that he could manage to spend more time in her presence without overreacting to what he felt was her critical behavior. We both realized that this was a great deal to attempt on this visit and that Bob himself might have many intense emotional reactions. We then devised a plan for Bob to deal with these reactions without acting them out within the family. He would find some way to extract himself from the emotional atmosphere by taking a walk or a ride by himself, during which he would think about and/or write down his emotional reactions so that he could regain his perspective. He also thought it best to only spend a limited time with his family.

Upon his return Bob reported some interesting new experiences with his family. He actually found that he was able to spend a great deal of time with his mother and had little trouble getting perspective on what he previously experienced as her critical behavior. They did not talk much, but he was able to accompany her on some errands and basically enjoy some companionable silence.

He had more trouble with Al. He was unable to remove himself from being father's confidant by simply taking the position that he had no ideas of how to be helpful. When father started to complain about mother, Bob found that nothing would stop him. Finally, Bob blurted out that he did not want to talk about mother anymore. Bob was frustrated that he couldn't be as calm as he would he would have liked, but in fact he accomplished what he wanted to do. Al immediately backed off, saying that he had no idea that Bob was upset by this and that he would try to not talk to him about this in the future. Although this commitment didn't last long, Bob's ability to make that statement to his father was actually important to him. He had much less trouble afterwards changing the subject when father wanted to talk about mother or simply saying he didn't want to talk about it.

The most interesting consequence of this shift from Bob's point of view was what happened with Joel, his brother. Without understanding how it happened, Bob found himself sharing his worries about his life in New York with him. Joel responded warmly and for the first time in a number of years they had a real conversation.

After rehashing the events of the weekend, Bob could see that he no longer had to be so isolated. He could share his feelings. By taking himself out of the role of father's helper, he saw that he didn't have to take the all-knowing position. Also, looking at mother's "self-sufficiency" from the point of view of her role in her family, he realized that she never really questioned whether it worked for her or not. The more she devalued father for his need for friends, the more she locked herself into an isolated, "self-sufficient" position. Bob was amazed that he had followed this position so automatically.

Over the next few months Bob reviewed the ramifications of this visit in therapy. He stayed in regular contact with his mother, asking specifically to speak to her if father answered the phone. He also spoke to Joel regularly. In his contacts with father, he maintained the same warm connection but made sure not to discuss his mother. He was surprised to find that, without discussing father's problems or mother's personality, they had a hard time making conversation. Bob felt good enough about his father, however, to explore other ways to connect with him.

The following winter Sonia told Bob that she was going alone to Florida to visit her mother, since Al couldn't get away at the time. Bob took this opportunity to make arrangements to spend a few days with her. He was aware that there would be some awkwardness, but he was committed to spend time with her nonetheless. He thought he could just do things with her when she wanted and share some of what was going on with his work. He was careful not to put himself in a position of complaining – his father's position. Since he would be with his mother and grandmother, he could also observe their relationship.

Bob returned from this trip ecstatic. Having put few expectations on his mother, he actually spent a good deal of time with her. As a result of Bob's accepting, nondemanding position, and emotions that were triggered while spending time with her own mother, Sonia began opening up to Bob about her life. She ultimately talked to him about her loneliness as a child and her own mother's admonitions to be self-sufficient. She told him that because her mother had lost her own mother at birth, she grew up in a series of foster homes. She accommodated to this situation by learning to be self-sufficient. She believed that teaching her daughter this skill would help Sonia survive in a difficult world. Bob was amazed to hear Sonia confirm that she was attracted to Al because of his warmth and availability. After this discussion he had a completely different feeling about his parents' marriage. He realized that, while Sonia was attracted to Al's warmth, it probably frightened her at the same time. Bob felt emotionally connected to his mother for the first time on this trip and committed himself to remaining so.

We talked about the possibility of her pulling back after this experience. Bob realized that this might happen and understood that it had very little to do with him personally. With this knowledge Bob was prepared to stay connected to her despite the vicissitudes of the next few encounters. He remained true to his convictions and when mother became critical or didn't want to speak to him on the telephone, he remained nonreactive and just called back later.

Bob remained in treatment for the next few months, essentially sorting through the changes he had made. When he realized that he did not have to live his life "on automatic," he lost the urge to pull away from people. Bob began attending neighborhood church socials and felt infinitely more comfortable meeting people. At the beginning of the summer, Bob took a young adult tour to France for a month. When he returned, he told me that this experience had shown him that he could reach out to people and that he had indeed made important changes in his life.

12

The Thirties: Susan's Story

ON A BEAUTIFUL SUNNY DAY in mid May, an attractive, elegantly dressed woman came into the office for a consultation session. She introduced herself as Susan Fishkind, she was 36 and single. As if startled by the abruptness of her introduction, she paused for a moment and started softly crying. She then continued, "The day is so beautiful and I hate it. The nicer the day, the more I get depressed. I can't bear to see couples walking hand in hand looking happy. I hate the fact that on the nicest day of the year I should feel so miserable."

Slightly embarrassed, Susan told me (NS) that she was terribly upset at not being married. She had increasing been feeling desperate, and the years since her thirtieth birthday had been fraught with anxiety about her single state. She saw her problem as being out of sync with the rest of the world. Though she went out regularly to socials, weekend resorts, and bars to meet men, she was unable to develop a lasting relationship.

To make matters worse, family members, who had previously tried to be considerately low-key when asking about her social life, had recently stepped up their concerns. When she herself was not worried, she had been able to tolerate these questions, assuming they came with the territory of belonging to a Jewish family. However, as she became increasingly concerned about her unmarried state, she also became more sensitive to these questions. She found herself responding with belligerence or withdrawing altogether. As a result, she was beginning to distance herself from family. This was in itself a problem, since they had always been a major support in her life.

Susan began to worry all the time about not ever getting married. She experienced herself as deeply lonely and terrified that this loneliness would never go away. The fear could get so overwhelming that she frequently woke up in the middle of the night panicked about being alone. She woke up early every morning, always thinking about her isolation.

Lately, Susan was unable to pursue any activity without the thought of her unmarried state somehow creeping in. She told me that she recently decided to take up the flute. As she was practicing she became gripped with an acute sense of sadness, realizing that if she were married and had children she would not have time for this activity. Suddenly she was no longer interested in practicing as she now saw the whole endeavor as an empty pursuit.

When relating this experience to a friend, she found herself embarrassed by her display of vulnerability. It didn't help much that the friend thought she was overreacting and wondered if she should see a psychiatrist. She found herself becoming more uncomfortable sharing her innermost feelings with people, as she thought most would react with insensitivity or, worse yet, pity.

Susan had a small studio apartment in a trendy section of New York City. She had a reasonably well paying job as an entertainment lawyer, and until recently she enjoyed the travel it necessitated, as well as the meetings with interesting and glamorous people. Now she saw these trips as merely delays in her major pursuit of finding a man. She was acutely aware of her biological clock and, when she let herself think about it, profoundly upset at the idea of not marrying in time to have a child.

At the same time, Susan felt ashamed of being so depressed over what she believed was a trivial problem in comparison to what other people had to contend with. She knew that many people's lives were a lot worse than hers. The bind she therefore put herself in — of being acutely depressed but also being ashamed of herself for feeling this way — just made her feel increasingly worthless.

When I commented that of course she wanted to get married, that her feelings were completely normal, she felt tremendously relieved. She was understandably responding to the sense that everyone else but her was moving on in life. I continued, telling her that many people at her age responded similarly when they noticed the increase in married couples in their circle. Some felt increasingly anxious and, as a result, felt obliged to increase their efforts to find a mate.

In our experience this very normal response, unfortunately, just adds to the sense of desperation already being experienced. When people focus on marriage to the exclusion of everything else, they lose the opportunity to work on the developmental tasks that are essential for maturing adults to accomplish. As a result many single people wind up stuck in a state of perennial adolescence, where neither they nor the people around them regard them as fully functioning adults.

By seeing the acute despair that Susan was feeling as a normal reaction to inner and societal pressures, we were able to legitimize her feelings. At the same time, demonstrating that this very reaction was preventing her from moving forward in life opened up opportunities for future work.

Susan, for the most part, responded positively to framing the problem in this way. At the same time, however, she wasn't exactly happy about being seen as in a category with other singles. She was very sensitive to any implication that there was a permanence to this state, since at this point she needed to believe that she would soon be married. Therefore, the prospect of working on developmental issues, although intriguing, also had its depressing side. She was hoping that we would be working more directly on looking at what prevented her from finding a husband.

Susan's ambivalence about the idea of having developmental work to do is quite common. Like Susan, most single people who enter therapy with this problem want to work on issues that keep them from getting married. Normalizing their feelings can be tricky. Sometimes people want to feel there is something wrong with them that can be fixed through therapy.

Although it may be true that for some people emotional problems interfere with connecting with a potential spouse, the panic that they feel about being out of sync with their peers often prevents them from dealing with these problems. Also, like Susan, many single people find the very notion that there is a single state abhorrent, since it implies a permanence that is unacceptable. At the same time, the only way they can gain a sense of a substantial life is to work on issues that open up possibilities for fulfillment and security at each phase of adulthood. They will be more likely to work on these issues if they believe that the therapist is in no way ruling out the possibility of marriage.

Susan was not fully convinced that this work would be useful to her, but she was interested enough to explore it further with me. She told me that she was the younger of two daughters in an upper-middle-class observant Jewish family. Her father, Jack, was the comptroller of a large hospital and was described as a dignified and highly scrupulous person. Yet he was experienced by Susan as distant and condescending toward women in general and particularly toward the women in his family. Her mother, Diane, was warm and supportive to the children but self-effacing in the extreme. Memories of the dinner table always included father putting mother down and both daughters feeling terrible about it. They experienced their mother as a loving parent and an important role model, and were disturbed at the way she was treated in the home.

Susan's older sister Norma was only 18 months her senior, and until recently her best friend. While Norma and she hung out together, they never thought much about whether or not they would marry. Although their parents expressed concern, Norma and Susan weren't actively worried. They felt they had each other, and felt safe in this relationship. Often they would conspiratorially talk about their dates, supporting each other if they felt rejected and helping each other gain perspective. They would often laugh about their experiences with the opposite sex.

When Norma met and fell in love with a professor at graduate school, Susan suddenly panicked. While she had many other caring friends, she experienced Norma as her closest ally. In fact, they typically looked to each other in the family for validation and self-esteem.

When Norma announced that she was getting married, Susan tried to be supportive but became suddenly very sad. Feeling abandoned, she was acutely sensitive to what she experienced as slights while the family was planning the wedding. She attributed these slights to Norma's fiance Allen and developed a dislike for him. Norma sensed the feelings Susan had towards Allen and pulled back from her sister because of them. Although the sisters remained friends after the marriage, the tension remained in the relationship. This contributed to the sense of loneliness in Susan's life.

Not only did Susan feel badly as a result of the change in relationship with her sister after the marriage, but she also became aware of the new status Norma enjoyed in the family. Before this event, both Susan and Norma regularly went to synagogue with their parents and attended holiday functions in the family home. With Norma's marriage and subsequent move to Long Island, she now attended services with her husband in their new community. This left Susan spending the holidays alone with her parents. It seemed to her that Jack and Diane were particularly focused on questioning her about her social life at these occasions. When Susan went to Norma's home for Thanksgiving, she became acutely aware of feeling like a grown-up "child." This just added to her loss of self-esteem.

Susan had a large and loving circle of friends, mostly professional people, men as well as women. Recently two of her friends had married. While there certainly was a significant number of friends who remained single in her group, these events had the catalytic effect of refocusing the attention of the remaining people onto marriage. The women, in particular, talked about nothing else but men and the ratio of men to women in New York City.

Most of Susan's activities with her friends now focused primarily on meeting men. Although previously she had attended the theater, concerts, and lectures, her present pursuits were mainly directed towards socializing. We began to look at how her activities had added to the depression as her world had become significantly narrower in the past year. It would make sense for her to feel empty if the only the only thing filling her life was the pursuit of a mate. Susan was somewhat intrigued by the direction of the consultation but still worried that I was interested in convincing her that she should stop looking for a man.

In trying to understand how marriage was experienced in her family, we agreed to meet again with this as an agenda. In the second session she came in with a tape from a sequence of a television show called *Thirtysomething*. She was a little defiant but not nearly as depressed as in the first session. She said that she had come away from the first session feeling much better and that she was interested in working on the issues that would help her emotional development. Yet it was important that she illustrate to me how terrible it was to be single. To prove her point she wanted me to see this sequence, which focused on Mellissa, a successful "thirtyish" photographer who presented her work in a one-woman show. Despite the accolades she received for the show, she ended up crying in the bathroom because a young man she fantasized as possibly being her intended showed up with a date.

Contrary to Susan's expectations about my reaction, I pointed out how this particular sequence illustrated the media's participation in devaluing women's accomplishments. It subtly gave the message that the only true achievement for a woman was marriage. I said that it is very difficult to live in a society where the message one gets from all over is that marriage is the only acceptable state for women. It would be helpful for Susan to distinguish between the vision of singlehood portrayed by her family and the media and her own lived experience, since this experience had been quite good in many ways. I wondered whether it would be possible for Susan to allow herself to recognize this and to explore the possibilities of expanding her life, despite what the larger system saw as normal. I was quick to reassure her that this in no way meant that she would not marry. It might, in fact, help her to be more emotionally ready for marriage, since she would be less desperate, less depressed, and more genuinely open to people. Susan was now very interested.

We next looked at the reality of single life from the point of view of the larger system, starting with the *Thirtysomething* tape. It was clear to Susan that, despite changes in society, being single was still seen as not only unacceptable but also dysfunctional. She believed people wondered what unresolved emotional problems contributed to her remaining single. She chuckled ruefully when I pointed out that her married friends probably had plenty of problems, but marriage automatically conferred on them a clean bill of mental health.

Susan realized, when she thought about it, that she was angry about the lower status she experienced as a single woman. She gave me many examples of how that played out in her daily life. I pointed out that, although society may have imposed this on her, she cooperated with this vision by accepting this low status.

We looked at the actuality of the life she was leading, as opposed to the picture that the media presented to the world — that of the pathetic, lonely, single woman. People at her job seemed to think she was pretty capable, and until recently she enjoyed the glamour of it quite a bit. Her friends, both male and female, seemed to admire and love her. She enjoyed hiking and camping as well as traveling to different parts of the world. Overall she seemed to be an exceptional person, attractive both in appearance and personality. Why was she allowing herself to be defined by any other criteria but her own?

She thought for a minute and wondered if it would be possible to stop herself from doing this. This was just a fleeting thought. However, it was the beginning of a process in which she learned to distinguish between her perception of the view imposed upon her by the larger system and her own self evaluation. Susan would have to examine this idea in many different arenas before she could fully embrace it.

In the third session she described an incident that illustrated the difficulty of removing herself from her role as the family failure. During a discussion with her mother about the possibility of a promotion at her job, Susan realized her mother wasn't listening. Finally, Diane sighed and said she wondered if Susan was being a little too picky about her male friends: "Maybe if you would accept someone who wasn't so accomplished, you could get married."

"How can I see myself as a complete person," Susan said, "if my parents see me as a failure because I'm single?" This revealing question brought us to our next step in the assessment process. It indicated not only how much Susan was dependent on her family's opinions for her self esteem but also brought the meaning of marriage in her family to the fore.

As a result, I asked Susan to examine her family's relation to this institution. Did they venerate marriage? Did they see it as the only possible success for a woman? How intensely did they feel about its role in their life experience? What were the myths and folklore surrounding it? Susan laughed and said, "OK, but don't forget — this is a Jewish family." I agreed that culturally Jewish people highly valued marriage. At the same time each family superimposes its own issues onto cultural values. By family, I explained, I meant not only her nuclear family but also the preceding generations.

Jack, Susan's father, was the only child born to Leo and his wife Rose. Leo, who had been a bookkeeper, died in a traffic accident when Jack was four, without having made long-term financial provisions for the family.

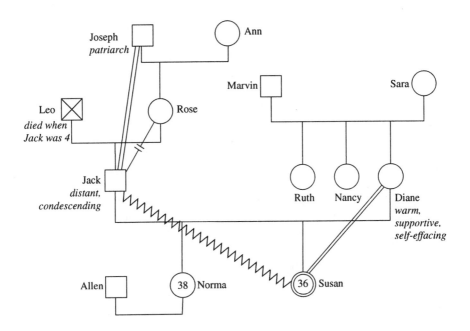

FIGURE 12.1 Susan Fishkind's Genogram

As a result, Jack's mother Rose moved in with her parents. Jack's youth was spent in surroundings that always felt rather solemn to him.

After Leo's death Rose was depressed and withdrawn. Jack became close to his grandfather, who, while being a taciturn and demanding man, always had a special feeling for Jack. Later, when Rose emerged from her depression and wanted to resume Jack's parenting, her father, Joseph, tended to ignore her wishes. He often indulged Jack while bypassing Rose's judgments about what was right for her son. Although Ann, Jack's grandmother, frequently tried to intercede, she was no match for her husband. Rose ultimately stopped objecting to Joseph's interference and spent most of her time with her mother. As a result, Jack and his mother grew distant from each other.

Jack grew up feeling guilty about his privileged position, especially when he observed his mother being ignored in the family. At the same time he was unwilling to give up his special relationship with his grandfather. He found himself mimicking his grandfather's attitude towards Rose, but simultaneously feeling terrified that she wouldn't love him anymore. He prayed for Rose to marry again so that they could leave this situation.

Diane, Susan's mother, was the youngest of three girls. Her father was a tailor who worked long hours to support the family and was usually exhausted when he returned home. Diane grew up knowing her family was desperate for money. She remembered, with humiliation, her father scolding her mother for spending too much money on the children. Susan remembered her mother describing how she and her sisters would huddle in fear while their parents fought.

Diane's parents, Marvin and Sara, ultimately took in boarders to help support the family. Sometimes the men would be seductive toward Diane, who was a particularly attractive adolescent. When Diane complained about this to her mother, Sara would either tell her she was imagining it or implored her not to take these advances too seriously since they needed these boarders to make ends meet. Diane felt unprotected and usually hid in her room at night or went to the library. Humiliated, she vowed that when she grew up she would never again allow herself to be in such a desperate financial situation.

Both parents wanted their daughters to marry well, as they saw marriage as the only opportunity for girls to raise their financial status. Diane took stenography and typing in high school so that she could work as soon as she graduated. At 18 she began working for an accounting firm where she met Jack, one of the younger accountants in the firm. When she married him two years later, Diane felt relieved. Not only did she love him, but she could now feel secure about her financial future.

When Susan told me about her parents' lives it was clear that she had always been aware of her mother's deference to her father. Diane would rise an hour before everyone else so that the girls would be dressed and have breakfast before Jack came down to eat. Dinner was always on time and there was never a complaint when Jack was late. The girls were asked to play quietly in their room at night so that their father could relax.

As we talked, the themes in both families emerged clearly. Diane's dependence on Jack stood out, as well as her veneration of marriage. Susan wistfully recalled passing her first grade teacher while walking with her mother. "What a sweet person Miss Krensky is," Diane had remarked, "what a pity she didn't marry." As a result of her own life experiences she genuinely believed that nothing in a woman's life had any value if she didn't marry.

Jack's experiences also led him to think that marriage was critical for women. He believed that the only way his mother could have been treated like an adult was to marry again. In fact, when he talked about his mother, which was rare, he always blamed her single state for the estrangement in their relationship.

Susan was able to see how the dynamics on both sides of her family contributed to an anxiety-laden overvaluation of the institution of marriage. The intense focus on Susan's social life was understandable in this context. She was finally able to see that everybody's anxiety about marriage was the problem, not her normal desire to seek a mate.

Separating out the normal wish for marriage, from the high intensity that her family brought to this subject was an important beginning step for Susan. This helped to reduce her overall tension and plan treatment. It also relieved Susan because she was able to see that therapy was not going to be about giving up on marriage. Work with Susan needed to proceed on three levels. Although these levels could be seen as separate segments, frequently they were dealt with simultaneously:

1. What actually happened in Susan's relationships with men
2. How Susan functioned in her family and in her peer network emotional system
3. What life steps would help Susan feel fulfilled as an adult

I was surprised to hear that Susan's experiences with men were often curtailed after one or two dates. She had no idea why these men never called her back and assumed that they had so many women to choose from in New York that they had no reason to ask her out again. Not only did this imply a lack of understanding of what relationships were about, but it also said that she did not have a good idea of her own behavior when with a date. By tracking some of her experiences, we quickly learned that she was quite defensive and self-protective. Often she would engage in joking repartee bordering on hostility. Interestingly enough, this did not occur with her male friends.

Susan was able to look at herself honestly. She admitted that she was furious with every man she found attractive. As soon as she realized she was attracted to a man she felt that he had power over her. She resented this intensely. Although she tried to hide it, her anger had to emerge on some level. She also saw how very frightened she was; often the anger kept her from feeling the fear.

Although Susan's response to these discussions bordered on hopelessness, I pointed out that the awareness of her behavior was significant, since it would help her to change the destructive interactions. We looked at how Susan's reactions might have emerged from her role in the family's emotional system.

She told me that she tended to identify with her mother and often would get furious when she observed her father humiliating Diane. She was terrified of putting herself in a position where this might happen to her. Susan remembered always being in a fury at her father. She was saddened by the fact that she and her father seemed always to be in a battle, while Norma had found a way to be close to him.

We then talked about how emotional systems worked in families and how she and her sister had been caught in the relationship between her mother and father. Norma allied herself with her father, and Susan was closer to her mother. Despite their different loyalties, both sisters reacted strongly to the tension in the family and forged a close link as a protective mechanism.

Susan saw that she always acted automatically as her mother's advocate. She was unable to stop long enough to get close to her father. We looked together at the fact that father had been in similar situation when he found himself unable to get close to his mother, despite his intense desire to do so. Did she really want follow her father's footsteps and spend a lifetime without a close relationship with a parent? Could she see herself dropping the role of her mother's protector with her father? This would be the only way she could develop her own relationship with him. Susan saw clearly how her role in the emotional system stood in the way of her relationship with her father, but she worried that her mother was too vulnerable to deal with him on her own.

At the same time Susan was determined to change things and realized how her relationships with her family affected her life. In truth, she was less motivated by a real desire to change her relationship with her family than by a sudden awareness of how this might directly affect her relationships with men. Regardless of her motivation, the fact that this work would ultimately benefit her was a good enough reason to proceed.

Because the family system was so rigid and so reactive, she needed more objectivity before proceeding to change her role within it. We spent the next few months tracking all the relationship systems in her family, so that she could get a better perspective on her family. As this process unfolded, Susan not only found herself having softer feelings towards her father but also realized that she was less depressed. She felt, at last, that she was "on the right track."

The women's positions in the family stood out for her, in that they all were seen as somewhat helpless and less important than the men. The fact that father was seen as coming from a family of a higher socio-economic status than mother's added to this perception. Since Susan identified with her mother, she realized that her feelings of inferiority and helplessness around men could have something to do with how she perceived women in her family.

As Susan was exploring her role in her family more deeply, the Jewish holidays arrived. Susan, once again, found herself going to her parent's synagogue and feeling like a child. Though she attended services regularly in the area close to her home, her parents wanted her to join them for the holidays. This meant that she had to sleep at their house. Even though her friends joined together to form a surrogate family for the holidays, Susan felt compelled to return home. Her feeling of childishness was accentuated by the fact that she slept in the room she had as a child.

Two months later, as Thanksgiving approached, Susan was determined to change something in the interaction. Norma would not be in the city for the holiday, and Susan did not want to be a child once again in her parents' home. She wanted to have her first Thanksgiving at her home.

Diane objected immediately. Susan's apartment was much too small to hold everybody—after all, Susan only had a studio. Her father seconded Diane's objection, adding that it was a completely ridiculous idea.

Susan came to the next session shaken but determined. She decided this was so important to her that she would have Thanksgiving at her home even if she were to eat alone.

Susan's determination was so strong that she realized that this decision would hold. She was able to maintain her position with her parents in a loving, clear, and nonreactive way. As each objection surfaced, she found a workable reply. The struggle persisted until the week before the holiday. Both Susan and I realized that her investment in it represented a profound desire to grow up. At one point she said to me, "I don't know if you realized it but I never really wanted to do this work for any other reason than to find a man. This is different. I want to do it for my own sense of self."

Susan held out, and the family came to her house for Thanksgiving. Elated, she brought in pictures of the celebration. There were roses on the table. Everyone came dressed for the occasion. The food, which she made in her own tiny kitchen, was delicious. Her parents called the next day to tell her how wonderful it was, and the struggle they had was never mentioned again.

This interaction, which on the surface had nothing to do with what Susan had come into therapy for, marked a turning point in her treatment. She felt that she had taken a very important stand with her parents and that she had been prepared for the consequences of that stand. Realizing that she had the ability to know what was right for her and articulate it clearly gave her the sense of feeling like an adult. She knew then that she had the ability to work towards changing her interactions in her family and in other areas of her life. The relationship Susan wanted to shift the most in her family was the one involving her, her mother, and her father. She felt that she could become closer to her sister Norma on her own, now that she understood that the intensity they experienced together was really a way for them to deal with the tension in the family. Susan knew they could develop a different intimacy now. In some ways it could be stronger than before, since it would not be based on being each other's protector.

The relationship with her father bothered her. As a result of our work Susan stopped being intensely angry with him. Without the anger she realized how much she had longed for a real relationship with him. She decided to try and spend some time with him without reacting in her typical way. We talked about how different this would feel to the rest of the family, contemplating what she could expect in the way of reactions. Susan thought that Norma most likely wouldn't care, since she was now involved with her husband. Mother, however, might be bewildered. Although she always professed to want Susan and Jack to have a better relationship, Susan believed that on some level mother might feel abandoned.

To her great disappointment our conversation about these relationships raised tremendous anxiety in Susan. She believed she had done her homework, had a good perspective on the family dynamics, and was ready for a change. So why was she anxious? I pointed out about how understandable her reaction was, in light of the rigid patterns in her family. Actually, her anxiety was a positive sign, since it meant that she was moving in the right direction. If she did change her position, she and everyone else in the family would experience discomfort for a period of time. Could she live with this discomfort? Susan laughed and said, "If it meant I would get married, yes." Although this was always on the periphery of her thoughts, she could at least laugh about it now. At the same time, it was quite clear that Susan's own self-respect was at stake.

This discussion was, in actuality, the beginning of Susan's struggle around her role in her family. She used the strength she found in herself on Thanksgiving as a reminder that she could withstand pressures and find the power within herself to change. During the next six months she made significant changes. She learned to understand and respect her father, and began spending limited periods of time with him. There was initially some tension with her mother, but not as much as Susan had expected. She managed to remain nonreactive and to convey to her mother that she still loved her despite her wish to have a separate relationship with her father. What really seemed to have changed for Susan was that she no longer needed to be approved of by everyone. This shift in her sense of self allowed her to begin to feel that she could enjoy life without being married.

Susan still was sensitive to her single state and thought about it frequently. She continued attending social functions geared towards finding romance. Our sessions were spent talking about what happened when she went out with men, as well as about her family work. Tracking the interactions with men was useful, since it revealed behavior patterns which resulted in her distancing herself from possible mates. She realized that she was so terrified of being rejected that she didn't let anybody know her real thoughts. As a result, she appeared flip and insensitive. She was able to radically change this behavior and ultimately saw a change in her relationships.

Susan began to have longer and more enjoyable experiences with men, and tolerated the disappointments when they ended without feeling devastated. This was a big, tough step. Ultimately, it enabled her to take risks and to place her in situations where she met and formed relationships with men she could actually envision marrying. She felt good about the progress she had made, even though she had not yet married.

As Susan broadened her perspective, she made time in her schedule for pursuits that appealed to her. For example, she joined a chamber music group, laughing as she told me she was playing the flute instead of waiting for the phone to ring Monday nights.

She joined a temple two blocks from her home. Soon she not only became part of the fabric of the surrounding community, but also found herself being valued as an important member. She specifically chose a temple that was not for singles only; instead it provided a mix of singles and families, so that she felt part of a normal community. She decided that she would visit her parents' temple for some part of the high holy days but attend her own services as well. This action made a profound difference in her feelings of alienation, and she wondered why she hadn't done this sooner.

Although Susan was no longer depressed, she was somewhat apprehensive about leaving treatment, since she had hoped that she would be married by then. Even though she knew it was irrational, she sometimes thought that she would give up some magical tie to the possibility of finding a husband if she stopped seeing me. What ultimately convinced her that she was ready to leave was the realization that she was no longer pushing men away. Generally content with herself and her life, she allowed herself to entertain the terrifying thought that she probably could lead a rich life if she didn't marry — at least on her good days.

She was also aware that her work on herself would not stop just because she was not officially coming to therapy. She knew, for example, that she had to continue to work on her relationship with her father. In the back of her mind she knew she had to address the idea of how to bring children into her life, but she wanted to wrestle with that issue a bit on her own. After Susan stopped treatment, she dropped me a note from time to time to tell me what was going on in her life. For the most part she seemed content.

About two years later Susan called me again. Her life continued to be rich. She had dramatically changed her relationships with her family. The previous winter she had had a serious relationship with a man and, although it didn't work out because of religious differences, she felt good about the experience. She and her friend had stayed in contact and, though the end of the relationship was painful, she was glad it happened.

Susan came back to therapy because she needed help sorting out her feelings about bringing children into her life. This issue loomed much larger than marriage for her at this point. She was convinced that she would probably marry someday, but was not convinced that she would be able to have children unless she dealt with it now.

Because of her profound desire to be around children, she had become a "big sister" to Emma, a troubled teenager. This had worked out quite well; she had weathered the storms of the first six months with Emma, and now they enjoyed their Sundays together. Emma had gotten into college and would be moving away in the fall. Susan was thrilled about this, since she felt that her relationship with Emma had contributed to her success. She knew she would miss Emma and pondered other ways to bring children into her life. These ranged from having another "little sister" to volunteering at a hospital for sick children to tutoring failing students. None of these choices seemed right.

I supported and encouraged her struggle, since she was dealing with a critical developmental task.

It ultimately became clear to Susan that she wanted to have her own child. This decision, while unexpected, seemed to have emerged out of her developing work towards autonomy. Since she had been intensely focused on clarifying her own needs and sense of self, she had in essence been building the courage that carrying out this decision would require. Susan allowed herself to examine the reasons for this decision in detail. In fact, she went back and forth over this decision for months before becoming absolutely sure that was what she wanted to do.

The most difficult part of the decision was wondering how having a child would affect her chances of ultimately marrying. Susan found it amazing that she had entered therapy desperate to marry, and here she was contemplating a decision that might, in fact, lower her possibilities for marriage. Finally, she realized that she could not postpone important decisions in her life on that basis. Actually, she knew single mothers her age who had a child while married but were now in the same situation she was contemplating. None of these women regretted having their children. Ultimately she decided she would be willing to take the risk of having a more difficult time finding a mate; having a child was critical at this point.

In carrying out her plan, Susan tried to look realistically at as many pitfalls as she could. She knew it would be extremely difficult to discuss this with her parents and Norma. If she were married she would not think of discussing the matter with her family; at the same time she knew her parents were conservative and a prior discussion would help them accept her plan. She was clear that she was not asking for her parents' permission. She did, however, want them to be an ongoing part of her child's life. Discussing the plan with them beforehand would help them to accept it.

There were a host of other problems she needed to deal with, including deciding whether she wanted to have this child through artificial insemination or adoption, how to make financial plans, how to set up a support system for herself, and how to include men as well as other parents with children in her life. Nevertheless, she felt the most difficult step would be the discussion with her family. Susan prepared to tell her parents by anticipating how very difficult it would be for them and by readying herself for every possible reaction. She didn't think Norma would have a problem with her plan, but felt she should also share it with her in advance. Meanwhile, she discovered a support group for women who either were contemplating having children on their own or already had them. She began to attend meetings and found herself sharing with them her thoughts about her parents. She found them to be extremely helpful, since they had gone through similar experiences.

When Susan finally approached her parents with this matter, their first reaction was horror that she would even contemplate such an action. Since she had prepared for this, Susan was able to respond with compassion. She told her father that she knew this was difficult for him. She had thought about it long and hard and had, in fact, hesitated out of concern about his reaction. She did not want to hurt him, but this was something she had to do for herself. After a long afternoon of struggle, her father finally accepted that this was what she was going to do. Her mother, though quieter, was no less determined in her opinion; ultimately, however, she too accepted Susan's decision.

Susan then proceeded to call her parents regularly, with a good deal of warmth. She managed to bring in news about her plans in each conversation. After a few weeks, her father unexpectedly asked Susan if she needed any money for this plan. Relieved, Susan felt as if she and the child would be accepted by the family. She told him that she didn't need money now, but if she was successful in having a child she would like to set up a trust fund and at that point his financial help would be welcome.

Susan found that her mother remained a bit more conflicted about the situation. This was puzzling to her and somewhat hurtful, since she felt that her mother should be "on her side."

As we talked this over, I speculated that Susan's mother might feel more responsible for Susan's upbringing and consequently for her unconventional life choice. Since she spent a good part of her marriage being blamed by her husband for not controlling her daughters, she might feel that he was right — that she had failed as parent. This helped Susan to be more understanding of her mother's position. As a result, she decided to spend some private time with her mother. During the day they spent together she shared her happiness about her choice to have a child. She told Diane that she knew her choice was unconventional and would take a great deal of strength. It was only because she saw her mother as having been such a good parent that she believed she had the strength to proceed with this plan. She hoped she would be as good a parent to her child as her mother had been to her. Mother was moved by Susan's genuine statement. They didn't talk more about this subject, but felt very close to each other for the rest of the day.

A few weeks later Diane called Susan and without discussing the previous conversation asked how Susan was doing with her attempts to have a child. Susan was grateful for her mother's change of heart. She believed she had dealt with the first major hurdle in her plan to have a child.

Shortly after this Susan decided to leave treatment. She felt she was comfortable in her life; she was on a path that she knew would provide her with the fulfillment she had always wanted. She was dating someone seriously and, while she was not at all sure where this would lead, she was confidant she would be able to handle whatever might happen. She had a support network to help her deal with the future child, and also felt that her family could be included in this group. She would call me from time to time to let me know what was happening with her plan.

13

Midlife: George's Story

I (DJ) FIRST MET GEORGE as his marriage of two years' duration to Mary was coming to an end. He was then 39 years old, and this was his first experience of therapy. At this time George and Mary were already living separately, but they wanted to make a last attempt to see if things might work — or at least to understand why things hadn't. Both were very conscientious people, and also religious. They took divorce very seriously.

George pretty much took Mary's lead; the sessions had been her idea. She was also much clearer about the difficulties between them. George seemed dazed by the events. The difference between Mary's and George's conceptions of how he should fit into the family were indeed enormous. George had married with the strong desire to be part of a family, including being a father. Mary, a mother of two who had been widowed for eight years, acknowledged that she mainly wanted George as her lover, someone special just for her and separate from "her" children and responsibilities. She did not want to change this; she drew a firm line around what she regarded as *her* family.

This helped George clarify the basis for his feelings. He had always felt like an outsider in the family and disrespected as a man. He was faced with a clear choice: could he accept this special but peripheral role or not? George felt that he could not. They moved toward formulating a separation agreement. George had become very fond of Mary's son, Tom, now age 12, and was saddened to be losing him. Mary also felt it would be a loss for Tom, and so the separation agreement also included visitation.

They left, and I did not see George until five years later. He was 45 years old and coming for individual therapy. Because George's marriage was a brief period in his adult life, we are including his story as a single person here.

THE PROBLEM

George was living alone, in an apartment he had bought shortly after our last meeting, and feeling depressed. It was getting hard for him to go to work each day, although he felt better once he got there. What was worse, however, was that he had lost his belief that he would ever feel happy again. His life stretched out in front of him "like a gray, cheerless fog." He was rightly worried about his drinking: his usual beer after work was now a six-pack. He was gaining weight, feeling "old," and concerned about becoming an alcoholic. George was also having an upsurge of physical ailments: back pain, stomach pain, and hemorrhoids (about which he felt so embarrassed that he never mentioned them to his doctor). He did not exercise regularly. He was convinced that his life and his feelings indicated his basic abnormality as a person.

THE CURRENT CONTEXT

The process of inquiring carefully about the connections in a client's current life often helps him frame his feelings differently. George was dating a woman whom he liked well enough, but she was extremely busy with her work and her three children. They saw each other only on Saturday evenings, if then. She did not invite him to her home, as she did not want to upset her children unless the relationship was serious. George did not want it to be serious. "Once burnt, twice shy" about marriage, he did not want to remarry until he was absolutely sure it would work.

He and Mary were now divorced, although they remained amicable and chatted occasionally. George's relationship with Tom, predictably enough, had drifted and finally faded. It had been difficult to maintain visitation because Tom had wanted to spend the time with his friends, not with his ex-stepfather. George had found it awkward "entertaining" Tom in his apartment as well.

George had worked as an accountant for the same large firm for twenty years. He had risen to be a supervisor of a group of younger men, while still doing hands-on accounting. He was now in some trouble at work, as a couple of the younger men had complained to his boss that he was "too irritable, too demanding, and too autocratic." George felt that these younger men were too careless about their work, and that he should not give in to the "slipshod standards tolerated today." He was also very angry that they had gone over his head. Nevertheless, he had told his boss he would approach his supervisees more sympathetically.

He spent holidays and special occasions with his family, who still lived in upstate New York. He had joined a Bible study group which met weekly.

The group was enjoyable, but impersonal. His two best friends, with whom he occasionally played tennis, were married with children. With all their responsibilities of work, nuclear family, and aging parents and in-laws, they had little "free" time to get together with George. Even if they did, there were few places to go. No one wanted to sit in a bar anymore, and it would be "ridiculous to invite them to my place for dinner. I don't want to tag along with their family, and they don't want me to either."

Even though he was a congenial person and enjoyed company, George was feeling the emotional isolation that single men often encounter in mid-life. Far from being the sought-after bachelor needed for those mythical dinner parties, he felt on the outside of life. While other men were rushing home to attend to family needs and home maintenance, George returned to emptiness. "I am even losing track of the fact that I am a person. I feel like a function."

A gender-specific factor within American culture—the discouragement of close male relationships—also contributes to George's isolation. Men generally avoid getting together for companionship outside the contexts of business, sports, gambling, or going to a bar. While women can deepen friendship in many ways, including spending an evening together, going to concerts or museums, having each other over for dinner, men who do so are likely to be viewed with some suspicion as possibly homosexual. Other cultures allow room for the expression of men's affection for each other (e.g., the English club, Italian coffee houses, Greek tavernas). George verbalized this societal proscription as "feeling funny" about inviting a male friend to his home.

The current context of George's life provided no buffer for his difficulties at work; he had no other life or even close enough relationships in which to anchor himself. When the relationships at work deteriorated, he was indeed alone. George himself remarked that anyone would probably be depressed with this amount of loneliness.

FAMILY HISTORY

George is one of four children of a working-class German Lutheran family from an upstate New York town. The family had endured difficult times before George's birth; his mother's first husband was an abusive drinker whom she (Ginny) finally threw out. At that time, she had two children, no money, and many debts. Ginny went to work as a waitress, and the children went to a "home." Ginny devoted the next years getting her family back together again—working long hours, paying off debts, and saving each penny. After three years, she had done it. It is a matter of great family pride that no charity was accepted, and all debts were paid off.

Shortly after the reunification with her children, Ginny remarried. Ralph (George's father) was a "quiet, steady person" who worked as a house painter. Ginny and Ralph had two children of their own. George was the youngest.

The emotional alliances in George's family coalesced to leave him on the periphery. His only brother, Allen, was 12 years older; by the time George came along he was most often out of the house with his friends, his after-school job, and school. The two middle girls formed a strong bond around interests that essentially excluded George. While they would help him with homework, they also regarded him as a bit of a nuisance. Ginny continued working long hours at the restaurant and came home to do more work. Ralph seemed content to sit in his armchair, watch TV, and sip his wine after his workday.

After Ginny's death ten years ago, Allen had drifted away from the family. George was unclear why this was so, and in his family you didn't ask. Marge, the oldest sister, had become the tenuous glue holding family members together. It was she who hosted the holidays, kept track of people's news, and knew where Allen was. George's father was alive and well, living contentedly by himself. He came to family affairs and, in old age as in middle life, watched TV and kept to himself. The children did not know him well as a person, but respected him as someone who "took on" a wife with two children. No one had ever heard from the first father.

George's siblings were all married with children. He had no living grand-parents and only one very elderly great-aunt. He had never known them well. George's mother, the youngest in her family, was 40 at the time of his birth, and her siblings were all elderly by the time George was old enough to remember them. Ralph had drifted away from his family long ago. George thought he had a sister in Seattle. The genogram in Figure 13.1 maps the family's emotional positions.

Growing up, George experienced life as crowded, lonely, and centered around work and church. George recalled that the only time he saw his mother relax was at the restaurant, where she kidded around with friends. She seemed driven to be sure to have enough food on the table and money in the bank. She cooked for weeks in advance—"She'd freeze everything and put dates on the packages for when we were supposed to eat them," since her work hours meant she was not home at dinnertime. Both his parents were exceedingly organized people. Ralph used to spend "hours in the garage getting his paints and brushes cleaned and lined up just right." Ginny, busy as she was, had fixed schedules for household chores which the whole family followed.

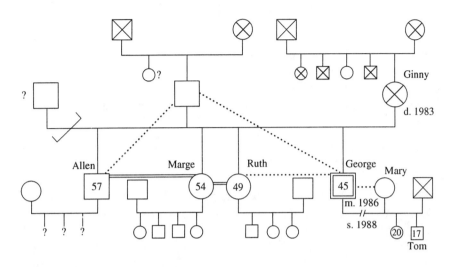

FIGURE 13 .1   George's Genogram

MULTIGENERATIONAL THEMES

Fear of poverty and split-up of the family were the driving forces in Ginny's life from the time that George knew her. Hard work was an important part of the German Lutheran tradition, but relaxation and enjoyment were possible "after the work was done." For Ginny, the work was never done, and there never could be enough savings. Ralph was not a counterbalancing force in the family life. He seemed grateful just to be there. Everyone appeared to be waiting for the time when Ginny would organize "fun" — that time never came.

All the children were taught respect for hierarchical authority. Adults were in charge and were not to be challenged. While children could ask for things, if the answer was "no" that was it. The church reinforced the value of this stoic acceptance.

The family pride in never accepting charity had continued with George in the form of not easily accepting help. A person should be able to do things on his own; needing help implied personal failure. Marge was the same; she wouldn't "let" George contribute food to the family holiday dinners, even though he was a pretty fair cook.

George had never personally experienced a home in which a man was anywhere near a central figure. The first father played a central role in family memory only as the cause of much misery. George had no idea what was expected or possible from a husband/father, beyond not causing trouble and being a reliable breadwinner. He only knew that he very much wanted to be a part of a family, and that women were the core.

As the youngest, George the child watched all the busy, more mature people go about their activities; now George the adult felt much the same. He was dealing with it in a similar way as well — waiting politely (with mounting inner anger and feelings of abnormality) for something to change or for a woman to "invite him in," while conscientiously trying to do his work. Now his work life was in jeopardy.

THE THERAPY: INITIAL PHASE

We first focused on George's work problems, the escalation of his drinking, and his inattention to his physical health.

Since George was the kind of person who needed to get a cognitive handle on issues before he could make changes, tracking his family themes and their impact on his work life was exceedingly useful to him. The multi-generational context enabled him to see other possibilities, while before when things went wrong he saw it as either his own failure, or as others' disrespect for him. Now he could contemplate change as change, not as capitulation or acknowledgment that he was wrong.

Accounting as a profession fit George well in some ways. Controlling money was still a central focus, and George never felt his work was meaningless. The fit was poor, however, in that money was also associated with great anxiety. The second theme, the meaning of accepting help, had kept George from going to his boss for advice before the troubles escalated. The third interlocking theme, that authority should be unilateral and unchallenged, led to rage at the younger men for first complaining to him and then going over his head.

We sensed that anxiety around controlling money would possibly always be a toxic issue for George. Any increase in his anxiety would cut into what objectivity about money he had. Tracking the vicious cycle that had developed as a flow chart helped George visualize his emotions and behavior, and it anchored them in a language he could understand. As his supervisees got "out of control," and his control of his own anger was strained, his mounting anxiety led him to become more demanding, leading to his supervisees' becoming even more "out of his control," raising his anxiety higher, and so on. Ways of relating to money and authority that worked in his earlier days were now causing him stress and interpersonal problems.

It was too big a step (i.e., aroused too much anxiety) for George to ask his boss for advice. He decided to ask a colleague in another firm about how much leeway he could give his supervisees and still do good accounting. George was surprised to find that his colleague was glad to talk about the issue and even asked George for his opinions. This helped George clarify his thoughts and lower his reactivity enough to go to his own boss. Although he now had some suggestions of his own, he was glad to leave many policy decisions to his boss. Clearing the air with his boss and feeling that he had his backing, George was enormously relieved. He had also seen what a cooperative process between boss and employee (rather than chief-follower) was like. Characteristically, he used this experience to beat up on himself: "I should have been able to think of doing this on my own."

Reducing his work stress helped George relax enough to be able to contemplate not filling his time with drinking. Drinking had never been an issue until recently, and he was ashamed of it. He made an appointment for a general physical and joined a health club to work out during the dangerous after-work hours. His life had become enough like his father's (work, go home, watch TV, and drink) to impel him to change.

Talking about what coming home at the end of the day felt like to George revealed what may be a gender difference. Women often view home as a nest, a reflection of self, a place to relax and not have to "put on a face." George didn't even call it his "home"; he called it his "apartment." He regarded it primarily as a financial investment and a place to store his stuff. A *home* was put together by a woman. Even worse, George was ashamed of his home—dust balls everywhere and minimal furniture. He felt he didn't know enough about himself to even begin making it his. One of the big benefits of singlehood—autonomy in the use of personal space— was a concept George had never considered. His home was indeed a reflection of his feelings—empty. His orientation was that men are not the core of anything, not even their own personal space. As we talked about how he could think of extending himself into his space, he realized how difficult it would be for him to spend money on something just for pleasure. At the same time, he was intrigued with the idea of letting loose a little. Until now he had relied on women to access the fun-loving side of himself; he had needed them to signal that it was time for pleasure. Eventually he did go to an art store and buy a poster he liked. George was never able to view his space as a canvas on which he could paint, but he did in time come to fill it with more things that gave him pleasure. Even though his space felt less like a waiting room, he continued to feel that to have a home one needed a woman.

George was a "good" client in that he respected authority and automatically looked to women to guide relationships. His shame about seeking help was somewhat lessened by talking about it; eventually he could even joke about it. The confidentiality of therapy was an aid; George told no one he was coming. This made for a good enough fit in the beginning as we were collecting information and I was giving direct advice on how to move toward change.

A more profound problem for George was that his relationship with his own feelings and thoughts was essentially adversarial. He very much depended on me to tell him whether they were "normal" or not. Since his deepest fear was that he was abnormal, he carefully hid his reactions so that people wouldn't discover them. We couldn't begin work on his connectedness to others without working on his connectedness to himself. As long as he needed an authority's mental health seal of approval for each thought and feeling, he could not be his own center. Nor could he begin to figure out what he wanted his position with people to be.

THE THERAPY: INTERMEDIATE PHASE

One piece of George's sense of abnormality stemmed from his family's custom of never talking about anything emotionally intimate. He had no idea what others' inner experiences were. He had assumed that the outer presentation reflected the inner life. Calling Marge and Ruth to ask for information about family life before he was born, he gained some inkling that they had deep feelings. They, too, kept emotional expression to a minimum and moved to level emotional intensity when it arose. They were still the "older sisters" and did not confide much to him. Neither did anyone else in the family. His father actively discouraged talk about personal feelings.

George's attitude toward feelings was that they were disorganized and messy and needed to be cleaned up or at least controlled. As a first step toward a friendlier relationship with his inner life, George's job was to try to label his feelings to himself as he went through his day. He found that he had been unaware of any feeling other than anger. Now he began to notice moments of pleasure and satisfaction, as well as other nuances. He was willing to entertain the idea that feelings might be used as valuable clues for personal direction.

His attempts to control not only feelings but also events became more apparent to George. For example, he mentioned with much embarrassment that he spent a long time mentally organizing errands in the most efficient way possible. He would estimate how long each should take and the driving time in between. George left no room for the unexpected (traffic jams, interesting encounters, or whims) and became furious if he was thrown off schedule. He felt this was evidence of his mental abnormality and went to great lengths to pretend to be carefree when with other people. A corollary of his method was that it insured failure; he was never able to make his ideal plan work. But it did keep him on "the straight and narrow."

Working with a person like George, who had always stayed on the emotional periphery of relationship systems, presents some therapeutic difficulties. Much of the clinical work presented throughout the book describes the process of helping clients move out of intense and/or rigid positions within emotional triangles. A person like George, however, suffers from the opposite—a lack of involvement. The initial task given—to call his older sisters and get more information about family life—had evolved into weekly chats, and this was a pleasure to George. However, the sibling relationships still remained pretty much on the surface of emotional life. The therapy was George's first and, as yet, only emotionally open relationship with another person.

What distinguishes a family systems approach is the belief that it is best to focus therapeutic efforts toward change on existing relationships in the ongoing context of the clients' life, rather than primarily on the therapist-client emotional system. George's lack of involvement with others in the context of his life was a distinct problem in planning the therapy from a systems frame of reference. George was, however, a deeply religious person, and he viewed his own life and its worth from the Lutheran perspective. It occurred to me that George *did* have one intense relationship—his relationship with God.

Luckily, I had chanced to hear a sermon some months previously in which the minister likened a person's relationship with God as similar to his relationship with his parents. People's conceptions of God can become frozen in their development over time, just as their relationships with people can. Thinking of God as an extended family member opened up the possibility of working on this relationship in the same way as family-of-origin work. For George, as a religious Protestant, being in the right relationship to God had always been central to his self-worth. Because the language of religion was more comfortable than the language of feelings or family, we chose this pathway toward George's becoming able to connect inner with outer life. When we started, George was not only hiding many of his feelings from himself but trying to hide them from God as well.

In the sermon I had heard, the minister had invited the congregation to visually imagine meeting God, to picture very concretely what this would look like. How would God be standing: Facing you? His back turned? What expression would he have: Loving? Stern? Indifferent? What would God look like: An old man? A young woman? A child? What would God be asking of you: Obedience? Penance? Joy? George was encouraged to talk about his image of meeting God. It was a fearsome and very sad one. His vision was of God turned away from him in disgust, a God who had almost given up on him and was no longer giving any messages about how he could redeem himself. George saw God as huge in comparison to himself—old, but very strong. He saw himself as a child, on his knees trying to hug God's legs. God was trying to shake him off.

The impact of this terrible vision was profound for us both. George began to sob. When he was able to speak, he described feeling connected to his inner life for the first time in many years. The feelings were hard to bear—alienation, guilt, and shame—but they were his and they felt real. Years of faithful church attendance and Bible study had not diminished or modified them.

We began reworking this relationship in the same way family-of-origin work would be done. George needed to broaden his information about who God was. He first went to his minister to talk about general images of God, from a cognitive point of view. He felt too vulnerable to begin on a more personal level. The minister reminded him of Jesus as the compassionate and loving link between God and his people. George had not really taken Jesus into account. I suggested that as a way to begin a relationship, he might carry a small picture of Jesus that reflected these qualities, and look at it during the day.

The next step was for George to talk with other people about his spiritual journey. With great trepidation, George brought up this issue (of images of God in personal relationship) with his Bible study group. It led to a stimulating and revealing discussion for most members, and George found there were as many images as people who spoke. He learned that those people whom he thought of as most "Christian" in their actions were those who had the most loving images. This gave him the permission he felt he needed to rework his view. George also experienced feeling a part of the group for the first time; he felt that if he were to miss a meeting his absence would be noticed. This experience also showed him very clearly that his feelings of connection to others depended on how much he was willing to reveal himself to them. This was the beginning of what will probably be a lifelong journey for George, as he continues to work on his relationship to God. Now the journey can take place with other people who are also seeking spiritual connections.

In the therapy sessions, George now began "confessing" to a host of "sins" for which he thought God could never forgive him: stealing from a department store as a child, cheating on a final exam, masturbating, and (most ashamedly) having sexual play with two other boys when he was 12. He had enjoyed it and believed this meant that he was "really" homosexual, even though he was attracted to women and enjoyed sexual relations with them. Having kept these things a secret all these years had increased their toxicity. George had no knowledge of the usual range of "sins" and sexual exploration. Education about these issues relieved his mind somewhat, although he definitely doubted the rectitude of the mental health field's position. He was encouraged to talk to his minister and to God about this as well. His minister turned out to be very reassuring; George then told him he was in therapy. As luck would have it, the minister confided that he himself had gone for therapy during a troubled time.

Chipping away at the walls of isolation and shame that George had built, while connecting the people involved in his spiritual life to each other and to him, helped George to quit hiding in his practiced ways. He was now in a position to take a more active and differentiated position with other people in his life.

THE THERAPY: FINAL PHASE

George needed to deepen his emotional intensity with his family and others. Those who have stayed on the periphery of emotional systems need to learn to heighten anxiety (rather than automatically moving to lower it). Understanding his family's culture (which valued personal privacy to an extreme) and having seen the effect of this code on his own isolation and depression, George prepared for change outside the religious context. He had always been in contact with his family; it had just been kept to a rather superficial level, even though they cared for each other quite deeply. Not having to work around intense triangles allowed us to move simultaneously in several different directions. George had also begun dating a woman, Barbara, some time earlier; he cared for her very much. This new relationship gave him an emotional anchor for the coming work with his own family, as well as a lot of enjoyment.

George's deepest felt losses were in really never knowing his older brother Allen and in feeling that he had never known his mother. He had mourned her death, but still felt a vacuum in not knowing who she was. It was George's idea to carry her picture with him (as he had that of Jesus) and speak to her occasionally as he went through his day. Gaining more knowledge necessitated talking to Marge, Ruth, Allen, and his father. George wanted to start with Marge and with meeting Allen.

Since Marge had always been very protective about revealing Allen's whereabouts, we predicted that this would be an area where George would have to push her (raise anxiety). We went over various ways he could hang in with this until he was ready to make the call. He happened to make his call shortly after Marge's son had been arrested for dealing drugs, and she was openly distraught for the first time in George's experience. George had known nothing about his nephew's drug use, and he and Marge had their first direct and emotional exchange with each other. He learned that her husband also had a drug problem. George's natural predilection was to appreciate the knowledge he'd been given but to do nothing. He was encouraged to continue calling Marge and to offer her his support. Through the ensuing phone calls, George came to know her much better, and in the process of giving her his support and advice, he lifted himself somewhat out of the "baby brother" position. When George did ask for Allen's address, Marge readily gave it. She warned him not to expect too much. It turned out that Allen lived about a mile from George's office. George then crafted a brief letter to Allen, telling a little about himself, and asking if they could meet.

A side benefit of George's focus on the relationships of his inner process and his spiritual and family life was a reduction in his intense anxiety around controlling money and controlling his supervisees. His anxiety had been shifted to the family-of-origin work. This lessened intensity helped George to be less autocratic; as a result, work relationships improved. He could now more easily go to his boss for direction on how to handle the continuing problems, such as lateness, work inaccuracies, and so forth. While George's standards were still quite rigid (there was *no* excuse for any inaccuracy or lateness), he now viewed his standards as ideals that didn't allow for human frailty. He was beginning to loosen up.

George offered to help Marge out during her troubles with her son and husband by taking more responsibility for Ralph. She was the sibling who had visited him regularly, and accompanied him on doctor visits. Now George picked up doing some of this "for her." The distance meant that George would have to stay overnight at his father's. For the first time in their lives, George and Ralph began spending time alone together. He went up about once a month.

The idea of visiting helped George feel like a bona fide family member and lessened his guilt about not doing enough for his father through the years. The actuality of time together with Ralph resulted in an extremely important personal discovery for George. Ralph was still primarily involved in keeping his possessions tidy. This time it was not paints and brushes, but pills and doctors' appointments. George spent a lot of time listening to his father talk about his organizational systems.

Ralph's knowledge of who Ginny was as a person was almost totally limited to "she was a good Christian woman and a hard worker." While he remembered family picnics that George had forgotten, Ralph seemed to know as little about Ginny as George did. Ralph's experience of his life in the family was of grateful contentment; he felt that Ginny had treated him well, and so had all the children (although Allen had given them some "trouble" that Ralph would not detail). Ralph likewise had very little to say about his life before marriage. George learned only that Ralph's parents had died when he was a teenager, and he was grateful to be taken on as a helper by a neighboring painter. Mostly their visits were filled with silence, as they watched TV together. George always left with relief and some depression.

It took about four visits for George to attach his feelings to his discovery: he was different from his father. The life that his father apparently found reassuring and sufficient felt overwhelmingly empty to George. This individuating step from his father was key in freeing George to envision other ways of being a man and of being part of a family. Until this time, contemplating a different life had been experienced as guilty disloyalty to his father. Now he could see that there was room for each to live his own kind of life.

Our sessions during this time were on a monthly basis—occasions to touch base and coalesce thoughts and ideas for development. Time had passed and George had still not heard from Allen. On an impulse he looked up his number in the phone book and just dialed it. Allen's wife was warmly welcoming and immediately invited him to dinner. She had long been wanting to know Allen's family. George accepted.

His impression was of a warm family life, with Allen attached to his children in a very real way. He learned that Allen was still extremely bitter about being sent to a home as a child, had loved his own father, and had never accepted his new family so quickly assembled. He had avoided contact because he didn't want to dredge up "old business"; he was very happy with his current life. Allen, too, knew little about Ginny, and still felt she had abandoned him. He seemed glad to meet George, however, and his wife began to invite George occasionally for dinner.

George and I had been working together about two and a half years. George had been going with Barbara for over a year now, and the relationship was at a stage where decisions about what would happen next were timely. Barbara, a single mother with three teenage children, had begun to push George for some clarity. George, in his meticulous way, had been trying to head off any future problems by reading everything he could get his hands on about remarried family life. He cared for Barbara very much and had developed a good bond with her youngest boy, but he was exceedingly anxious about marriage itself. The casual camaraderie of the household bothered him, and he felt the oldest girl showed too little respect for Barbara. He didn't know what to do with his anger about some of what went on.

George suggested that he ask Barbara to come to a session with him so he could develop some guidelines for discussing these things with her. It had sounded to me as though they were doing a good job on their own, but the fact that George no longer tried to keep his therapy hidden was a great step. He also was willing to risk bringing up issues which might be conflictual, and furthermore, be the one to articulate them. George's old emotional position of staying on the periphery and trying not to make waves as the "price" of being in a romantic relationship had changed. In the joint sessions it was clear that Barbara was looking for a partner in life, not a peripheral breadwinner or lover, and regarded these discussions as natural in a relationship. George's work in therapy opened the way for him to hold onto who he was as a person even at times when tensions increased between them. They did become engaged two months later.

Remarriage had never been a goal of the therapy work; George had been too fearful of another failure when he began treatment. Our work enabled George to live more comfortably as a single person who was more meaningfully connected to the people in his life. This time his choice to pursue marriage was not grounded in flight from the isolation of singlehood.

14

Later Life: Lina's Story

LINA, BORN IN Czechoslovakia and now in her late fifties, was still a striking woman. She dressed elegantly and walked with the loose confident stride of those used to power or beauty. She would have been intimidating were it not for her smile which transformed her cool elegance into a warm, welcoming openness. The intensity that characterized everything she undertook communicated itself across the waiting room, as she sat working on papers she had brought.

THE PROBLEM

Lina came for therapy wanting to "finally" get rid of the feelings of loneliness, anxiety, and depression that had plagued her much of her life. She described going through life "not totally present. I feel disconnected from my feelings, numb. I only feel connected and present when I am in love." The immediate precipitant for deciding on therapy now was that she had angered a very close friend and was feeling very scared. She was unclear about what she had done and was completely at sea about how to go about making amends. Lina, who was very bright and articulate, said she "knew nothing about how to do relationships. When people are angry at me, I just go home, sit in the corner, and cry."

The real problem, she finally revealed, was that, without a husband, nothing she had meant anything to her. She felt empty and so did her life; she wanted to work on getting married. Lina was experiencing a kind of double deficit whammy—she felt a failure because she had not married, and also a failure because, as a feminist, she "shouldn't" be having these feelings about needing marriage.

Since it is important to address the immediate issues that people bring, we first spent some time on her current fear: that her friend would never speak to her again. We went over things she could do and say to her friend, with Lina taking detailed notes as if all this were a foreign language. After she felt she had some tools to work with we looked at the current context of her life. Lina had been in therapy twice previously, and so was prepared with her story.

THE CURRENT CONTEXT

Lina was vice-president of personnel in a large American bank, worked long hours, and was very successful. Recently she had been given the task of organizing new offices for Central and South America, and so she spent quite a bit of time traveling. Even with all her achievement, however, she felt she was working "below her level." Even though she was successfully holding her own in a male-dominated, highly competitive field, Lina was plagued with the constant fear that she would be "thrown out for something she did wrong."

Although she earned an excellent salary, Lina had no savings. She had a close platonic relationship with Jeffrey, an older, very wealthy divorced man who "took care" of her finances. On his advice she had recently purchased a condo, and on her own had gone into debt to have it completely remodeled. Since it was her first home she wanted it to be "perfect." She also spent considerable money on clothes. Lina felt she didn't have to worry about her money situation, however, as "he's very good with money and will take care of things." This extended even to his bookkeeper paying Lina's bills and balancing her checkbook for her. She and her friend were very companionable, went on vacations together, and talked at least twice a day. But she was not in love with him. She thought he loved her and was just waiting for her to give up her search for love and settle down with him.

She had a wide friendship network with other women and remained in touch with friends from earlier years as well as those more recent. Most were married. Lina also sometimes provided a home for young women coming to New York from the Midwest, letting them stay in her apartment as they found jobs and got settled. It was good for them, and it was good for her: "I don't like to be alone." She was always very generous with her advice and help to them.

From the outside Lina's life looked full and even exotic; she had a prestigious job, good friends, young people she was mentoring, a home of her own that many would envy, and the friendship of a wealthy and powerful man. With the exception of taking responsibility for her own financial planning, Lina appeared to have done well at tasks of mastery and competence. Her friends found her feelings of emptiness and meaninglessness both incomprehensible and unshakable, and were frustrated at hearing about them. This was creating resentment on both sides and increasing the emotional distance between Lina and her friends.

Because of her particular history, Lina had not pursued the issue of marriage in the same chronological sequencing as had her peer group. Confronting it now in the later life phase increased the difficulties for her: the urgency of time running out, the developmental gap with her friends, and the sense that she was doubly "out of step" (not only unmarried but also "out of sync" with her friends) contributed to her feelings of deviance and failure. Lina could not begin to take pleasure in what she had until the American "ideal family" fantasy had been worked through.

LINA'S DEVELOPMENTAL RHYTHM

Time had had an atypical impact on Lina. In her twenties she had observed wives, clearly secondary to their husbands, working in the kitchen at dinner parties while the men had interesting conversations in the livingroom. She decided then that "work would be her salvation." In her thirties she did indeed work hard and took pride in her accomplishments; in addition, she felt connected to the feminist movement around her. She had liaisons with men, but always became fearful about "losing herself" and terminated them as soon as marriage was broached. She described "losing all her feelings for the man in question. I would feel nothing." In her forties she suffered a depression for which she sought therapy. She educated herself about medications and worked out a regime with her psychopharmacologist. What "really" brought her out of it, however, was a love affair. She and the man became engaged, but Lina broke it off when she discovered he was having an affair with someone else. In her fifties, Lina felt she was finally ready for marriage and was desperate because she might be too late.

There was no way to bypass her fixed solution to her experienced emptiness (i.e., getting married). Lina was adamant about this being the next step in her development. The intensity of her focus was actually keeping her from growing, however. We were able to agree that it would be better to deal with her problem of holding onto her "self" in relationships before marriage rather than after. Since there was no man she loved in her current life, we could "practice" on the relationships she did have. Having been in therapy before, Lina was aware of operating from old themes and positions, and was very willing to work on changing them, as long as it was helping her with men. The best route to achieving this is often by reworking the client's emotional position within the family of origin.

FAMILY HISTORY

Lina was born in 1936 in Czechoslovakia of a wealthy aristocratic family. The older of two sisters, she lived with her family in a large house in Prague. She spent as much time as she could at her maternal grandmother's country home. Her memories of her parents (Alex and Nina) were of "beautiful people dressed always for parties. They would come in and give me a goodnight kiss before leaving." It was her grandmother who brought her up, together with her fun-loving and eccentric great-aunt: "She never married, traveled a lot, did whatever she pleased, and was very good to me." Although the children had a nanny in Prague, Lina thought of her grandmother as her mother. Her younger sister, Vera, was "sly and mean. She would tear up my paintings." The sisters never changed this early pattern. Lina lived surrounded by women; the only man in the entire household was her father, who was rarely there. But when he was, "he and I would go off for good walks together. I loved him very much." Lina's mother has described her as a happy child whom she never worried about.

Lina's sense of the relationship between her mother and her grandmother was that it was very "prickly"; she thought her grandmother disapproved of Nina's frivolity. They were not close. Lina was certain that her grandmother was more attached to her sister (the great-aunt) than she was to her daughter Nina.

Becoming Refugees

As World War II was drawing to a close and the Russians were approaching Prague, Lina's father was advised to leave the country, since it was thought that the Russians would be arresting liberal, artistic people with ties to the old aristocracy. Assuming that it would not be for long, the family left with very few possessions. Lina waved good-bye to her grandmother and the other relatives; everyone thought they would be reunited in the near future. Lina was never to see them again. The family escaped to Austria, where they spent the next two years in a displaced persons camp. Lina was nine when she left Prague and her memories of the camp years were sad and difficult: her father became very withdrawn and her mother became like a "crazy person," screaming at her and then sobbing, while cuddling Vera. Lina remembers the townspeople being very kind, offering cast-off clothing. A soldier once wanted to give her a coin for a candy machine, but she refused out of pride. To be penniless and accept charity was a bitter pill; she felt no one was aware of her family's "worth."

Coming to America

As it became clear that the Allies were not going to free Czechoslovakia, the family obtained papers to emigrate to America. Lina remembers the boat trip over as the time when she first began to feel empty. Her father continued to be withdrawn, her mother to be openly angry at him and everyone. Lina herself only cried. They settled in Chicago. Lina was 12.

This involuntary emigration was devastating for her parents, and thus for the children as well. Coming to America did not represent the chosen search for freedom or opportunity that it did for other emigrants. Rather, it represented the final step in being forced to take leave of all that was loved and safe. Throughout their lives her parents would continue to keep their faces turned toward the past, mourning (in her father's case) or railing at the fate which had brought them down (in her mother's).

Establishing a New Life

Lina's parents were ill-prepared for their new life in America. Neither had been educated for a trade or profession, and both were used to servants doing all the physical labor. Through connections, Lina's father obtained a job as a bookkeeper for a manufacturing company. Her mother became a housewife. The girls were enrolled in public school. Alex continued to be quiet and withdrawn, although he developed a great love for gardening and spent many hours tending his plants. Nina had more energy, and spent it keeping the house, angrily shouting at Lina, hovering over Vera, and attempting to recoup the family position.

Solidifying Themes and Positions

Lina's younger sister Vera, being the "pretty one," was chosen to be the one who would redeem the family. She was literally groomed to find a wealthy and highly placed husband in the future. Any extra family money was spent on her clothing and music or dance lessons. She was told from an early age that her task was to marry well. Assuming the mantle of reclaiming the family's lost world, Vera became the focus of all her mother's efforts. No one was allowed to discipline or oppose her. In disputes between sisters, her mother took Vera's side. Lina was the "strong" one, who helped her mother with the work, and her father remained emotionally apart from it all.

Although Lina was aware that he sympathized with her position, he was unwilling to tangle with her mother on her behalf.

Lina's relationship with her mother was openly hostile, tempered only by Lina's fear of being hit. The relationships of all three women were enmeshed and fused. Vera existed for Nina as an extension of her dream, and Lina was to be Nina's coworker in making this possible. Nina and Lina together were expected to sacrifice their own needs in the "greater service" of regaining status through Vera's marriage. Counting so heavily on Vera to live out her dream, Nina avoided any upset with her. Thus, Vera became the undisputed queen on whose shoulders the family's fortune rested.

Lina enjoyed school and did well. She made a close friend and spent as much time out of the house as she could.

Multi-Generational Themes

Most families have several themes around which family life is organized. In Lina's family one theme dominated: recouping the family identity through marriage to a highly placed man. All the women's lives were lived in service to this goal. While pleasure might be possible for the next generation, it was "lost" to Nina and Lina. Hard work was their lot. Other themes included the belief that women's achievement was not only negligible but even a selfish deviation from the main goal. Men were never viewed as people; they were gatekeepers to status and the good life but written off as undependable in emergencies (as Alex was regarded). The emotional positions that solidified so quickly after the move to Chicago remained unchanged for the next 45 years.

Through the intervening years, Lina's grandmother and great-aunt had died. Alex's four siblings had been arrested, and their whereabouts were not known. Vera *had* married her wealthy businessman, who traveled frequently, and they had a daughter, Sonia, who was now 14 years old. Vera lived in a large country home with her husband (when he was there) and her housekeeper. Sonia lived with her grandparents, so that she could attend a prestigious private school in Chicago. Vera had cut off all contact with Lina and insisted that Sonia do the same. The event which precipitated the cut-off was Lina's insistence that she should have half the family silver (the only remnant of their former life). Lina took her half, her mother siding with her for once, and Vera did not speak to Lina again. Nina continued to avoid angering Vera — now because she was afraid her granddaughter would be taken from her. The genogram in Figure 14.1 illustrates these rigidly fixed relational patterns.

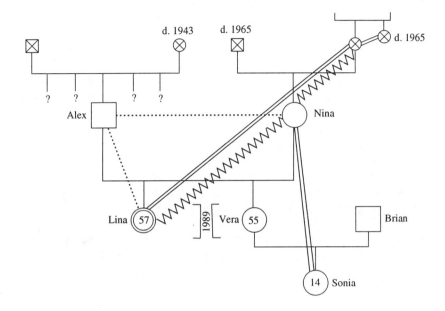

FIGURE 14.1 Lina's Genogram

THE THERAPY: INITIAL MOVES

It is very useful for some clients to have their own genogram in front of them. Seeing her family position visually mapped enhanced Lina's clarity about her sense of being outside and alone. She could see her current feelings in context: she *was* outside the main emotional life of her family. She could also see that her mother had been on the "outside" of the close relationship between her own mother and aunt. Noting that her entire adolescence was spent in service to the belief that marriage to the right kind of man is the sole goal of women's "development" made her current urgency more comprehensible. Lina was still obedient to the family message; all that had changed was that she had decided that now it was her turn. While her leap for survival in leaving Chicago and immersing herself in work in New York had served her well in many ways, her family relationships had essentially remained as they were (fused). Her fear of getting "sucked back in" and "losing herself" was as strong as ever. Her experience of being cut off after angering her sister also placed her extreme anxiety about upsetting people in its context.

At this point, Lina felt only hurt, anger, and rejection by her family;

she was unable to see any benefit to being in the "outside" position. Our family-of-origin work was framed as learning to be more connected without losing oneself. This, she could see, was relevant to her desire to "be a person" after marriage.

I (DJ) wondered whether Lina — or any forced emigrant — could ever feel truly at home (i.e., not an "outsider") anywhere. The impact of being torn from a loved homeland and family to which return is literally blocked is tremendous. Lina and I had differing views; she felt that with enough work — and a husband — this could be accomplished. Such was her seemingly unshakable belief in the power of marriage.

Aside from getting information about her earlier years, we did not focus on that part of her life. Lina had spent "countless hours in her previous therapy going over it" and felt that she had mourned those losses. However, we thought that hanging up photographs from her earlier life might be a way to get to the other side of the loss and feel some of the happiness and connection around her again. Lina had been keeping her pictures buried in a box. She also continued to work with her psychopharmacologist to adjust her medication for anxiety and depression.

Her father's failing health meant that Lina's first move with her family of origin would be to connect with him. That was the relationship that genuinely was in danger of being too late. Just deciding to take a different approach will often release stuck feelings. As she thought about what she would say to her father, long buried feelings surfaced: her anger at him for not standing up for her or to her mother, her great sadness for his life, her fear that he would not want to speak with her, and her continued love for him. She also felt considerable guilt about not making attempts to get closer to him; she had passively and helplessly waited for him to make a move. She did not want to ask him about his family of origin, although she knew little, as this had always been a taboo topic.

The purpose of making shifts with one's family is *not* to dump one's anger on them; rather, it is genuinely to act differently. Lina decided that she wanted simply to let him know how much she cared, to talk of early happy memories, and to let him know about her job and her pride in her accomplishments. Through the planning process her anger and her guilt had diminished enough so that she was open to a new experience.

The enmeshed nature of the family relationships and the sensitivity to being the "one left out" meant that her mother needed to be included in the planning as well. Indeed, Lina felt that her mother had always been jealous of her father's feeling for her and might not let her be alone with him now. Lina's usual style was either to crumple helplessly in a corner or to come out blasting and intimidate others into compliance. It initially went against her grain to ask for her mother's help. "Why should I? She should let me see my father if I want to." Lina was willing to include her mother only because we predicted that the ensuing conflict if she didn't would take up all the emotional space, and leave little left over for her father. We planned that Lina would ask her mother to help her overcome her nervousness about talking alone with her father and say that she wanted to give her mother a day off from care-taking responsibilities.

Part of this work with anyone, but particularly with Lina, involves going over in great detail what to say and do given different possible reactions. Lina's experience in her family was that there was no way to negotiate conflict, and she had never developed this skill in subsequent relationships. One person prevailed while the other one crumpled. We went over how to hold one's position without attacking the other.

Once she understood the reasoning behind something, Lina was indefatigable in following it out. When she went to Chicago, the visit went almost as planned. She and her father had a wonderful talk, and he told her how proud he was of what she'd done. Most astonishing to Lina, her father couldn't get over the fact that such an "important" person as she had taken the time for him. Lina had previously thought that she was the only one in the family who felt unworthy. She felt connected to him — and to herself — for the first time in a long time. Her mother had wanted to know in detail what had been said during their visit, and Lina joyfully told her. When Nina reacted with anger and attack (e.g., "You just upset your father telling him about your tramp's life"), Lina's anxiety went sky high. Feeling the shift was a failure, her knee-jerk reaction was to apologize to her mother and not try to speak with her father when she called home.

We had experienced the intensity of that parental triangle. The price of connection to her father appeared to be abandonment and verbal abuse by her mother. The amount of anxiety in Lina's family when a woman was on the "outside" of a warm two-person relationship was enormous. The task here was for Lina to control her reactivity, not attack or crumble, but to stay connected to her mother and continue to talk separately with her father. It was important that mother and daughter develop a conversation that didn't include a third person. The first step was to give Lina a concrete way to respond when her mother attacked. Lina chose to just keep repeating, "I'm sorry you feel that way. Now let's talk about something else." Nina soon stopped attacking, but called less frequently. The next step involved the longer process of giving up the fantasy that she could change her mother. This work eventually allowed Lina to place her mother's attacks in a less personal context and see her as a person with her own troubles.

Making these shifts revealed the source of some of Lina's profound fears about marriage. While closeness with her father was desperately yearned for, he was at the same time a weak reed to lean on. If the price of closeness was such attack by her mother, it was understandable why Lina had not pursued it. Her mother, for all her faults, was the energy of the family. Forming an alliance with a man had the emotional significance of being in a truly precarious position.

THE THERAPY: INTERMEDIATE MOVES

Lina was still feeing shaky, but was clearer about how her intense dilemma about marriage had developed. She had some respect for her strength in moving away from her family. Her work life was going well, and she had received a raise. Friendships were a little smoother; she had begun to be able to acknowledge her friends' problems with her without interrupting and attacking. Most importantly, she had learned that she didn't have to talk endlessly with her mother and apologize to stay connected. Her mother had not cut her off. She could now sit with some anxiety, and not leap to get rid of it. Her desperation about finding a man to marry was almost as intense as ever, however, and she still saw her satisfactions as meaningless without it.

Lina's experience in dealing differently in the parental triangle and not crumbling in the face of attack lessened her need for constant reassurance in relationships. She now began to feel some irritation with Jeffrey, her friend. His frequent phone calls during her workday were now annoying. Their unspoken agreement seemed to have been that she would be available to help him with his needs, while he would pay for luxuries she enjoyed and take care of her money for her. Lina was understandably anxious about upsetting this balance; Jeffrey was a powerful man and very used to having people make themselves available for him. She was able to request a small change—to have two scheduled daytime calls that she could plan for, instead of instant availability. This decreased somewhat her feelings of being "smothered" by him. Jeffrey remained annoyed by these limits and soon began to call whenever he wished again. Lina was unwilling to risk more upset with him, but her attempt to shift the power balance helped her see Jeffrey more clearly as a person who definitely enjoyed control.

Lina's tendency to obsess over detail and decisions continued to be troublesome in her daily life. Her need to be perfect and not cause any upset in her family of origin, the disastrous impact of the emigration, and a possible mild attention deficit disorder contributed to this focus on control. We worked on using strategies that would help her get less bogged down. For Lina the most useful ones were concrete. Visualization techniques felt too hazy. We chose two: writing the possibilities on pieces of paper, putting them into a hat, and picking one at random (i.e., let fate decide); and/or sorting decisions into two categories—those she *must* worry about today, and those she could postpone for a week. The postponed decision box was checked each week and brought up-to-date.

Using these kinds of strategies creates considerable anxiety at first, but if clients can stick with it, it allows enough room for them to experience a less disastrous view of life. They can see that terrible things don't happen if every detail is not totally planned for or controlled. With time, Lina was able to let go of some of the minor issues.

At this time fate provided a love experience to "practice" on. She heard that Piero, a former love, was about to remarry, and Lina experienced an overwhelming rush of loving and tender feelings for him. He had loved her for some years, but she had felt "nothing" for him after the first few months and had let the relationship drift. Now that he was to belong to someone else, she was intensely in love again. The experience of intense desire fanning up at times when she was about to lose a man was an old pattern of Lina's, and she was understandably leery of trusting these feelings. At the same time, she wanted him very much, and with her intense approach to life saw him as her last chance at happiness. Lina's desperation was too great for her to be able to pause long enough to challenge this old pattern; she needed to contact Piero immediately. This meant the work of therapy would hinge around pushing her to confront her previous assumptions about the centrality of marriage. It also provided a needed opportunity for Lina to learn how to hold onto her "self" as she tried to negotiate this romantic relationship.

Lina had never had to lay herself open for possible rejection. Because of her beauty, she was used to having men approach her. She wrote Piero a letter telling him how she felt and inviting him to spend some time with her before he decided to remarry. She viewed herself as very much the underdog in this triangle. In his response, Piero agreed to spend time together if she would come to Italy. He himself was leery of her constancy.

What followed over the next months was the development of Lina's first relationship in which she worked hard to hang in and deal with (not flee) the uncomfortable feelings: despair when she heard that he was still seeing the "other woman," exaltation when Piero finally acknowledged that she was "the one," and then the new work of dealing with Piero as a person once the initial triangle was eliminated. This was the point at which previously she would begin to feel "nothing" and end the relationship.

In contrast to the past, Lina stayed closely connected to her friends during the ups and downs of this relationship. Her family-of-origin experience was that connecting with a man jeopardized her relationship with her mother and sister. It was important to experience women's solidarity rather than jealousy and anxiety. Her friends were a genuine help in providing advice on dealing with relationships, and allowed Lina the experience of staying connected to a man and women at the same time.

Once the triangle with the "other woman" was eliminated, the emotional task was to learn to relate to a man as a person, someone with his own strengths and liabilities, not a projection of her fantasies. Piero did not call her as often as she wanted, for example, and Lina at first saw this as his lack of love for her. Later she was to see it as his frugality.

During this time, Lina's father died. She was able to genuinely mourn for him, as she had begun to know him as a person, not a mythological being. She decided that she wanted to be an integral part of the funeral, not just a guest. Brian, her brother-in-law, was in charge of funeral arrangements. Knowing her mother's sensitivity to being "on the outside", she first told her she wanted to call Brian. This was Lina's beginning effort at challenging the five-year cut-off. Nina was exceedingly anxious about possible conflict, but did not forbid Lina from contacting Brian. Lina then spoke to Brian about her desire to give a eulogy. Brian's response was that he was giving the eulogy and hers was irrelevant. Lina decided to prepare one and just stand up and give it without Brian's permission. This decision reflected her growing feeling that she was a member of the family—she didn't need to be invited in. The therapy work was around not just acting impulsively in her old "Damn the Torpedoes" style. She needed to build on the changing relationship with her mother by including her—not by raging at her because she didn't stand up to Brian for her. She consulted with Nina in preparing the eulogy. She gave a very wonderful eulogy that was filled with memories of Czechoslovakia. Predictably Brian was very angry that she had changed his plan, and her mother's anxiety, as we had anticipated, was expressed by attacking Lina (for "being selfish and ruining her father's funeral"). Nina calmed down as soon as she saw that Brian would not retaliate by removing Sonia from her home.

When Vera did not attend the funeral, Lina learned some very important information from her mother. Vera, who had not left her home for two years, was suffering from severe agoraphobia and possibly substance abuse. Thus collapsed the fantasies that Lina had nurtured over the years of Vera's magical life, beloved by husband and daughter, on her beautiful country estate. Their mother had kept this a secret at Vera's request.

Lina attempted to bridge the cut-off by writing to her sister, describing the funeral and telling her how sorry she was that she wasn't there. Vera's reply came through their mother: she did not want Lina ever to get in touch with her again. The fuel behind the power of this cut-off continues to remain a mystery; our hypothesis was that Vera had continued to live out the family message. Once she was married, her life no longer had purpose. She had not gone on to become a person. Knowing of Lina's career success, she might be unable to face the great differences in who the sisters had become. There had been nothing in their earlier relationship to suggest the possibility of mutual support.

The fact that Nina had trusted Lina with this information was evidence of the shifting relationship between them. Now Lina had to face the emotional importance for her of maintaining the fantasy of Vera's magical life. She had to either deny reality or view herself as the better off of the two. After a lifetime of feeling like the Little Match Girl, Lina began to revise her vision—but not without considerable resistance. There had been comfort in seeing herself as the poor outsider.

Lina's mother, meanwhile, began to treat her with more respect. She had always viewed Lina's life as one of selfish pursuit and profligate spending (similar to her own mother's view of her), but now she ceased attacking her for it. Lina, for her part, was able to see her mother's opinion in its context and separate from herself.

As people change, the relationships around have to either shift or founder. The tension in her friendship with Jeffrey had reached the point of no return: he did not want to be her friend if she was involved with Piero. Not only would he no longer take care of her finances, but he presented her with a bill for many of the luxuries that Lina had thought were gifts. This loss was a big one—a friend and a wealthy, powerful man who was gatekeeper to the social world that the sisters had been trained to seek. Now she had to learn to handle her money herself. She did it surprisingly quickly and easily. Her biggest decision, taken on her own, was to rent out her apartment and move in with a woman friend. She was not earning enough to pay for her condo, and have a life besides. The feared position, being "alone and homeless" (which for Lina meant being unmarried and not in her own home), was now her life. This time she had chosen it. Lina experienced it as feeling free and began to use her extra time and money to resume painting, which she had not done since childhood.

We had been working together for approximately two years. Some things had changed; Lina no longer saw herself as a pitiful, deviant failure. She had learned to live with uncomfortable feelings and not try to disperse them by attacking others or by apologizing abjectly. She had a clearer understanding of her family's themes and their continued impact on her. She no longer needed to play her life always in contrast to her imagined sister's, but could see it as separate. And she was learning, through the arduous process of the relationship with Piero, how to let some things go, negotiate others, and not budge on still others. What remained unchanged

was Lina's continued drive for a married life—not with the same desperation, but still with an intensity that detracted from contentment with what
she had.

She still had trouble with periods of depression, but we had come to link
these with shifts in biochemistry as much as with psychological factors.
Going off estrogen replacement, for example, had set off a serious bout of
anxiety and sleeplessness. Continuing to work with her psychopharmacologist was an important element throughout the therapy process.

THE THERAPY: FINAL PHASE

Our meetings were now on an irregular basis, whenever Lina felt the need.
As she worked hard on the relationship with Piero, practical difficulties
(she would have to move to Italy and find a job there), as well as growing
disenchantment with his limitations as a person (his frugality and irritabil-
ity with the usual discomforts of life), made sacrificing her own work and
friends less palatable. The growing awareness of the differences between
them and the real problems in talking directly to Piero about them in a
way that might have led to some negotiation eventually overburdened the
relationship and it ended. This ending was of a new character, however.
Lina, while saddened, did not experience the devastation of former endings.
She retained her affection for Piero, while choosing to stay with the life she
had.

Another connection was made in her first trip back to Czechoslovakia
together with her mother. Both family homes were still there—the city
house was a restaurant, the country house intact but dilapidated after being
used by the Russians. Both women met former friends, distant relatives,
and visited the graves of their family. Nina and Lina together mourned the
loss of their mother/grandmother. Now that Czechoslovakia was open to
them, neither felt a desire to return to live there. Lina was surprised that the
visit was less intense for her than she had anticipated; it was a nostalgic visit
to a loved life in the distant past. It was a different country now.

Sonia, Lina's niece, was now 16 years old and increasingly independent.
When Lina called home now, Sonia actively sought conversation, and they
were coming to know each other in spite of continued parental opposition.
Nina supported this new relationship.

Lina continued to see her life as inferior without marriage, but the desperation had diminished considerably. After all, she did choose not to
marry Piero. The examples of her great-aunt's wonderful single life and her
mother's not-so-wonderful married life did not change her view. She was,
however, now able to feel that the other parts of her life also had value and
meaning. She also felt that while her life might be "inferior," *she* was not

inferior. The total focus on marriage in her family of origin, combined with a lack of counterbalancing societal visions of life for single women in her earlier years, had left a powerful template. Some life experiences are so powerfully desired that there seems no way over, around, or through the regret if they are not accomplished. For Lina, marriage was *it* at this point in time. However, her drive toward self-development has always taken precedence over her desire to belong to someone, so she may revise her vision of the necessity of marriage in the future.

15

Stories from Gay and Lesbian Singles

BETSY: YOUNG ADULT ISSUES

To identify herself as both lesbian and single for the first time in her life at age 29 was an unnerving experience for Betsy. With no familiar signposts on how to behave, she found herself increasingly anxious and sought therapy.

Betsy had grown up thinking of herself as heterosexual, but with very little dating experience or time on her own, she married her high school boy friend. She had done so against the wishes of her family, and the relationship had remained conflicted. From the beginning, her husband was extremely violent toward her and she struggled for five years to extract herself from the marriage. The divorce, like the marriage, was very bitter, with lawyers battling where the spouses had left off.

Dealing with the aftermath of the marriage and divorce and fearful of being on her own for the first time, Betsy became romantically involved with a woman and had her first homosexual encounter. The sense of comfort that came with this relationship was so intense that the relationship quickly became all-consuming. Six months later, Betsy fled the relationship, anxious about her sexuality, depressed over the losses in her life, and isolated from friends because she had cut off from everyone. This is when she entered therapy.

Although in her late twenties, Betsy faced many issues of the young adult. Marrying so young, she had never really been on her own and had yet to have the experience of taking care of herself. She needed to gain confidence in her ability to take charge of her finances and become self-supporting. She had never had a "single" moment in her adult life and had no idea what is was like to have casual relationships or date as a way to gain experience in relationships. Her connection to her family had also remained strained throughout the marriage. Even though they approved of the divorce, she had not really negotiated an adult self with them.

Her newly acknowledged attraction and sexual comfort with women added another dimension to all the young adult tasks facing Betsy. She questioned what she truly knew about herself and whether she could trust herself to make good decisions. She knew few lesbian or gay people, and therefore had no adult homosexual role models. Struggling with the issue of sexual identity, being unsure of herself in relationships, and feeling truly alone at age 29 were all parts of Betsy's depression. Rather than seeing herself as moving through a transition to defining a fuller self, she felt like a failure.

The first step in therapy was to create a framework with Betsy that would allow her to take a different position. While it was hard not to see her marriage as a derailment and a waste of time, she could see how the experience had allowed her to marshal her resources and learn to stand up for herself. She also believed if she had had any inkling of her interest in homosexual relationships as an adolescent, there would have been no safe place to express her sexuality. Her mother and stepfather, staunch Catholics, would have thought she was sick or bad. At least at this point in her life, she could locate times in the past when she had taken a firm position (to end the marriage) and dealt with the consequences. Given the homophobia in our society and her family, she needed to know she could be strong. She also realized that she had ended the marriage when she had been ready to do so. This reinforced her ability to go at her own pace.

As Betsy began to see herself as a "work in progress" rather than the product of many mistakes, she began to experiment with relationships and being single. Again, this was complicated. She wanted to do this with women but was totally uneducated about "rules" of same-sex relationships. Her first steps included joining a woman's political action group whose members were both lesbian and straight. She also connected with a lesbian social club, where she found a safe environment to begin to date. Her biggest challenge was to manage her anxiety without jumping into a relationship.

While Betsy worked on expanding her network of friends, the conflicts in her family hung over her head. In addition to her marriage bypassing her adolescence and young adulthood with respect to forming relationships, it had also allowed her to bypass negotiating her relationship with her parents. Her "jailbreak" marriage, and then the uproar that had accompanied it, had frozen in time her struggle for autonomy. She still responded to her parents from a reactive adolescent position. They also shared her old depressed assessment of herself, as someone who made many mistakes. Most encounters with her mother and stepfather ended in some form of disagreement, with Betsy bridling at their attempts to be "helpful." As she identified herself more comfortably as a lesbian, she claimed a "secret" that further increased her sense of being misunderstood.

Betsy was motivated to change her relationship with her parents. The pressure of having a "secret" that might diminish her further in her parents' eyes, along with her need to validate her newly emerging sexuality, increased her anxiety to an uncomfortable level. With her new view of herself as someone who stands up for herself, she unexpectedly told her mother that she was a lesbian. If her mother didn't like it, then Betsy would have nothing to do with her. While the information was new, Betsy's rebellious position with her mother was a familiar one. Her mother responded in her predictable fashion, which disqualified Betsy's experience and questioned her certainty regarding her sexuality. Her mother also refused to tell her stepfather out of fear that he would cut Betsy off because of his religious views. The mother now had a "secret" from the stepfather. This exchange reactivated a common stepfamily triangle, which kept her mother in a position of divided loyalty, and Betsy and her stepfather at a distance.

Unfortunately the manner of Betsy's disclosure of her homosexuality had been "more of the same," and therefore it did not further her work on differentiating from her family. Clearly, for Betsy to reconnect to her family in a more adult position, she needed to decrease her own anger and reactivity to her mother and stepfather. She also needed other supports to deal with her anxiety regarding her sexuality.

The therapy followed two threads, very much interwoven during young adulthood: working on competence in the outside world, which for Betsy included finding a community of support, and taking a more responsible adult position with family. To accomplish the latter task, Betsy needed to put aside the hurts of her childhood. She had come from a middle-class, Protestant background. Her biological father had died when she was very young, and she had been completely cut off from his side of the family. Her mother had remarried several times, with each new marriage bringing the hope that they would at last finally become a "family"—a hope shattered when each marriage ended. The current stepfather had been on the scene since Betsy was a young adolescent. Betsy felt her mother had made many compromises to make this marriage work. Her own intense involvement with her boyfriend and early marriage were, she felt, her attempt to deal with her mother's preoccupation with the marriage.

To decrease her reactivity to the family, she needed to understand her parents better. She did this by exploring their families of origin, and the roles they played in the extended family. As she thought about her family more objectively, she became clearer on what part she played in keeping her relationship with her mother, stepfather, and siblings in an adolescent position. To move out of that role, Betsy needed to become a more active presence with her family. This would involve sharing more about her life, even if all the details were not settled.

Before approaching her mother again, Betsy decided to disclose her sexuality to her brother and sister, who she felt fairly certain would not reject her. When this turned out to be the case, she took the plunge and invited her mother into therapy. With her own feelings somewhat under control, she felt much better prepared for this meeting. Not only had she been coached in therapy, but she had also learned from gay friends that she needed to allow her mother to come to terms with her daughter's lesbianism in her own time. Betsy would have to be patient with this. The mother joined Betsy for several sessions and went through many stages that other parents experience. This included wishing for it not to be so, blaming herself and her bad marriages, worrying about her daughter's future without a husband (despite the bad marriages), and assuming there would be no grandchildren.

The other important discussion that Betsy and her mother had was about the role marriage had played in the family. For women it had always represented a trade-off between security and loss of self. Betsy's marriage, it turned out, had not been all that different from her mother's first marriage. Her own quest for a relationship that would protect her was not unlike her mother's quest. In Betsy's current stepfather, the mother finally felt like she had found the right person. Part of her wanted Betsy to keep pursuing until she found the right person. In the face of her mother's anxiety about her future, Betsy was able to hold onto her position that she needed time to be on her own now, and that, if she did connect in the future, it would be with a woman.

Hardest for Betsy was her mother's struggle about whether to tell the stepfather about her lesbianism. Here was a man whom her mother finally felt could be a "father" to Betsy. However, she was convinced that his religious beliefs would never allow him to accept a gay stepdaughter. She was also not sure what demands he would make on her to cut off from her daughter. While it was hard for Betsy not to feel rejected, her sense of compassion for her mother mitigated the impact. In addition, Betsy was clear that, although she would have liked to have had a relationship with her stepfather, she was not looking for a "father." Her mother could give up that burden.

Betsy's position, in a way, allowed the mother to take the risk of disclosing Betsy's homosexuality to the stepfather. Mirroring Betsy's "I" position, she told the step father that if he could not be around Betsy now that he knew, that was his decision. She, as Betsy's mother, would continue her relationship with her daughter. Surprising the mother, the stepfather did not respond with an absolute rejection of Betsy and did not try to impose his religious views. For Betsy and her family this was the first step toward learning to connect in a new way that allowed for differences. Given that Betsy had come out to her family in the 1990s, her mother and stepfather were lucky enough to find a support group for parents of homosexual children within their religious community. This provided a forum in which they could work through their feelings.

EDWARDO: CULTURAL IMPLICATIONS

Edwardo, age 28, requested therapy soon after learning that his father had cancer. As a gay Puerto Rican man, he had never felt comfortable sharing his sexual orientation with anyone in his family, least of all his father. He had fended off questions regarding his love life with jokes but experienced the father's pressure for him to marry as his unspoken concern about whether Edwardo was a real man. His father's illness intensified the father's pressure on Edwardo to settle down and Edwardo's sadness that his father would never really know him. Through therapy, Edwardo was hoping to find the tools to come out to his father and other members of the family.

Accompanying his concern regarding his relationship with his father was Edwardo's unhappiness about not being in a relationship. On some level he shared his father's concern about not being in a long-term love relationship, although for different reasons. While he had a wide circle of friends, gay and straight, and had dated many men, not having a primary love relationship contributed to his sense of fragmentation about his life. The "family," which had been so important to him growing up, was part of the straight Puerto Rican world. He wanted the same sense of family closeness and ritual in his gay world.

Edwardo was the oldest of three, with two younger sisters. His parents had immigrated from Puerto Rico for economic reasons before the children were born, but returned to the island for frequent visits with extended family. Edwardo's father had done very well and maintained a job in a union shop that allowed him to support his immediate family and send money home to help support his parents.

Quite suddenly, Edwardo's mother died of an undiagnosed cancer, when he was 15. Shortly after his mother's death, he and his sisters returned to Puerto Rico to live with a maternal aunt and maternal grandparents. Although he saw his father regularly, Edwardo never returned to live with his father. His father also started a long term alliance with a woman, whom the extended family never accepted as a replacement for Edwardo's mother. When Edwardo returned to New York to enter college, he hoped to have more contact with his father, but their relationship had become quite formal. Edwardo was also just coming to terms with his sexual identity and felt very uncomfortable being around his father, whom he felt certain would not approve.

Over the next ten years, with respect to his relationships with his father and mother's extended family, Edwardo struggled with the gender training and expectations of men in the Puerto Rican culture. Manliness was to be demonstrated not only by being a heterosexually active man but also by becoming a responsible family man. His educational and professional accomplishments, which were considerable, were always a little suspect because he had not become a traditional head of family. In his own mind, he questioned his "manliness" because he did not have the courage to stand up to his father and say who he was. Throughout the struggle, he kept in touch with the family but emotionally distant.

The first phase of therapy was spent in trying to create a framework that might allow him to a have a fuller relationship with his father before he died. This included gaining understanding about the father as a person, not just head of the family. It included spending more actual time with his father and finding aspects of his life that he could safely share. It also involved revisiting the loss of his mother and its impact on the family with respect to shutting down feelings. He began to see how the death of his mother and the subsequent withdrawal of his father made him very cautious in relationships, including with his father. He felt this directly connected to his difficulties in relationships with both friends and lovers.

As a preparatory step to talking to his father, Edwardo also explored how he imagined his mother would have reacted. Because he had always felt more emotionally connected to his mother, the thought of talking about his homosexuality to her did not seem so frightening. He also felt that the mother-son connection would override the cultural prescriptions regarding how a man was supposed to be. Perhaps if his mother had been able to accept him, it would have relieved some of the intensity with his father. He wrote a long letter to her. It began with the loss and loneliness he experienced as an adolescent. He then tried to detail those aspects of her he remembered and carried with him to comfort himself, like her songs and stories, and memories of her cooking. In the course of describing who he was now, and the aspects of his life he valued, he found many similarities with his mother. They had a similar sense of humor. They loved good food. With these feelings of connection, he allowed his childhood anger at his mother for leaving him to dissipate. His mother had been buried in Puerto

Rico, so Edwardo chose a symbolic site to read the letter to her. Near his old neighborhood, there was a park were they had spent many hours as children. He sensed he would feel close to his mother there.

Edwardo also attempted to be in better touch with his sisters. One had recently moved to New York, freshly divorced, and was experiencing some similar issues about trying to have a life of her own in a traditional Hispanic family, although from a woman's point of view. She seemed to be a prime candidate for Edwardo to talk to first. She was indeed accepting of her brother but agreed that their father would never accept his son as a homosexual.

Feeling better connected to his mother and sister, Edwardo felt less cautious about trying to reach out to his father. There was less at stake. He began by being available to help him with doctor visits. However, whenever he thought about sharing more of his life and telling his father about his homosexuality, he would panic. He would then be furious in his certainty that his own father would not accept him. His anger would activate a cycle of distance not just from his father but from friends. Having grown up with the message that family is everything, it was hard for him to value his friendships and use them as an alternative family, as many gay men do. The distance from family and from friends made his single life much more difficult. He clearly needed help altering his model of what constituted a valid life.

Several months into therapy, his father entered the hospital for surgery and family members were asked to donate blood. As part of this, Edwardo was tested for the AIDS virus and was found to be HIV positive. In some ways, this was very difficult information for him to absorb, because he had no symptoms whatsoever; at the same time, the frequency with which this was happening to friends and acquaintances took away its surprise. The focus of therapy shifted to processing the impact of this news. Because on some level his mortality seemed so remote, his initial concern was about the potential loss of the love relationship he longed for. To be single and HIV positive felt like being sentenced to isolation forever. It also placed him in the position of having to rethink everything he had assumed would occur in his life. As a significant step, Edwardo joined an HIV positive gay men's support group, which gave him a network of other HIV positive men who were knowledgeable about the illness and willing to serve as role models for coping. Through his work in this group, and by becoming politically active in response to his own illness, he realized that the rest of his life was up to him — there was no waiting (for my prince or anyone).

The diagnosis also caused him to rethink what he wanted out of telling his father that he was gay, and whether he would reveal his HIV status to the rest of the family. A part of him came to believe that his father would never be able to overcome his cultural conditioning about what it means to be a man and, as a piece of this, his revulsion toward gay men. For Edwardo to come to some peace for himself, he had to accept that about his father. It did not make sense to back his father into a corner by directly disclosing his homosexuality, so that the father would have to choose whether or not to reject his son. At the same time, he felt he wanted to communicate that he had learned from his father what it meant to be a "good man," a phrase his father often used to judge others. He had a career that he liked, not just a job. He knew this was important to his father, who didn't want his children to be held back by the discrimination he experienced in breaking into the unions. Through his HIV status, Edwardo was developing a social and political consciousness, something his father had tried to instill in him. He also felt he was beginning to have a community of friends, for whom he felt responsibility, and who would be there for him when he needed them.

During his father's illness, Edwardo had a chance to get to know the father's girl friend. He began to feel an alliance with her, which changed his position in an old triangle, where the ghost of his mother kept him from acknowledging this important aspect of his father's life. Indeed, Edwardo's fledgling relationship with the girlfriend, enabled Edwardo and his father to discuss the mother for the first time. It was in the course of a conversation about the mother and the early years of the family that Edwardo made his most direct reference to the areas of his life that were hidden from his father. He had rehearsed the conversation many times in therapy and to himself. When the moment arose, he put it very simply, saying he wished his father could know him better. The father responded, with what Edwardo heard as real clarity, by saying, "I know who you are—you are a good man." In this conversation, Edward felt acknowledged and he believed that his father did truly know him. The issue of disclosure felt resolved for him.

TOM: DEFINING A SINGLE GAY IDENTITY

At age 33, Tom had just come out of his first real relationship, which had lasted a year, and was quite depressed about being alone again. Before this relationship, he had been isolated socially as well as professionally. While he had known he was gay for most of his life, he had only come to accept it in recent years. It still felt like an invisible part of his life.

He felt his parents knew, without asking, that he was gay, but they chose not to talk about it. Before he had become involved with this first lover, he had shared little about his life with them and he continued this pattern when he was in the relationship. No one in his family, for example, had met his lover. This "don't ask, don't tell" policy kept his homosexuality invisible in the family. At least outwardly, his parents did not have to confront their feelings about his homosexuality. He was also not "out" at his work in the banking industry, since he was convinced that his firm was much too conservative. He had been hoping that the relationship he was just in would be his bridge to a "normal life." Not surprisingly, it had collapsed under the intensity.

The first part of therapy dealt with mourning the loss of the relationship and confronting what it meant for him to be single again. As he pulled himself out of the relationship, Tom resumed frequenting bars, the one venue he had for meeting people. While his bar encounters rarely lasted beyond the night, he found them exciting, and this temporarily lifted his depression. He initially felt reluctant to discuss this form of socializing and ascribed this to his discomfort discussing his sexuality with a straight woman therapist (although he could not imagine discussing his sexuality with anyone, gay or straight). In examining this issue, it became clear that he was also doing an excessive amount of drinking during these times and was protective of this behavior as well. While he reluctantly acknowledged he might have a drinking problem, he could not imagine going to the bars and not drinking, and if he stopped going to the bars, he would become very isolated again. At this point he believed that the bars and alcohol were his only means to relieve his depression and meet other gay men. Tom had no sense of being able to affect his life in a more direct way.

Two issues had to be addressed: (1) his gay identity was so circumscribed that the only place he could feel himself was in the bar scene, and (2) the alcohol, which was medicating his depression, had an addictive life of its own. The alcohol use also affected the regularity with which he practiced safe sex, so potentially the consequences were lethal. To deal with the first issue, the alcohol abuse, had to be confronted. As a condition of therapy, Tom had to attend AA meetings. It was strongly suggested that he go to a gay AA group. The commitment to AA was very shaky for several months, and so his alcohol use remained the primary focus of treatment. The final impetus to own up to the alcohol abuse came when he had a car accident after drinking and lost his drivers license. Once Tom really connected to AA, it immediately cut into his sense of isolation and challenged his view that he could not affect change in his life. With the support of the AA meetings, he began to take his sobriety seriously and was ready to deal with other issues.

As a single man in his thirties, Tom's difficulty in coming to terms with his sexual identification as a gay man had immobilized him with respect to other developmental tasks. These included forming significant attachments outside the family (lovers or friends), sharing adult aspects of himself with his family, which left him cut off and isolated, and perhaps most importantly, beginning to feel he could have a life vision that took into account all aspects of himself. The one area where he felt successful was work. As long as he stayed in the closet, his male gender training regarding work behavior served him in good stead. There was, however, a cost, in that he always had to keep certain aspects of himself invisible. Part of him longed for and romanticized his old relationship, despite its faults, as an island in his sea of disconnection.

Looking at Tom's background, it was not surprising that he had difficulty forming a positive gay identity. He had come from a small town in the Midwest, the youngest of three sons, where the homogeneity of experience was stifling to anyone who felt out of step. His parents had both been raised in the same community and were active in the church, where his family had been members for generations. His older brothers were married with families and lived within an hour's drive of the parents. The family norm was geared toward sameness and continuity. He was the first family member to move away.

Tom's exile from the family, while self-imposed, was not challenged by any family member. While he paid ritualized visits home around holiday time, no one had ever visited him in the city where he lived. Because Tom's difference was unspoken, it could be tolerated, as long as everyone participated in the family rule regarding the avoidance of conflict. This rule was reinforced by the example of cut-offs in the extended family. For example, Tom's father had a brother who didn't "fit" and hadn't been heard from in years.

When Tom moved away from home after college, he assumed he would magically find his place; however, his own ambivalence about expressing his sexuality held him back. In his mind, it seemed that once his sexuality was fully expressed he could never go "home" again — and he wasn't sure if he would find a new home. For a long time, he used drinking as a way to handle his conflict.

Tom's therapy focused on how his sense of not belonging anywhere was preventing him from leading an authentic life. Critical to that sense of not belonging was his own lack of acceptance of himself and the difficulty he was having forming an identity that would allow him to have a full life whether single or in a relationship. As a way to explore his identity, participation in gay groups, both political and supportive, was suggested. Tom resisted each suggestion, complaining of being ghettoized. In fact, his own internalized homophobia was forcing him into a constricted life.

Nevertheless, maintaining his sobriety convinced Tom that he could begin to take charge of his life. Building from this, he began to confront how society's homophobia and heterosexism had drastically cramped his life, and to plot ways to escape from their hold on him. As he began to take charge of this process, the issue of whether a gay therapist might be a better co-conspirator became relevant. He realized that switching to a gay therapist would be a major step in validating himself. This phase of his therapy ended as Tom transferred to a gay therapist.

VALERIE: HAVING A CHILD

Valerie, age 45, called requesting family therapy, although she wasn't sure she could get the family members to come to therapy. She had just informed her family that she was planning to have a baby through artificial insemination, and the negative reaction of her sister and mother had hurt her. She felt some urgency about the family meeting because she wanted to confront them about what she saw as a resurgence of their homophobia before the baby came. Because the intensity of her own anger had likely already scared them off, she agreed to come for a few sessions to prepare for a family meeting.

Valerie had been single for most of her adult life. She had come out to her parents, both liberals and nonreligious Jews, in the late 1960s. They had understood and accepted her homosexualty as part of the general rebelliousness of the times, secretly hoping that time and perhaps the "right" man would change her mind. In her twenties and thirties, her job as an international journalist became the primary focus of her life. It kept her out of the country for significant periods of time. When her single status came up with relatives and friends, her parents would point to her career success. She had always suspected that the absence of long-term relationships in her life had made it easier for her parents to tolerate her lesbian identity, because they had never had to integrate a "partner" into their system. In this family, being single was a step up from being a lesbian.

The older of two girls in middle-class family, Valerie had always had a special closeness with her father, who had passed away the previous year. He had been particularly supportive of her career and her adventuresome spirit, which took her on treks around the world. Her sister's life had mirrored her mother's suburban life, filled with caring for children. The dissimilarity between her life and her mother's had kept them distant. Valerie had felt removed from her sister's children, not only because she was not around much, but also because she felt out of the "club" of parenthood when she was around family.

When she was traveling, she often wished she was in a relationship, but she never quite found time for the commitment it required. She had also valued her freedom and work far more than the demands and comfort of a settled relationship. Not being in a relationship, she never imagined raising a child.

By age 40, however, her nomadic, workaholic life had taken its toll and become less appealing. She found a state side job that allowed her to switch her journalistic focus to an area that made far fewer demands on her time.

Her own desire to have a child took her by surprise when she articulated it to herself in her early forties. She had adjusted to living in one place, had developed a decent social life, but felt there was one area in her life that she had never really given any thought to — having a child. Her father's illness and death forced her, as a death of a parent often does, to think about what she wanted to make of the rest of her life. Finding a relationship might be nice, but seemed like only one piece of the puzzle. The thought of raising a child allowed her to open parts of herself she had never explored or validated, such as nurturing others. Valerie had shared little of this desire with her sister or mother because their experience of motherhood seemed so different from what hers was likely to be. She had a number of lesbian friends, single and in couples, who had biologic and adopted children, and used them as a support system in making her decision.

Valerie was furious with her sister and mother over their negative reaction to her decision to have a child. She felt the message from the family was that she could be gay, she could be single, but only if she stayed in the little box of acceptability, which did not advertise her situation. Having a child would certainly expose her lack of a partner. Her sexuality might also become more public. Despite her anger, she was not willing to write her family off. She wanted her child to have a connection to a grandmother, an aunt and uncle, and cousins as well.

Using a life cycle frame, Valerie began to track how her own feelings regarding her lesbianism, her singleness, and her connection to her family had evolved over the years. Indeed, she believed that the idea of having a child at midlife only emerged after she had evolved a strong identity for herself in the outside world. Both her lesbianism and singleness, however, had forestalled the development of a more mature identity in the family. Because Valerie kept her life so separate, her parents and sister had frozen their the image of her in a young adult, experimental phase. She could see that her wanting a child challenged that notion of who she was in the family and pushed her mother in particular to rework her feelings about having a daughter who was a lesbian. She also realized that by having a child she might be encroaching on her sister's territory and closeness with their mother. Because she had chosen such a different life path from her mother and sister, she had never taken the trouble to discern which apsects of their lives she could relate to and admire.

Because Valerie had let the relationships with her family become pro forma over the years, she did not have a bond strong enough to withstand a confrontation over their reaction to her choice as a lesbian to have a child.

Her first task, then, was to find ways to build her connection to her sister and mother. She decided to approach them with an eye toward learning more about their lives as mothers. With her sister, she began with the basics of just spending some relationship time and getting to know her children. They slowly began to build a relationship. She felt much less successful with her mother. Every time she approached the subject of motherhood, her mother would either change the subject or talk about her sister's children.

Feeling she was getting nowhere, she again asked her mother if she would join her in therapy. Because Valerie was much calmer, this time her mother was more receptive. Valerie's goal for the session was to broach the issue of her homosexuality, something she felt had never been truly aired in the family. In the course of the session, it was clear that her parents had tolerated her lesbianism only by viewing it as phase. Valerie's decision to have a child now brought home to mother the reality of her daughter's life.

Her mother also discussed how at other points in her life, when her husband was alive, she had less difficulty with her daughter being different. Now she was more involved with and dependent on friends for her social life. Exposing this aspect of her life was very uncomfortable. Even Valerie's choice to be artificially inseminated was distasteful to the mother. If she wanted a child so badly, couldn't she at least find some guy, any guy, to have a baby with? She had even wondered at times if Valerie was a lesbian because she was unsuccessful in relationships with men. Wasn't that something she could fix in therapy?

Valerie was clear with her mother that she did not need "to be fixed." The session was the first time she had tried to describe to her mother what it meant for her to be lesbian and that it was a positive experience, except for dealing with the homophobia and heterosexism of the culture. She also did not disguise the loneliness she had felt at times and how she often wished for a long-term relationship (with a woman) like her parents'. She even imagined it would probably be easier to raise a child with two parents, even if they were both women. She was not willing, however, to postpone any longer doing what she wanted in her life.

Valerie and her mother talking about relationships was, to some extent, like two people talking about apples and oranges. Differences in generation, marital status, and sexual preference had conspired to keep them distant and often confused about each other's lives. If Valerie had chosen to keep her lesbianism closeted when she decided to have a child, a grandchild could have possibly been the bridge for mother and daughter to connect more comfortably. However, Valerie was not willing to let a grandchild become the focus of her relationship with her mother. Inviting her mother into therapy to talk about her homosexuality was the first step of many in an ongoing discussion regarding their differences and their points of connection that would eventually lead to a fuller relationship.

Epilogue

FROM THE "Metropolitan Diary" of *The New York Times*, November 23, 1994: Overheard by William Pordy at a downtown watering hole: three 30-ish executive types discussing the advent of therapy in the 90's.

WOMAN 1:   I just started going back to my therapist.
WOMAN 2:   Why had you stopped?
WOMAN 1:   She just turned into my mother.
MAN: That's what's supposed to happen. It's called transference.
WOMAN 1:   No, no, you just don't understand. She used to say things like: "What's wrong with him?" "You're not getting any younger." "No one's perfect." Therapy got so stressful, I started calling my mother for relief.

To be single in a married world is to be out of step with the prevailing definition of what constitutes a meaningful life. In this book, we have looked at the way meaning regarding marital status has been imposed by society, our culture, and our families. As therapists, we must also remain aware of the way the "helping process" can become infected by the ideas of the surrounding milieu regarding the normalcy of marriage and pathology of singlehood. The single person continues to be viewed as disabled or at least disadvantaged in our culture. Unlike other "disabilities," however, the single state is frequently viewed as being correctable — with a little work a single person can become "normal" by marriage.

When marriage is held as the ideal by society, culture, family, and the mental health establishment, how far can any individual move toward elevating other definitions of self? Clients vary in their ability and desire to evolve personal meaning in the face of social stigma. Perhaps those who pride themselves on being different — on charting their own course — have an advantage. For the majority of us, however, personal change is difficult without a receptive social context. We firmly believe that for any major change to occur there has to be greater societal tolerance and respect for the diversity of people's lives.

Having said that, we also believe that the therapeutic context can help start the process moving. Following the thinking of Michael White and David Epston (1990), we suggest that when therapist and client take a step back from the "truths" of the dominant story regarding marital status, alternative versions of a client's life may emerge. These versions may give value to the experience of the present, the single person's experience of life as it is actually lived. Taking a step back is often a gradual process, where therapist and client bit by bit deconstruct the surrounding belief systems that maintain the negative perception of the single self. This has been at the core of our work with single people.

We also want to emphasize that in this process of defining other versions of a fulfilled life, we are not trying to elevate the single life over marriage, but, rather, to put them on an even par. It does no one any good to romanticize singlehood — or marriage for that matter. In our experience, the majority of people would choose to be in a good marriage over being single. Our job as therapists is not to argue them out of that but to help them stop postponing their lives. As in Susan's case, when she finally could accept that she might not ever marry, she started taking care of the things she wanted in her life (like having a child). While Lina remained frustrated about not marrying, she did stop romanticizing married life and validated the life she had. When single persons can find meaning in life as it is currently lived, whether marriage is in the future or not, they stop cooperating with the imposition of meaning from the outside and start evolving meaning from their own lives.

References

AARP Bulletin (Dec. 1994). Vol. 35, No. 11, Washington, DC, pp. 1, 12, & 13.

Adam, B. D. (1987). *The rise of a gay and lesbian movement.* Boston: Twayne Publishers.

Adams, M. (1981). Living singly. In P. Stein (Ed.), *Single life* (pp. 221–234). New York: St. Martin's Press.

Ahrons, C. R. (1994). *The good divorce.* New York: HarperCollins.

Anderson, C. M., Stewart, S., & Dimidjian, S. (1994). *Flying solo.* New York: Norton.

Aylmer, R. C. (1989). The launching of the single adult. In B. Carter & M. McGoldrick (Eds.), *The changing family life cycle: A framework for family therapy* (2nd ed., pp. 191–208). Boston: Allyn & Bacon.

Bergquist, W. H., Greenberg, E. M., & Klaum, G. A. (1993). *In our fifties: Voices of men and women reinventing their lives.* San Francisco: Jossey-Bass.

Bernard, J. (1982). *The future of marriage.* New Haven, CT: Yale University Press.

Berzon, B. (1988). *Permanent partners.* New York: Penguin.

Birren, J. E. (1983). Aging in America: Roles for psychology. *American Psychologist, 38,* 298–299.

Bowen, M. (1978). *Family theory in clinical practice.* New York: Jason Aronson.

Boyd-Franklin, N. (1989). *Black families in therapy: A multisystems approach.* New York: Guilford.

Brodbar-Nemzer, J. Y. (1986). Jewish marital relationships and self-esteem. *Journal of Marriage and the Family, 48,* 89–98.

Brown, H. (1962). *Sex and the single girl.* New York: Simon & Schuster.

Brown, B. B. (1981). The relation of age to friendship. In H. Z. Lopata & D. Maines (Eds.), *Research on the interweave of social roles* (vol. 2). Greenwich, CT: JAI Press.

Bureau of the Census. (1992). *Marital status and living arrangements: 1991.* Washington, DC: U.S. Government Printing Office.

Carl, D.(1990). *Counseling same-sex couples.* New York: Norton.

Carlsen, M. B. (1991). *Creative aging.* New York: Norton.

Carter, B. (1994). *Clincial dilemmas in marriage: The search for equal partnership* [Videotape]. (Available from Equal Partners Productions. Topeka, KS)

Carter, B., & McGoldrick Orfanidis, M. (1976). Family therapy with one person and the family therapist's own family. In P. J. Guerin (Ed.), *Family therapy* (pp. 193–219). New York: Gardner Press.

Carter, B., & McGoldrick, M. (1989). *The changing family life cycle: A framework for family therapy* (2nd ed.). Boston: Allyn & Bacon.

Cass, V. (1979). Homosexual identity formation: A theoretical model. *Journal of Homosexuality, 4* (3), Spring, 219–235.

Clark, D. (1977). *Loving someone gay.* Millbrae, CA: Celestial Arts.

Cockrum, J. S. (1983). *Gender differences between never-married adults: Sociodemographic, psychological and social support factors.* Unpublished doctoral dissertation, University of Tennessee, Knoxville.

Cole, J. B. (1995). Commonalities and differences. In M. L. Anderson & P. H. Collins (Eds.), *Race, class, gender: An anthology* (2nd ed., pp. 148–154). Belmont CA: Wadsworth.

Combrinck-Graham, L. (1985). A developmental model for family systems. *Family Process, 24,* 139–150.

Conner, K., Powers, E. A., & Bultena, G. L. (1979). Social interaction and life satisfaction: An empirical assessment of late-life patterns. *Journal of Gerontology, 34,* 116–121.

Coontz, S. (1992). *The way we never were.* New York: Basic Books.

Cramer D., & Roach, A. (1988). Coming out to mom and dad: A study of gay males and their relationships with their parents. *Journal of Homosexuality, 15* (3/4), 79–91.

Dalheimer, D., & Feigal, J. (1991, Jan/Feb). Bridging the gap. *Networker,* 44–53.

Dunne, E. (1993). *Single adults.* Paper presented at The Family Institute of Westchester, Mt. Vernon, New York.

Duvall, E. M. (1977). *Marriage and family development* (5th ed.). Philadelphia: Lippincott.

Ehrenreich, B. (1983). *The hearts of men.* New York: Anchor Books.

Ehrenreich, B., & English, D. (1978). *For her own good.* New York: Doubleday.

Eisler, B. (1986). *Private lives.* New York: Franklin Watts.

Erikson, E. (1950). *Childhood and society.* New York: Norton.

Erikson, E. H. (1968). *Identity, youth and crisis.* New York: Norton.

Erikson, E. (1982). *The life cycle completed.* New York: Norton.

Erikson, E., Erikson, J., & Kivnick, H. (1986). *Vital involvement in old age.* New York: Norton.

Essex, M. J., & Nam, S. (1987). Marital status and loneliness among older women: The differential importance of close family and friends. *Journal of Marriage and the Family, 49,* 93–106.

Falicov, C. J. (1988). *Family transitions: Continuity and change over the life cycle.* New York: Guilford.

Faludi, S. (1991). *Backlash.* New York: Crown.

Farber, B., Mindel, C. H., & Lazerwitz, B. (1988). The Jewish American family. In C. Mindel, R. W. Habenstein, & R. Wright, Jr. (Eds.), *Ethnic families in America: Patterns and variations* (3rd ed., pp. 400–437). New York: Elsevier.

Franklin, J. H. (1988). A historical note on Black famlies. In H. P. McAdoo (Ed.), *Black families* (2nd ed., pp. 23–26). Newbury Park, CA: Sage Publications.

Friedan, B. (1963). *The feminine mystique.* New York: Norton.

Friedman, E. (1982). The myth of the shiksa. In M. McGoldrick, J. K. Pierce, & J. Giordano (Eds.), *Ethnicity and family therapy* (pp. 499–526). New York: Guilford.

Friend, R. A. (1987). The individual social psychology of aging: clinical implications for lesbians and gay men. *Journal of Homosexuality, 14* (1/2), 307–331.

Gans, H. (1962). *The urban villagers.* Glencoe, IL: Free Press.

Gans, H. J. (1979). Symbolic ethnicity: The future of ethnic groups and cultures. *Ethnic and Racial Studies, 2,* 1–20.

Garcia Preto, N. (1982). Puerto Rican families. In M. McGoldrick, J. K. Pierce, J. Giordano (Eds.), *Ethnicity and family therapy* (pp. 164–186). New York: Guilford.

Gilligan, C. (1982). *In a different voice.* Cambridge, MA: Harvard University Press.

Glick, P. C. (1984). Marriage, divorce, and living arrangements. *Journal of Social Issues, 5,* 7–26.

Goodrich, T. (1991). *Women and power.* New York: Norton.

Gordon, B., & Meth, R. (1990). Men as husbands. In R. Meth & R. Pasick (Eds.), *Men in therapy: The challenge of change* (pp. 54–87). New York: Guilford.

Griffin, C., Wirth, M., & Wirth, A. (1986). *Beyond acceptance.* Englewood Cliffs NJ: Prentice-Hall.

Haley, J. (1973). *Uncommon therapy: The psychiatric techniques of Milton H. Erickson.* New York: Norton.

Hammersmith, S. (1987). A sociological approach to counseling homosexual clients and their families. *Journal of Homosexuality, 14* (1/2), 173–190.

Heiss, J. (1988). Women's values regarding marriage and the family. In H. P. McAdoo (Ed.), *Black families* (2nd ed., pp. 201–214). Newbury Park, CA: Sage Publications.

Herz, F. M., & Rosen, E. J. (1982). Jewish families. In M. McGoldrick, J. K. Pierce, & J. Giordano (Eds.), *Ethnicity and family therapy* (pp. 364–392). New York: Guilford.

Herz Brown, F. (1989). The post divorce family. In B. Carter & M. McGoldrick (Eds.), *The changing family life cycle: A framework for family therapy* (2nd ed., pp. 371–398). Boston: Allyn & Bacon.

Herz Brown, F. (1991). *Reweaving the family tapestry: A multigenerational approach to families.* New York: Norton.

Hicks, S., & Anderson, C. M. (1989). Women on their own. In M. McGoldrick, C. M. Anderson, & F. Walsh (Eds.), *Women in families: A framework for family therapy* (pp. 308–334). New York: Norton.

Higginbotham, E., & Weber, L. (1995). Moving up with kin and community: Upward social mobility for black and white women. In M. L. Anderson & P. H. Collins (Eds.), *Race, class, & gender: An anthology* (2nd ed., pp. 134–147). Belmont, CA: Wadsworth.

Hill, R., & Rodgers, R. (1964). The developmental approach. In H. Christensen (Ed.), *Handbook of marriage and the family.* Chicago: Rand McNally.

Hill, R. (1971). Modern systems theory and the family: A confrontation. *Social Science Information, 10,* 7–26.

Hochschild, A., & Machung, A. (1989). *The second shift: Working parents and the revolution at home.* New York: Viking.

Hoffman, L. (1989). The family life cycle and discontinuous change. In B. Carter & M. McGoldrick (Eds.), *The changing family life cycle: A framework for family therapy* (2nd ed., pp. 91–106). Boston: Allyn & Bacon.

Holder, D. P., & Anderson, C. M. (1989). Women, work, and the family. In M. McGoldrick, C. M. Anderson, & F. Walsh (Eds.), *Women in families: A framework for family therapy* (pp. 357–380). New York: Norton.

Holland, B. (1992). *One's Company.* New York: Ballantine.

Holloway, L. (1993, August 16). What? No Husband? *The New York Times,* pp. B1, B5.

Jacob, D. (1991). Families in later life. In F. Herz Brown (Ed.), *Reweaving the family tapestry* (pp. 169–188). New York: Norton.

Jacoby, S. (1974, February 17). 49 million singles can't all be right. *The New York Times Magazine,* pp. 41–46.

Kegan, R. (1982). *The evolving self.* Cambridge MA: Harvard University Press.

Keith, P. M. (1989). *The unmarried in later life.* New York: Praeger.

Kerr, M., & Bowen, M. (1988). *Family evaluation: An approach based on bowen theory.* New York: Norton.

Kitano, H. H. (1988). The Japanese American family. In C. H. Mindel, R. W. Habenstein, & R. Wright, Jr. (Eds.), *Ethnic families in America: Patterns and variations* (3rd ed., pp. 258–275). New York: Elsevier.

Klinkenberg, D., & Rose, S. (1994). Dating scripts of gay men and lesbians. *Journal of Homosexuality, 26* (4), 23–35.

Kochman, A. (1994). *The lesbian and gay elderly.* Unpublished paper available from S.A.G.E., New York.

Krestan, J. (1988). Lesbian daughters and lesbian mothers: The crisis of disclosure. *Journal of Psychotherapy and the Family, 3* (7), 113–130.

Krout, J. A. (1986). *The aged in rural America.* Westport, CT: Greenwood Press.

Lang, S. (1991). *Women without children.* New York: Pharos.

Lawson, C. (1993, August 5). Single but Mothers by Choice: "Who is my Daddy?" can be answered in different ways. *The New York Times,* p. C1.

Lehne, G. (1976). Homophobia among men. In R. Brannon & D. David (Eds.), *The forty-nine percent majority: The male sex* (pp. 66–68). Reading, MA: Addison-Wesley.

Lever, J. (1994, August). Sexual revelations. *The Advocate,* 15-24.

Levinson, D. (1978). *The seasons of a man's life.* New York: Ballantine Books.

Lucco, A. J. (1987). Planned retirement housing preferences of older homosexuals. *Journal of Homosexuality, 14* (3/4), 35-36.

Manchester, W. (1973). *The glory and the dream. A narrative history of America 1932-1972.* New York: Bantam.

Manuel, R. (1982). *Minority aging.* Westport, CT: Greenwood Press.

Martin, A. (1993). *The lesbian and gay parenting handbook: Creating and raising our families.* New York: Harper Perennial.

May, E. (1988). *Homeword bound: American families in the cold war era.* New York: Basic Books.

McDonald, H., & Steinhorn, A. (1990) *Homosexuality: A practical guide to counseling lesbians, gay men and their families.* New York: Continuum.

McGill, D., & Pierce, K. (1982). British Families. In M. McGoldrick, J. K. Pierce, & J. Giordano (Eds.), *Ethnicity and family therapy* (pp. 457-482). New York: Guilford.

McGoldrick, M., Pearce, J. K., & Giordano, J. (Eds.) (1982). *Ethnicity and family therapy.* New York: Guilford.

McGoldrick, M., & Rohrbaugh, M. (1987). Researching ethnic family stereotypes. *Family Process, 26,* 89-99.

McGoldrick, M., & Carter, B. (1989). Forming a remarried family. In B. Carter, M. McGoldrick (Eds.), *The changing family life cycle* (2nd ed., pp. 399-429). Boston: Allyn & Bacon.

McGoldrick, M., Anderson, C. M., & Walsh, F. (Eds.) (1989). *Women in families: A framework for family therapy.* New York: Norton.

McGoldrick, M., Garcia-Preto, N., Hines, P. M., & Lee, E. (1989). Ethnicity and women. In M. McGoldrick, C. M. Anderson, & F. Walsh (Eds.), *Women in families: A framework for family therapy* (pp. 169-199). New York: Norton.

Meth, R. (1990a). Men and sexuality. In R. Meth & R. Pasick (Eds.), *Men in therapy: The challenge of change* (pp. 209-223). New York: Guilford.

Meth, R. (1990b). The road to masculinity. In R. Meth & R. Pasick (Eds.), *Men in therapy: The challenge of change* (pp. 3-34).

Meth, R., & Pasick, R. (1990). *Men in therapy.* New York: Guilford.

Michener, J. (1993, January 11). After the war: The victories at home. *Newsweek, 2,* 26-27.

Mindel, C. H., Habenstein, R. W., & Wright, R. (1988). *Ethnic families in America: Patterns and variations* (3rd ed.). New York: Elsevier.

Mindel, C., & Wright, R. (1982). Differential living arrangements among the elderly and their subjective well-being. *Activities, Adaptation, and Aging, 3* (2), 25-34.

Mishel, L., & Frankel, D. (1991). *The state of working America.* (Armonk, NY: M. E. Sharpe.)

Nichols, M. (1989). Sex therapy with lesbian, gay men, and bisexuals. In S. Leiblum & R. Rosen (Eds.), *Principles and practice of sex therapy* (pp. 269-297). New York: Guilford.

Pasick, R. (1990). Friendships between men. In R. Meth & R. Pasick (Eds.), *Men in therapy: The challenge of change* (pp. 108-127). New York: Guilford.

Peplau, L., Bikson, T. K., Rook, K. S., & Goodchilds, J. D. (1982). Being old and living alone. In L. Peplau & D. Perlman (Eds.), *Lonelinesss: A sourcebook of current theory, research, and therapy.* New York: Wiley.

Popenjoe, P. (1968). Mate selection. In T. Judsen & M. Glandis (Eds.), *Building a successful marriage* (p. 48). Englewood Cliffs, NJ: Prentice-Hall.

Ragucci, A. T. (1981). Italian Americans. In A. Hargood (Ed.), *Ethnicity and medical care.* Cambridge, MA: Harvard University Press.

Rosenheck, S. (1992). *Sex therapy with difficult couples.* Paper presented at the Ackerman Institute for Family Therapy. New York.

Rotunno, M., & McGoldrick, M. (1982). Italian families. In M. McGoldrick, J. K. Pierce, & J. Giordano (Eds.), *Ethnicity and family therapy* (pp. 340-363). New York: Guilford.

Roybal, J. (1988). Mental health and aging. *American Psychologist, 43* (3), 189-194.

Rubenstein, C. M., & Shaver, P. (1982). The experience of loneliness. In L. Peplau, & D. Perlman (Eds.), *Loneliness: A sourcebook of current theory, research, and therapy.* New York: Wiley.

Rubenstein, R. (1986). *Singular paths: Old men living alone.* New York: Columbia University Press.

Scallon, R. (1982). *An investigation of paternal attitudes and behavior in homosexual and heterosexual fathers.* Unpublished doctoral dissertation, California School of Professional Psychology, Los Angeles.

Schaie, K. W., & Willis, S. L. (1986). *Adult development and aging.* Boston: Little, Brown.

Scherz, F. H. (1971). Maturational crisis and parent-child interaction. *Social Casework, 52,* 363–369.

Schnarch, D. (1992). *Constructing the sexual crucible.* New York: Norton.

Schoofs, M. (1994, August). Love stories in the age of AIDS. *The Village Voice,* pp. 21–28.

Schwartzberg, N. (1991). Single young adults. In F. Herz Brown (Ed.), *Reweaving the family tapestry* (pp. 77–93). New York: Norton.

Shapiro, E. (1988). Individual change and family development. In C. Falicov (Ed.), *Family transitions* (pp. 159–180). New York: Guilford.

Shon, S. P., & Ja, D. Y. (1982). Asian families. In M. McGoldrick, J. K. Pierce, & J. Giordano (Eds.), *Ethnicity and family therapy* (pp. 208–228). New York: Guilford.

Silverstein, B., & Hyman, H. (1982). *You and your aging parent.* New York: Pantheon.

Silverstein, C. (1991). Psychotherapy and psychotherapists: A history. In C. Silverstein (Ed.), *Gays, lesbians, and their therapists* (pp. 1–14). New York: Norton.

Simon, B. L. (1987). *Never married women.* Philadelphia: Temple University Press.

Simon, R. M. (1989). Family life cycle issues in the therapy system. In B. Carter & M. McGoldrick (Eds.), *The changing family life cycle: A framework for family therapy* (2nd ed., pp. 107–108). Boston: Allyn & Bacon.

Simpson, R. (1976). *From the closet to the courts: The lesbian transition.* New York: Viking.

Solomon, M. (1973). A developmental conceptual premise for family therapy. *Family Process, 12,* 179–188.

Spordone, A. (1993). *Gay men choosing fatherhood.* Unpublished doctoral dissertation, City University of New York, New York.

Staples, R. (1988). An overview of race and marital status. In H. P. McAdoo (Ed.), *Black Families* (2nd ed., pp. 187–189). Newbury Park, CA: Sage Publications.

Staples, R., & Johnson, L. B. (1993). *Black families at the crossroads: Challenges and prospects.* San Francisco: Jossey-Bass.

Stein, P. (1981). Understanding single adulthood. In P. Stein (Ed.), *Single life: Unmarried adults in social contexts* (pp. 9–20). New York: St. Martin's Press.

Steinberg, S. (1989). *The ethnic myth: Race, ethnicity, and class in America.* Boston: Beacon Press.

Stoller, R. (1964). A contribution to the study of gender identity. *International Journal of Psycho-Analysis, 45,* 220–226.

Szapocznik, J., & Kurtines, W. M. (1993). Family psychology and cultural diversity: Opportunities for theory, research, and application. *American Psychologist, April,* 400–407.

Taylor, E. (1989). *Prime time families.* Berkeley, CA: University of California Press.

Tischler, B. (1989). Voices of protest. In B. Tischler (Ed.), *Sights on the sixties* (pp. 197–209). New York: Penguin.

Van Horn, S. (1988). *Women, work, and fertility, 1900 to 1986.* New York: New York University Press.

Walters, M., Carter, B., Papp, P., & Silverstein, O. (1988). *The invisible web.* New York: Guilford.

Weston, K. (1991). *Families we choose.* New York: Columbia University Press.

White, M., & Epston, D. (1990). *Narrative means to therapeutic ends.* New York: Norton.

Whitman, D. (1990, October 15). The rise of the hyper poor. *U.S. News and World Report,* 40–42.

Williams, L. (1994, May 29). Childless workers demand equality in the corporate world. *The New York Times,* pp. A1, A22.

Wolf, T. (1987). *Bonfire of the vanities.* New York: Farrar, Straus, & Giroux.

Zinn, M., & Eitzen, S. (1987). *Diversity in American families.* New York: Harper & Row.

Zollar, A.C., & Williams, J. S. (1987). Marriage and life satisfaction of Black adults. *Journal of Marriage and the Family, 49,* 87–92.

Index

acceptance
  of a homosexual identity, 133
  of one's own life, 122–24
Adam, B. D., 25, 127, 128, 129, 130
Adams, M., 76, 77
addiction, three-generational perspectives
  on, 150, *see also* alcoholism
adulthood
  pathways to, 44–46
  young, 58–68
adult role
  establishing with extended family, 97–98
  establishing with parents, 96–97
affiliation, as a goal for women, 64–67, 69–
  81
African-American communities
  changes in circumstances, 1970s, 21
  cultural context of, 38
  economic realities and expectations of mar-
    riage, 45
  homosexuality in, 138
  impact of economic instability of the
    1970s, 20
  meanings of marriage in, 42–43
ageism, defined, 117–24
age spans
  failing health to death, 117–24
  fifties to failing health, 99–116
  forties to mid-fifties, 82–98
  the thirties, 69–81
  young adulthood, 58–68
Ahrons, C. R., 25
AIDS
  and the gay rights movement, 129
  impact on dating behavior, 79–80, 129
  impact on gender roles, 135
  routine test for, 208
Alcoholics Anonymous, 210
alcoholism
  in the homosexual population, 130
    Tom, 210
alienation
  felt by singles, in the 1990s, 26–27
  singles industry responding to, 20
alternative scripts, 82–98, 216
  achieving through children, 122
American dream, the, 13–16
American Psychiatric Association, on homosexuality, 129
Anderson, C. M., 5, 7, 91, 95, 96, 102
anger, social, expressed in comedies of the
  1970s, 23–24
anxiety
  activation of a triangle resulting from, 33
  consulting a therapist about, 60–61
  about controlling money, 178–79
  in the emotional system of the family, 35–
    37
  family, over a woman outside a two-
    person relationship, 195
  in the gay community, engendered by
    AIDS, 129
  about getting married, 59–60
  heightening, with an unreactive client,
    183–84
  about managing same-sex relationships,
    203–4
  in the young adult period, 59

articulation, of the adult self in the family system, 71–74
authenticity
    defined, for a single adult, 90–96
    for a gay in the thirties, 211
    in homosexual identity, 138–39
autonomy
    as a goal for men, 64–67
    in a Korean family, 76–77
    struggle for, negotiation in the family, 203–4
    using in the retirement years, 115–16
    and a wish for children, 168–69
    work towards in the thirties, 170–72
Aylmer, R. C., 53, 61, 63, 64

backlash, to the Women's Movement, 19
belief systems, family versus personal, 153
Bergquist, W. J., 99
Bernard, J., 8, 21, 87, 88
Berzon, B., 36, 131
Bikson, T. K., 120
biological issues
    confronting mortality, 119–22
    in the timing of marriage, 9
Birren, J. E., 118
birth control methods, and the sexual revolution, 19
black community, see African-American communities
blame
    for singlehood, 9
blueprint, lack of, for single adults, 5
Bonfire of the Vanities, 25
boundaries
    between the family and the rest of the world, 39
        vignette, 40–41
    marriage as a means of setting, 35–36
    marriage as a ritual for making, 7–8
Bowen, M., 11, 31, 32, 33, 34, 36, 66
Boyd-Franklin, N., 31, 45, 46
Brodbar-Nemzer, J. Y., 44
Brown, B. B., 120
Brown, H., 20
Bultena, G. L., 120
Bush, Barbara, 14

career
    developing, 65
    and gender expectations, 8–9
    meaning of, in the forties, 89–90
    reevaluation of goals in the thirties, 69, 77
    and singlehood, 4
        for homosexuals, 141–42, 211
    stress of, resolving, 179

Carl, D., 128, 129, 133, 141
Carlsen, M. B., 117, 118
Carter, B., 7, 11, 23, 31, 32, 35, 36, 52, 53, 54, 55, 57, 82, 100, 118, 134, 137, 138, 139, 152, 153, 154
Cass, V., 132, 133
Cather, Willa, 28
celebrations, centered around family, 9
change
    versus awareness of a need for change, 62
    in family expectations about marriage of children, 30–31
    in an individual's culture over time, 37–38
    need for a receptive social context for, 216
    in relationships, and reorganization of the self, 63
    in social expectations about marriage for women, 23
    and stress, 55
    of work in midlife, 90
childlessness
    feelings about, in women in their forties, 86
    issue of, 81
    and satisfaction in the elderly years, 120
children
    birthrate of the 1970s, 23
    desire for, 170–71
        and a partnered relationship, 10–11
        by homosexuals, 142–43
        outside a partnered relationship, 80–81, 212–14
    effect on the emotional tasks of the family, and the life cycle, 53
    living with, in the elderly phase, 120
church communities, sensitivity to the needs of single people in, 28
Clark, D., 130
class
    emphasis on, in the 1980s, 24–26
    and homosexual dating patterns, 128
    and inclusion of singles as family, 83
    interaction with ethnicity in influencing values and identity, 37–38
coaching, of homosexuals, in therapy, 138
Cockrum, J. S., 100
Cole, J. B., 38
Colucci, Pat, 135
Combrinck-Graham, L., 53, 55
coming out, in the seventies, 128
communication, in the elderly phase, 123–24
community, search for, by homosexuals, 136
companionship, in the later years, 104
competence, defined for daughters in terms of service and marriage, 35

conflict
    family rule for avoiding, 211
    and fusion, 34
conformity, in American society, in the
        1950s, 16
connectedness
    Lina, in later life, 197–98
    to self, 180
connections
    with family, for a lesbian, 214
    with future generations, 92
    of gays and lesbians with other single peo-
        ple, 127–28
    through a long-term commitment, for ho-
        mosexuals, 141
    spiritual, 182
Conner, K., 120
consensus, and fusion, 34
consumerism
    and the need for two wages to support a
        family, 18
    portrayal in the popular culture, 1950s, 15
context
    of a life story, 123
    Lina, therapy in later life, 188–89
    social
        in the middle years, 174
        for personal change, 216
        and self-definition, ix–x
    sociocultural, and life cycles, 52
    see also historic context; multigenerational
        context
continuity, as a function of marriage, 39
    in Jewish families, 43–44
Coontz, S., 14, 15, 16, 17, 18, 19, 20, 24, 25,
        58, 128
couples culture, and the single adult, 13–29
Cramer, D., 140
culture
    broad issues of, informing therapy, 11
    context of therapist and of client, 9–10
    couples, 13–29
    dominant, relationships of ethnic or racial
        groups with, 47–48
    expectation about age of marriage, 59–60
    and family, 30–48
    of immigrant families, 47–48
    issues of ethnicity and race, 37–39
    polls on popular view of singles, 1950s, 16
    popular, failure to reflect social diversity,
        15
    Puerto Rican expectations about manli-
        ness, 207
    tolerance towards homosexuality in, 138,
        206–9
    see also ethnicity; race

cut-offs
    effect on homosexuals, 136
    effect on triangles, 33
    for enforcing family rules about conflict,
        211
    by siblings, Lina in later life, 192, 198–99
    by young adults
        in a lesbian relationship, 202–6
        and family relationships, 60
cynicism
    of the 1960s, 19
    of the 1980s, 25

Dalheimer, D., 126
dating
    impact of AIDS on, 129
    process for homosexuals, 131, 135
    structure of, 22
Daughters of Bilitis, 128
dependency, in marriage, 164–65
depression
    attributing to biochemistry, 200
    attributing to career choice, 4
    attributing to singlehood, 3, 158,
        203
    in singlehood, 174
    for a gay, 210
development, stages of, 53–55
    Lina in later life, 189–90
    see also age spans
developmental drivers, for single adults, 53–
        54
developmental tasks
    in home and family, popularized psycho-
        logical material, 15
    in the thirties, 158–59, 210–11
deviance
    in the 1980s, 25
    singlehood as, 5, 7
        exaggeration in the forties, 83
        for women, 16
Diamond, R., 80
differences, tolerating within the family, 63,
        206
differentiation, 33–34
    and life cycle, 55–57
    of self, by adults, 54
    work of, for homosexuals, 137
Dimidjian, S., 91, 95, 96, 102
disequilibrium, as an opportunity for renego-
        tiation, 54
dissatisfaction, social and cultural, in the
        1950s, 16
divorce, 173
divorce rate, 5
    in the 1970s, 22

dominant story, about marital status, 216
double standard, in sexual mores, 16
dropping out, of middle-class lives, 19
duality, in emotional processes, the fifties to
    failing health, 99
Dunne, E., 127, 128
Duvall, E. M., 52, 53

economic opportunities
    in the 1980s, and backlash against destruc-
        tion of the American family, 25
    declining, in the 1970s, 20–24
    earnings of single women, 7
    and living alone in the elderly phase, 119–
        20
    and marriage as adulthood, 45
    restrictions on choices for older adults,
        101
    for women
        view from the thirties, 69, 74
        and view of marriage, 5
education
    and marriage, in the 1950s, 14
    valuing of, in Japanese families, 48
Ehrenreich, B., 14, 15, 16, 18, 22, 64
Eisler, B., 14
Eitzen, S., 20
emotional crisis, on asserting homosexuality
    to the family of origin, 137–38
emotional development, in the elderly, 118–
    19
emotional links
    of gays and lesbians, 127–28
    through sharing possession before death,
        122
emotional system, family, 32, 166, 180
    role of anxiety in, 35–37
    see also family system
emotional tasks
    critical, in the homosexual's life span, 131–
        32
    of the young adult, 60
English, D., 15, 16, 18
enmeshment, of women in a family, Lina in
    later life, 192
Epston, D., 71, 216
Erikson, E. H., 118, 119, 122
Erikson, J., 118
Essex, M. J., 110, 115, 120, 121
esteem, built on accomplishment, 114–15,
    see also self-esteem
ethnicity
    and career choices, 65
    and inclusion of singles as family, 83
    and Italian family's view of gender roles
        and marriage, 40–41

evaluation, personal
    in terms of cultural expectations, 13
    in terms of marital status, 4
examples
    Allan Fried, a Jewish family's view of mar-
        riage, 43–44
    Ann, the "problem" of singlehood, 3, 10
    Anna Samperi, an Italian family, 40–41
    Barbara, in the forties, 85
    Betsy, young adult issues for a lesbian,
        202–6
    Betty, planning an adventure, 115
    Bob, the twenties, 149–56
    Brian Thomas, meaning of marriage, 42–
        43
    Carrie, giving during a lifetime, 107–8
    Christine, apathy in the later years, 115–
        16
    Eamon, lifetime within the family home,
        110
    Eduardo, a gay Puerto Rican, 206–9
    Frank, willing possessions, 106–7
    George, in midlife, 173–86
    Jacques, connecting with future genera-
        tions, 93
    Jenny, proactive adult in an Italian family,
        72–74
    Joanne, the "problem" of singlehood, 3–4,
        10
    Joe, network in the forties, 88–89
    Larry, developing relationships in the thir-
        ties, 77–78
    Letitia, career in young adulthood, 65–66
    Levines, single thirties, in a Jewish family,
        72
    Lina
        later life, 187–201
        regrets of the forties, 90–91
    Lorraine Sampson, an African-American
        family, 46, 123, 124
    Lucy
        disclosing contents of a will, 107
        young adults leaving home, 60–61
    Mary
        anxiety over marriage, 61–62
        need for family in the older years, 111
    Nancy, shifting work for older adults,
        102–3
    Peter, the "problem" of singlehood, 4, 11
    Richard, culture and family, 30, 32
    Rose, connecting with future generations,
        93
    Susan, the thirties, 157–72
    Susan Yatashi, fit of an ethnic or racial
        group with the dominant culture, 47–
        48

Tom
  in a parental triangle, 32–33
  defining a single gay identity, 209–12
  Valerie, lesbian motherhood, 212–14
  Young Soon, finding satisfaction in living
    single in context of family culture,
    76–77
experts, contribution to "normalcy" in the
  1950s, 15
extended family, establishing an adult role
  with, 97–98

Falicov, C. J., 54
Faludi, S., 19, 25
family
  communication with, through mate
    choice, 6
  culture and, 30–48
  definition of, 39–41
  isolation from, 3–4, 213–14
  living with in later years, 104, 105
  as a perceived cause for singlehood, 9
  renegotiating relationships with, 61
  sense of, in the gay world, 206
  single in the world of, 7–8
  view of marriage as experienced in, 161
  see also family of choice; family of origin
family history
  George in midlife, 175–76
  Lina, immigrant from Czechoslovakia,
    190–93
  and resolution of developmental tasks, 36–
    37
Family Institute of Westchester, ix
family of choice, developing, by homosexuals, 140
family of origin
  asserting homosexuality to, 136–40
  messages about personal enjoyment from,
    116
  relationships for a single lesbian, 204–5
  therapeutic work on, 194–96
family structure, number of "mother only"
  homes in the 1980s, 25
family system
  articulation of the adult self in, 71–74
  God as a member of, 181
  and the meaning of singlehood, 11–12
  operation of, 139
  see also emotional family system
family therapy, looking at previous generations, 13
family wage system, 14
fantasy, of the "ideal" family, 84–89
Farber, B., 44
Feigal, J., 126

Feminine Mystique, The, 18
feminism, questioning of the facts of family
  life, 18, see also Women's Movement
finances
  as a male preserve, 8–9
  personal, individual responsibility for, 61
financial planning
  in the forties and fifties, 95–96
  by gay or lesbian singles, 144–45
  by an older woman, 188–89
  for women, 77
fit
  of a subgroup with the dominant culture,
    47–48
  between therapist and client, 82, 212
Flying Solo, 95
forties to mid-fifties, 82–98
Frankel, D., 24
Franklin, J. H., 42
freedom
  of older adults to shift jobs, 102
  in the retirement years, 115–16
Friedan, B., 18
Friedman, E., 6
Friend, R. A., 145
friendships
  and community ties in the elderly phase,
    121–22
  as an expansion of family, 74–75
  in the forties and fifties, 94–95
  see also relationships
fulfillment, in the thirties, 70–81
fusion
  defined, 34
  of women in a family, Lina in later life, 192
Future of Marriage, The, 21

Gans, H. J., 37
Garcia-Preto, N., 38, 66
gay and lesbian movement, 25
  effect of coming out on the family life cy-
    cle, 36
gay rights groups, 129
gender, and suicide rates in the elderly phase,
  120–21
gender roles
  basis for the traditional family in, 18
  challenges to, in the 1970s, 22
  and effects of culture, class and race, 38
  expectation that single women are caregiv-
    ers, 113
  and gender identity for homosexuals, 134–36
  in making a home, 179
  self-definition in terms of, 134–35
  training in, and expectations about mar-
    riage, 8

generational issues
  as parents age, 111–12
  connections with future generations, 92
generational solidarity, 123
Gilligan, C., 64, 69, 134
Giordano, J., 31, 38, 39, 83, 115
Glick, P. C., 5
goals
  of men and of women, 64–67
    in their thirties, 69–81
  personal, marriage as, 8–9
  primary, of families for their children, 45
  socially sanctioned, 10
Goodchilds, J. D., 120
Gordon, B., 7
government
  changing view of, in the 1960s, 18
  impacts of cutbacks by, 20–21
Greenberg, E. M., 99
Greening of America, The, 17
Griffin, C., 137

Habenstein, R. W., 39
Haley, J., 53, 55
Hammersmith, S., 144
Havinghurst, R. J., 15
health
  and age, 117
  caring for oneself physically and emotion-
    ally, 108
  and marriage
    for men, 22, 88–89
    for women, 22
  of singles approaching sixty, 100
Heiss, J., 42
Herz, F. M., 45
Herz Brown, F., 32, 96, 118, 137, 151, 153
heterosexual privilege, straight women's re-
    luctance to surrender, 128
Hetrick Martin Institute, 142
Hicks, S., 5
Higginbotham, E., 45
Hill, R., 53
Hines, P. M., 38
historic context
  the 1950s, 13–16
  the 1960s, 17–20
  the 1970s, 20–24
  the 1980s, 24–26
  the 1990s, 26–29
  of reactions to homosexuality, 127–30
Hochschild, A., 21
Hoffman, L., 55
Holder, D. P., 7
Holland, B., 28, 83, 89, 91, 114
Holloway, L., 7

home
  in midlife, 179
  ownership of, as a rite of passage, 76
homophobia
  among men, 8
  as a normal male attribute, 134
homosexual community
  culture of, 38
  issues and opportunities, 125–45
  see also singles, homosexual
homosexual movement, in the 1960s, 19
hopelessness
  and accepting the single state, 75
  and dating behavior, 165
horizontal movement in families, 34–35
  defined, 35
hosting, as an adult role, 97–98, 167
husband hunting, 85–86
Hyman, H., 117

identity
  acceptance of, by homosexuals, 133
  comparison of, by homosexuals, 132–33
  confusion about, in homosexuals, 132
  family, 192
  homosexual, development and unfolding
    of, 132–34
  pride in, by homosexuals, 133
  secret, problematic consequences of, 130
  social, and ethnicity, 37
  synthesis of, by homosexuals, 133
  tolerance for, by homosexuals, 133
  work as a source of, for men, 11
immigrants, involuntary, 191–92
independent living, and definition of the el-
    derly period, 118
individuation
  family involvement in, 63
  from a parent, 185
Integrity vs. Despair, in the last stage of life,
    119
intellectual system, role in differentiation, 34
interconnectedness, emotional, of life cycles
    of family members, 51
intimacy
  encapsulated, 92
  patchwork, 68
intimacy issues, 64
  in midlife, 91
  in the thirties, 79
involvement, lack of, and the tasks of ther-
    apy, 181
isolation
  from family and married peers, 4
  of older homosexuals, 144–45
  see also cut-offs

issues
    attachment, in the family, 151–52
    developmental, for the single adult, 53
    entrenched, suggesting triangles, 32–33
    family, and urgency to develop a perma-
        nent relationship, 150
    of intimacy, 64
        in midlife, 91
        in the thirties, 79
Italian family
    proactive response of a single in, 72–74
    view of marriage, 40–41

Ja, D. Y., 47, 48, 76
Jacob, D., 113
Jacoby, S., 87
Jewish family
    meaning of marriage to, 43–44, 72
    Susan in the thirties, 159–72
Johnson, L. B., 6, 21, 38, 42, 43
joining, and gender difference between thera-
    pist and client, 82

Kegan, R., 66
Keith, P. M., 119, 120
Kennedy, John F., 17
Kerr, M., 32, 33, 34
King, Martin Luther, 17
Kitano, H. H., 47
Kivnick, H., 118
Klaum, G. A., 99
Klinkenberg, D., 135
Korean culture, role of the individual in, 76–
    77
Krestan, J., 130, 138, 139
Krout, J. A., 120
Kurtines, W. M., 31

labor force, women in, in the 1970s, 21
Ladies Home Journal, 15–16
Lang, S., 14, 23, 58, 81, 120
Lawson, C., 80
Lazerwitz, B., 44
leaving home, as a symbolic statement, 60–
    64
Lee, E., 38
legal rights, of homosexuals, 125
Lehne, G., 8
lesbians
    dating patterns of, 135
    expanding socially defined gender roles,
        136
    see also gay and lesbian movement; sin-
        gles, homosexual
Lever, J., 135
Levinson, D., 69, 118

life cycle
    and definition of emotional tasks, 53
    differentiation and, 55–57
    family, 11–12, 31, 34–35, 52–53
    of a lesbian in the forties, 213–14
    limbo of "between families," x
    marriage as a task of, 8–9
    overview of, 51–57
    unpredictable events in, affecting stress
        around marital status, 36
life expectancy, and singlehood, 5
life satisfactions, of men and of women in
        marriage, 22
lifespan, of the homosexual single, 131–45
life story
    familial and historical context, 123
    about the single status, 9
loneliness
    importance of friendships versus families
        in lessening feelings of, 110–11
    male view of, 11
loss, three-generational perspective on, 150–
    51
love, and marriage, reforging the connec-
        tion, 91–92
Lucco, A. J., 144

McDonald, H., 130, 138
McGill, D., 152
McGoldrick, M., 7, 11, 23, 31, 32, 35, 36,
    37, 38, 39, 40, 41, 52, 53, 54, 55, 57,
    82, 83, 115, 137, 138, 139, 152, 153,
    154
Machung, A., 21
Manchester, W., 14
map, for single clients, 5
marginalization, of gays and lesbians, 125–
    26
marriage
    as a concern in the thirties, 157–72
    as a family issue, interlocking triangles as-
        sociated with, 32–33
    "his" and "hers," 21–22
    homosexuals stuck in, 128
    living with a spouse in the elderly phase,
        120
    meanings and function of, 6
        Betsy's family, 205
        cultural variants, 39–41
        example of an African-American fam-
            ily, 42–43
        gender differences in the forties, 82
        median age for, change since 1950, 58–
            68
        premium on, and women's financial sta-
            tus, 14, 27

marriage (*continued*)
   prevalence of, 58
      1950s, 14
   as a solution for young adults lacking inde-
      pendence, 63
   as a transition to adulthood, 35
   and women's physical and emotional
      health, 115
married world, place of singles in, 4–7
Martin, A., 142
Mattachine Society, 128
maturity, marriage as proof of, 1950s view,
   15–16
May, E., 15
meanings, of singlehood, shifting in therapy,
   11–12
men
   awareness of loneliness, in the thirties, 69–
      81
   burden of lifetime family financial respon-
      sibility, 14
   culturally discouraged relationships
      among, 175
   fathering by gays, 143–44
   as gatekeepers to status, 192
   goals of the young adult period, 64
   homophobia and cultural expectations, 8,
      134
   prevalence of marriage, fifties and over,
      99–100
   single
      social view of, 7
      workplace view of, 27–28
   social network of, in the forties, 87–89
   sources of identity for, 11
Meth, R., 7, 11, 77, 79, 134
Michener, J., 17
midlife crisis, and longevity, 90
milestone
   of marriage
      in Jewish families, 44
      timing of, 4, 8, 12
   of parenthood, 51
   of revealing a homosexual identity in the
      family of origin, 136–37
Miller, J. B., 134
Mindel, C. H., 39, 44, 120
minorities, economic independence in the elderly phase, 119–20
Minuchin, S., 82
Mishel, L., 24
mobility, loss of, in the elderly phase, 121–22
money, control of, as a toxic issue, 178–79,
      see also finances; financial planning
moral correctness, in the 1960s, 18
mortality, confronting, 119–22

mourning
   for the child that will never be, 86–87
   of the disability and death of loved ones,
      109–13
   of a lost relationship, 210
multigenerational context, 11
   of a family's response to disclosure of ho-
      mosexuality, 139–40
   George in midlife, 177–78
   life story in, 123

Nam, S., 110, 115, 120, 121
Narvis, Joe, 126, 127
networks
   of emotional connections outside the fam-
      ily, 67–68, 140
   extended family, in the black community,
      45
   friendship, of single people, 28–29
   realigning relationships in, in the older
      years, 110–11
   social, devaluation of a single person's, 7
   see also relationships
Nichols, M., 136
normalcy
   experts' contribution to views of, in the
      1950s, 15
   restriction on the state's power to define,
      24
normalization, of identity exploration by ho-
      mosexuals, 133–34
normative framework
   for the family's reaction to singlehood, 38–
      39
   for nodal events in a family's life, 54
"not married yet" phase, 58–68

old age, vision of, formed by family experi-
      ence, 100–101
oppression, of people with homosexual iden-
      tities, 127
options, beyond normatively prescribed
      choices, 55
outsiders, men in the later years, 104

Papp, P., 31, 100, 134
parents
   accommodating changes in involvement
      by, 52–53
   aging, and generational issues, 111–12
   loss felt by, when children remain single,
      96
   relationship of adult children with, 62–63
   see also generational issues; multigenera-
      tional context
Parents Without Partners, 22

Pasick, R., 8, 134
past
    connecting with emotionally, through
        things, 106
    debt to, 92
patchwork intimacy, 68
path, life, 64–67
patriarchy, in Puerto Rican families, 66
Pearce, J. K., 31, 38, 39, 83, 115
Peplau, L., 120
personal growth, from accepting help in the
    elderly phase, 121
personal space, in midlife, 179
physical capacity, acknowledging future di-
    minishment of, 103–8
Pierce, K., 152
place, sense of, in terms of social expecta-
    tions, 4
planning
    of assertion of homosexual identity to the
        family of origin, 139–40
    of connection to the family of origin, 194–
        95
    detailed, and failure, 180
    for later life, by gay and lesbian single peo-
        ple, 144–45
    see also financial planning
Popenjoe, P., 15–16
poverty rate
    in the 1980s, 24–25
    for married couples with children, 1970s
        and 1980s, 20
power
    relationships between husbands and wives,
        21
    shifting between generations, as parents
        age, 112
Powers, E. A., 120
pride, in work, 102, see also self-esteem
process dimension, of negotiating the life cy-
    cle, 54
procreation, emphasizing the passage of
    time, 82
pseudo-autonomy, and fusion, 34
pseudo-independence, 63
psychiatric community, homosexuality as de-
    fined by, 128–29
psychological correctness, 16
Puerto Rican community
    cultural response to homosexuality in,
        138, 206–9
    family in, 65–66

race, as a cultural context, 38
    example of an African-American male,
        42–43

Ragucci, A. T., 41
reciprocity
    between generations, 53
    in a mutual support system, 46, 66
referent power, and single women, 7
relationships
    family, realigning on marriage of children,
        7–8
    gender, changes in the 1960s, 19
    in the larger community, 94
    sexual, as a bridge to intimacy, 11
    shifts in, 199–200
    skill in maintaining, for men in their thir-
        ties, 77
    social, place of marriage in, 6
    see also friendships; networks
responsibility
    for final living arrangements, 119–21
    financial, for oneself, 95–96
retirement
    changes in expectations, 104–5
    planning for, 103–5
retirement home living, satisfaction with,
    120
revolution, of the 1960s, 17–20
rites of passage, home ownership, 76
rituals
    boundary-making, marriage as, 7–8
    centered around family, 9
Roach, A., 140
Rodgers, R., 53
Rohrbaugh, M., 37
role models
    for being a husband/father, 177–78
    in cultural shifts among generations,
        41
    for divorced adults, in the 1970s, 23
    for single people, 10–11, 27
        in the 1960s, 19–20
        homosexual, 131, 203
Rook, K. S., 120
Rose, S., 135
Rosen, E. J., 45
Rosenheck, S., 137
Rotunno, M., 40, 41
Roybal, J., 117
Rubenstein, C. M., 104, 109, 110
rules, creating, for singles, 80–81

S.A.G.E. Foundation, 144–45
Scallon, R., 143
Schaie, K. W., 109, 118, 119, 120
Scherz, F. H., 53
Schnarch, D., 108
Schoofs, M., 141
Schwartzberg, N., 59, 63

secret
  of identity, problematic consequences of,
    130
  toxicity of, 182
segregation, between single and married peo-
    ple, 83
self
  adult, articulating in the family system,
    71–74
  defining, 57
    within a system, 33–34
    within a system, stages of development,
      53–55
  differentiation of, 54
  life beyond, 94
  reorganization of, in response to changing
    relationships, 63
self-blame, for not reaching work goals,
    102–3
self-definition, of singles, in a social context,
    ix, 5, 13
self-esteem
  depending on family for, 161–62
  finding new areas for, in the thirties, 70–
    81
selfhood, of women working outside the
    home, 21
self-support, need for young adults to de-
    velop, 64–67
separation and togetherness, balance in the
    family system, 33–34
setting, of homosexuality in society, 126–
    27
Sex and the Single Girl, 20
sexuality
  and intimacy issues, 79
  as an issue in the context of culture and
    family, 137
  messages of the church community about,
    28
  in the older years, 108
sexual mores
  in the 1950s, 16
  revolution of the 1960s, 18–19
sexual prime, 108
sexual relationships, and the quality of single
    life, 11
Shapiro, E., 63, 79
Shaver, P., 110
Shon, S. P., 47, 48, 76
siblings
  care for retarded, in the later years, 116
  relationships with
    distant, 152
    opening up in the older years, 112–14
  separation by marriage, 160

Silverstein, B., 117
Silverstein, C., 19
Silverstein, O., 31, 100, 134
Simon, B. L., 4, 101–2, 103–4, 109, 113,
    115, 120, 123
Simon, R. M., 82
Simpson, R., 127
singlehood
  for homosexuals, defined, 125
  open discussion of, 71
  the "problem" of, 3–12, 168–69
  skills developed in, use for the elderly
    phase, 121
  tasks of accepting, in the thirties, 75–
    80
singles
  couples culture and, 13–29
  homosexual, 130–31, 141–44
    stories from, 202–14
  previously married, 173–86
Singles Project, ix
skeleton, family, singlehood as, 84–89
skills, consolidating in the thirties, 71
social debt
  example, Lorraine Sampson, 46
  sense of, the black community, 45
social issues
  reflection in television of the 1970s, 23–24
  social equality, 24
socialization
  gender-related differences, and the lives of
    singles, 64–65
  scripts on dating behavior, 135
  socialized isolates, men in later years,
    104
  social power theory, and suicide, 120–21
social structure
  dismemberment of, in the 1960s, 17–20
  and status, 6
  supports of single men, versus single
    women, 8
socioeconomic variables
  comparing single men with single women
    in their forties, 87–89
  status and life satisfaction, for never-
    married adults, 100
Solomon, M., 52
solution, and problem, self-defeating goal of
    marriage, 10
spiritual connections, 182
Spordone, A., 143
spousal support staff, for executives, 27
Staples, R., 6, 21, 38, 42, 43
statistics
  estimates of prevalence of homosexuality,
    126

statistics (*continued*)
  on incomes
    in the 1980s, 24–25
    of men and of women over 65, 103–4
  on living alone, at advanced ages, 119
  on marriage
    in the 1950s, 14
    by age 24, 5
    after age 50, for women, 99–100
  on poverty, 1970s, 20
  on size of the singles population, 19
  on women in the work force, 21
status
  financial, for women, from a husband, 64
  of single men, 7
  of single women, 161–62
  social, authenticity of, 10
status quo, hypocrisy of, 1960s, 17
Stein, P., 6, 27, 54, 64, 68, 69
Steinberg, S., 37
Steinhorn, A., 130, 138
stereotypes
  about gays, 135–36
  gender, 18
  in roles acquired by young adults, 63
  about singles, 6
    in the workplace, 27–28
Stewart, S., 91, 95, 96, 102
Stoller, R., 134
Stonewall bar riots, 19, 128
stress, during times of change, 55
structure, of dating behavior, 22
suicide, among the elderly, 120–21
support group, for HIV positive gays, 208
system, *see* family system
Szapocznik, J., 31

Taylor, E., 15, 23, 24, 26
television
  questioning of authority on, 17
  transmission and creation of culture
    in the 1950s, 14–15
    in the 1970s, 23
    in the 1980s, 26
therapist
  cultural context of, 9–10
  gender of, and fit with clients, 82, 212
  role of, 215–16
    in examining intimacy issues, 79
    in redefining singlehood, 70–71
  sexual orientation of, 131
  values of, 92
therapy
  approaches to singlehood in, 12
  Betsy in young adulthood, initial phase,
    203

family, looking at previous generations, 13
George in midlife
  final phase, 183–86
  initial phase, 178–80
  intermediate phase, 180–83
Lina in later life
  final phase, 200–201
  initial phase, 193–96
  intermediate phase, 196–200
  singlehood as an issue for, 9–11
thirties, the, 69–81
time, emotional meaning of, in the forties,
  82
timing, of marriage
  biological issues for women, 9
  delays in the 1970s, 23
  delays reflected in census data, 5
  and sense of place, 4
Tischler, B., 18
togetherness, balance with separation, in the
  family system, 33–34
traditional family, questioning of, in the
  1990s, 26
transitions
  family, influence of multigenerational ex-
    perience on, 34–35
  life cycle, second order changes in, 55
triangles, 32–33
  and life transition problems in a previous
    generation, 36–37
  with parents, 153–54, 195
    and their ghosts, 209
  stepfamily, 204
"twilight zone" of singlehood, 69–81

upward mobility, and the family wage system, 14

values, social, family as a mirror of, 31
Van Horn, S., 21
vertical movement in families, 34–35
  defined, 35
Vietnam War, effect on the culture of the
  1960s, 17–18
violence, and cultural changes, 19
visibility, of singles, in popular culture, 29

wage earners, in the 1970s family, 21
Walters, M., 31, 100, 134
Weber, L., 45
Weston, K., 140
White, M., 71, 216
Whitman, D., 25
Williams, J. S., 42
Williams, L., 27
Willis, S. L., 109, 118, 119, 120

wills, 105-8
Wirth, A., 137
Wirth, M., 137
wisdom, defined, 124
withdrawal, of singles in families urging marriage, 72, *see also* cut-offs
Wolfe, Tom, 25
women
    black, expectation of working in marriage, 45
    blaming for decline in American family life, 25
    as caretakers, 115-16
    closing doors for, in the forties, 84-87
    competent, portrayal of in the 1970s, 24
    as daughters raised to accommodate others, 35
    declining loneliness in the older years, 110-11
    education and marriage, in the 1950s, 14
    entry into the work force
        1960s, 18
        1970s, 21
    goals of the young adult period, 64
    responsibility for friendship networks of couples, 149-50
    salaries of, 27

single
    feeling of failure in, 134
    increase in number with aging, 99-100
    social view of, defined by husband's status, 6-7
    status of
        defined by husband's status, 6-7
        in Japanese families, 47-48
    see also gender roles
Women's Movement, 5
    backlash to, 19
    joining of lesbian organizations with, 128
work, *see* career
work families, 23-24
work force, women's entry into, the 1960s, 18
work life, consolidating decisions about, 101-3
workplace shows, television, 26
work systems, organization of, around family life, 27
Wright, R., 39, 120

young adulthood, 58-68

Zinn, M., 20
Zollar, A. C., 42